XENOGLOSSY

A Review and Report of a Case

IAN STEVENSON, M.D.

School of Medicine, University of Virginia

University Press of Virginia
Charlottesville

The University Press of Virginia
Copyright © 1974 by Ian Stevenson
First published 1974

Also published as Volume 31 of
*Proceedings of the American
Society for Psychical Research*

ISBN: 0-8139-0443-9
Library of Congress Catalog Card Number: 73-77947

PRINTED IN GREAT BRITAIN BY JOHN WRIGHT & SONS LTD.,
AT THE STONEBRIDGE PRESS, BRISTOL BS4 5NU

Contents

iii

Acknowledgements

THIS investigation finally ended in an extensive collaborative effort to which many persons generously contributed their counsel and time in studying various aspects of the main case reported. I gratefully extend thanks to these persons.

I wish first to acknowledge the valuable assistance of several persons who acted as interpreters at the sessions at which the Swedish personality manifested or who listened to copies of the tape recordings of the sessions.

Dr. Nils G. Sahlin (a native of Sweden), formerly Director of the American Swedish Historical Museum, Philadelphia, and later President of Quinnipiac College, Hamden, Connecticut, acted as an interpreter and interviewer at one recorded session and gave much time and labor to a careful review of the tape recording of this session. In the later development of this book Dr. Sahlin read the entire typescript, including the Appendix with the transcription of the interview in which he participated. His additional comments about various details have further improved the text, transcription of the Swedish spoken, translation, and commentary.

Mr. Lennart Ekman of Stockholm, Sweden, in 1956 a graduate student at the University of Pennsylvania, attended the same session as Dr. Sahlin mentioned above and acted as an additional interpreter and interviewer. He has furnished some comments on the case, which I have quoted.

Mr. Oscar Sunday, also a native of Sweden, now residing in New York, acted as an interpreter and interviewer at a later session (number eight) and has given me his notes and opinions on that session.

Mrs. Eva Hellström, Honorary Secretary of the Swedish Society for Psychical Research, Stockholm, supervised the making of verbatim transcripts of four tape-recorded sessions, using copies of the original tapes sent to Sweden. She and Mr. Rolf Ejvegård, Professor of Swedish at the Högre Allmänna Läroverket i Enskede, Stockholm, then annotated these transcripts, offering comments on the language used and some other points that arose in connection with the life described by the Swedish personality manifesting. I am further indebted to Mr. Ejvegård for his careful reading of the Appendix and suggestions for its improvement.

Mr. W. G. Roll, Project Director, Psychical Research Foundation, Inc., Durham, North Carolina, who understands Scandinavian languages, studied the tape recording of session seven and gave helpful comments thereon for this report.

Dr. Nils Jacobson of Lund, Sweden, during a summer spent at the University of Virginia School of Medicine, made a careful study of the data of the case and especially of the Swedish language exhibited. He furnished valuable additional comments about the xenoglossy. Back in Sweden, Dr. Jacobson also uncovered some information relevant to the possible identity of the personality manifesting in the subject's hypnotic trances.

Dr. William A. Coates, Associate Professor of Modern Languages, Kansas State University, Manhattan, Kansas, made a thorough study of the Swedish xenoglossy and contributed valuable comments and suggestions for further analyses.

Docent Folke Hedblom of the Dialekt- och Folkminnesarkivet, Uppsala, Sweden, examined the tape recordings of the Swedish xenoglossy with regard to the question of whether the Jensen personality spoke an identifiable dialect of Swedish and I am grateful for his analysis and comments.

Mrs. Birgit Stanford (a native of Sweden) gave valuable assistance in the editing of the transcript of the Swedish xenoglossy published as an Appendix to this monograph. She also revised and improved my translation of the Swedish in the transcript.

Without the assistance of all these persons I would not have considered the present case worth publishing, because it is clear that the first point to establish is whether or not the manifesting personality did in fact speak a foreign language. I think it important to add, however, that my numerous collaborators have no responsibility for two other aspects of this paper. They have had nothing to do with the investigation of the subject's early life with regard to the possibility that she may have learned Swedish prior to the time of the sessions. And they have made no contribution to the various explanations of the xenoglossy which I discuss in the latter part of this monograph.

Dr. Carleton T. Hodge, School of Modern Languages, Foreign Service Institute, Department of State, Washington, D.C., suggested the use of the Modern Language Aptitude Test in the present case.

Dr. Karlis Osis, Director of Research, American Society for Psychical Research, suggested some additional inquiries concerning the case.

Dr. Burke Smith, Department of Psychiatry, University of Virginia School of Medicine, gave helpful suggestions about the psychological tests administered and furnished a report of the Minnesota Multiphasic Personality Inventory administered to the subject and to the hypnotist.

Dr. Jack D. Hain, Department of Psychiatry, Medical College of Alabama, also gave counsel about the use of psychological tests.

Mr. Richard O. Arther, 57 West 57th Street, New York, administered polygraph tests for lie detection to the subject and to the hypnotist.

Dr. Robert W. Laidlaw, of New York City, was a witness of session eight and placed his notes at my disposal; he also offered much helpful counsel during the investigation of the case.

Mr. John H. Wilkens, Director, American Swedish Historical Foundation, Philadelphia, made available to me the excellent library of that Foundation.

Dr. Erlendur Haraldsson of Reykjavik, Iceland, M. Reşat Bayer of Istanbul, Turkey, and Senhor Hernani G. Andrade of São Paulo, Brazil, furnished information about several cases with xenoglossies.

Miss Inger Teigland conducted some investigations into possible verifications of names in Norway.

I also acknowledge gratefully the excellent cooperation of the subject of the main case reported in this monograph and that of her late husband. They spared no effort to facilitate my inquiries and investigation of the case.

For her usual careful editorial assistance I am most grateful to Mrs. Laura A. Dale of the American Society for Psychical Research. Thanks are gladly given also to my colleagues, Dr. J. G. Pratt and Mr. C. Ransom, at the University of Virginia, and to Dr. Gertrude Schmeidler, City College of the City of New York, for valuable suggestions made after reading earlier versions of the monograph.

Heartfelt thanks go also to my secretaries, Miss Sione Ross, Mrs. Betty Heavener, and Mrs. Carole Harwell, for painstaking and uncomplaining labors in typing many revisions of the manuscript.

And finally I express thanks again to two anonymous donors of funds whose assistance has made this work possible and whose encouragement has been invaluable.

I.S.

University of Virginia
Charlottesville, Virginia

I Introduction

Glossolalia and xenoglossy

THE literature of religion and especially of spiritualism contains abundant records of claims that persons have spoken in languages ordinarily unknown to them. This phenomenon is known as glossolalia or "speaking in tongues". Cutten (18) reviewed the better known cases of this kind which have occurred from the time of the New Testament up to 1927. Kelsey (44) provided a further review, published in 1964, of the subject of glossolalia. Glossolalia holds much of interest for students of religion. Religious enthusiasts of "tongue speaking" can say that the miracle is in the listener rather than in the speaker, so that for their conviction of an inflowing of the holy spirit no known language needs to be identified.* Linguists also may find glossolalia relevant to their studies. Parapsychologists, however, usually interest themselves only in cases in which evidence appears of an ability to speak an identified language not normally known to the subject. If any miracle occurs in the hearer of glossolalia, it is private and unverifiable.

In the majority of recorded instances of glossolalia the language allegedly spoken has probably consisted of either (*a*) an incomprehensible and nonsensical gibberish or (*b*) a fictitious, if clever, invention of the subject's subconscious mind. The strange language invented and interpreted by LeBaron (48) provides an example of the first type and the "Martian" language (shown to be a derivative of French) spoken by Mlle Hélène Smith (32; 33) exemplifies the second type. Instances of a person's speaking a real language entirely unknown to him in his ordinary state are unfortunately rare and well-documented cases even rarer. Richet (69) coined the word "xenoglossy" to refer to cases of this type, and we further divide them into "recitative xenoglossy" and "responsive xenoglossy".

* "Now when this was noised abroad, the multitude came together, and were confounded, because that every man heard them speak in his own language.
"And they were all amazed and marveled, saying one to another, Behold, are not all these which speak Galileans?
"And how hear we every man in our own tongue, wherein we were born?" (Acts 2: 6–8.)

Recitative xenoglossy

By recitative xenoglossy we mean the expression of phrases and sometimes longer passages of a foreign language, usually learned earlier in
life, without the ability to converse in the language. In a number of
cases investigation has shown that the speaker learned fragments of a
language years before, forgot them in his ordinary condition, and
spoke them in some altered state, such as during sleep, delirium, or trance.

The earliest report known to me of a case of this type occurs in Lord
Monboddo's *Ancient Metaphysics* (51, vol. 1, pp. 217–220). A French
woman was noticed by her servants to speak, when sleeping, a language
quite unknown to them. They were sitting with her at night when she
was not well, but it does not seem that she was delirious. The woman
herself did not understand a word of what she was reported to have said
in her sleep when this was told to her when awake. After a time she
was attended during a delivery by a nurse from Brittany and this woman
immediately recognized the language spoken by the subject during her
sleep as Breton. She had been born in Brittany and during her infancy
had been cared for by a Breton family while away from her French
parents. The Breton language spoken by the subject was only that with
which a small child would be equipped. No one seems to have tried
conversing in Breton with the woman when she was sleeping. The
case seems one of recitative xenoglossy only.

Samuel T. Coleridge described a case of recitative xenoglossy of a
different origin (13, pp. 70–72). A young woman about twenty-five
years old spoke Latin, Greek, and Hebrew during a delirium. Subsequent study showed that she had learned something of these languages
many years before. When she was between nine and thirteen years old,
her foster father, a learned pastor, had declaimed in her presence from
his favorite books written in these languages. A young physician investigated the case and succeeded in tracing some of the utterances of the
woman to passages in books found in the library of the pastor, who
had since died.

Eckermann wrote that Goethe had mentioned such a case to him
(27, vol. 3, pp. 215–216). Eckermann gave it from Goethe as follows:

I know a case in which an old man, desperately ill and at death's door, began to
recite Greek sentences completely unexpectedly. Everyone was fully convinced
that this man understood no Greek whatever and called it a great wonder. The
cunning had already begun to exploit the credulity of simpletons when it was
unfortunately discovered that this old man had been obliged in his early youth
to learn a lot of Greek phrases by heart and in the presence of another boy of
aristocratic family whom it was hoped his example would stimulate. He had
learned this classical Greek quite mechanically without understanding it and had

not thought about it again for fifty years until, in his last illness, all this material with which he had been stuffed began to stir and come to life again. (*My translation.*)

Abercrombie reported several similar cases in the first part of the nineteenth century (1).

Herman Melville was acquainted with this kind of case and its explanation, for Starbuck in *Moby Dick* says: "I have heard that in violent fevers, men, all ignorance, have talked in ancient tongues; and that . . . in their wholly forgotten childhood those ancient tongues had been really spoken in their hearing by some lofty scholars" (50, p. 476).

Hélène Smith, the medium already mentioned, provided another example (almost certainly) of cryptomnesic recitative xenoglossy. She correctly wrote a phrase in Arabic, a language she had certainly never studied. The phrase, however, occurred in a book which she had probably (not certainly) seen, although perhaps just to glance at (32).

Freeborn reported (in 1902) a particularly instructive case of the recovery during illness in advanced years of a language (Hindustani) learned in early childhood but not spoken since (34). The patient was a woman, seventy years old, who had been born in India where she had lived until nearly four years of age. She was then brought to England. Up to the time of reaching England she had been entirely under the care of Indian servants, especially an ayah (Indian nursemaid), with whom she spoke only Hindustani. After separation from her ayah the patient had never again spoken Hindustani, but had begun to learn English.

During her illness with severe pneumonia the patient became delirious and was observed to be talking in a language unknown to those around her. She seemed to be conversing, or repeating conversations, in this language, and also to be reciting verses in it. "She repeated the same poem time after time." A person who had spent much time in India recognized the poem as one commonly used by the ayahs in India and she also translated some of the conversations the patient carried on in Hindustani.

During the patient's illness she moved forward chronologically in the memories of her life as she successively relived some of its earlier events. She first began to mix English with Hindustani, then dropped the Hindustani and after a time talked in English, French, and German. The latter two languages she had learned in later life. As she continued toward recovery the friends she spoke about were of progressively later dates in her life.

The following points in this case deserve emphasis:

1. In speaking Hindustani the patient seemed to be reliving (as if in the present for her) the period in childhood when she spoke that language. Thus one of

her translated remarks was a request to the servant to take her to the bazaar to buy sweets.

2. Although she recited verses spoken to her by an ayah, it is improbable that she herself had ever, as a child, spoken the verses which had been retained in her mind more or less passively.

3. The patient's memories seemed to lie in strata through which she progressed during the delirium from her earliest days to those of later life and eventually the present.

4. The patient had, after recovery, no ability to speak Hindustani (apart from a few words she knew consciously) and furthermore she had no recollection of ever having spoken the language.

5. Although the patient, when she was in the phase of speaking Hindustani, spoke as if she was then addressing other persons, these were actual persons of her past, e.g., the ayah. It is not recorded in the report, and presumably was not the case, that she could speak Hindustani responsively with persons present who could speak the language. For this reason I have classified the case with recitative xenoglossies.

Richet reported the case of a French medium, Mme X., who, in a state of partial dissociation, wrote long sentences in Greek, a language with which she was said to be entirely unacquainted under ordinary circumstances (69). Richet discovered that many of the Greek sentences came from a particular Greek–French dictionary. The medium seemed to write as if from a mental vision of this book and the errors she made were those likely to be made by someone who was copying something he understood imperfectly. Richet had no evidence that Mme X. had ever seen the relevant dictionary, nor any definite proof that she had not seen it. This case excited controversy and differences of opinion in those who examined the evidence critically (49). Richet studied a number of similar cases of apparent xenoglossy. He concluded that he had encountered none which had sufficiently rigorous documentation for acceptance as a paranormal phenomenon, but considered them examples of a type having great potential importance in psychical research.

Delanne cited an Italian case of recitative xenoglossy (21). A family named Battista, apparently inhabitants of Rome, lost a small child, Blanche, in 1902. Three years later Signora Battista was pregnant and had an apparitional experience in which the deceased Blanche said she was returning to the family. Signora Battista and her husband (who reported the case) named the new baby, born in February, 1906, Blanche also.

When the first Blanche was alive, the family had a Swiss domestic servant who spoke only French. This girl had taught a French lullaby to Blanche. After Blanche's death, the Swiss servant left the family and they had almost forgotten the lullaby which she used to sing to the child.

They were astonished therefore when one day they (Signor Battista and his wife together) heard the second Blanche (then about five years old) singing the old lullaby taught to the first Blanche by the Swiss servant. It had not been sung or heard in the family for nine years. When her parents asked the second Blanche who had taught her the song, she replied: "No one, I just know it by myself."

More recently Rosen has reported another example of the kind of case that we can explain as a subconscious remembering (74). A young man when hypnotized spoke words of a foreign language eventually found to be Oscan, an ancient language of Italy. Further investigation of this feat showed that this man had happened one day to read (and subconsciously remember) a passage of Oscan in a book which lay open within his view in a library.

Before leaving this review of cases of recitative xenoglossy I wish to add that although nearly all the cases so far studied can be best interpreted as instances of cryptomnesia, that is, the revival in adulthood of a language learned in childhood (usually) and later forgotten, other interpretations may apply to other cases. I shall in a later section of this monograph, for example, present a summary of a case of recitative xenoglossy (the case of Swarnlata Mishra) which I believe has a paranormal provenance. And I do not exclude the possibility that some instances of recitative xenoglossy may derive from telepathic communications. The distinction I emphasize between recitative and responsive xenoglossy does not relate to the presence or absence of paranormal components in their processes, but to the fact that I consider responsive xenoglossy evidence of a learned skill and recitative xenoglossy evidence only of information somehow acquired by the subject.

Responsive xenoglossy: Review of published cases

In *recitative* xenoglossy the subject repeats, without necessarily understanding, fragments of a strange language. He usually exhibits rote memory only. In contrast, in *responsive* xenoglossy the subject can converse intelligently in the foreign language. Authentic instances of this feat are even rarer than those of the simpler kind.

Aksakov published the earliest reports of responsive xenoglossy in the serious literature of psychical research (2). He summarized reports of J. W. Edmonds, who had earlier published letters in American newspapers about cases observed by him and others reported to him. Edmonds' daughter, Laura, was the medium for some of the cases cited by Aksakov. One episode occurred when a native of Greece reportedly conversed at length with a Greek communicator through Laura. Laura was stated to know no foreign languages except a little schoolgirl French. Yet on another occasion with another medium a communicator spoke French and Laura Edmonds, according to her father's report, conversed fluently with this communicator in Parisian French. This discrepancy about how much French Laura knew raises doubts about how much of any foreign language Edmonds himself knew and therefore about how well he understood exactly what languages were spoken. The reported Greek responsive xenoglossy might have been an auditory illusion of which I shall give a probable example later.

Aksakov cited other cases of reported responsive xenoglossy, including one conversational exchange between an American medium controlled by an Indian female communicator, "Springflower", and a man who had learned the Indian language spoken by "Springflower" during a period of duty as an Indian agent on the American frontier of the West. It is difficult to believe that the numerous cases reported to and by Edmonds and Aksakov included no genuine instance of responsive xenoglossy. At the same time, the reports regrettably provide insufficient documentation of essential points. Podmore reached the same conclusion about the Edmonds xenoglossies and other similar cases of nineteenth-century spiritualism (61, vol. 1, pp. 257–263).

In 1900 Whitaker (104) reported a case of xenoglossy which had occurred much earlier, in 1847–50. The subject, Ninfa Filiberto, was a sixteen-year-old Italian girl of Palermo, Sicily, who developed various hysterical symptoms, such as paralyses and convulsions. Her ability to speak languages shifted during her illness. On one occasion she seemed to forget Italian and comprehend only French. On another she failed to understand either French or Italian, but spoke "excellent English" and "carried on an easy conversation" with a Mr. Frederick Olway, an Englishman then staying in Palermo. The English xenoglossy was accompanied by a certain amount of personation of an Englishwoman. The patient was described as "well-educated" and she had been taught a little French. The informants denied, however, that she or the members of her family knew even the first elements of English. Unfortunately, the report gives no details of exactly what English Ninfa Filiberto actually spoke during her illness. And it gives only two words ("Fifteen September") of what she wrote in English. Nor does it include a statement from Mr. Olway himself about the English xenoglossy.

In the early years of this century, van Eeden published a case that was perhaps the first instance of responsive xenoglossy deserving serious attention (98). He reported conversing in Dutch with a communicator through the medium, Mrs. Rosalie Thompson, who knew no Dutch whatever. Although the communicator (ostensibly a deceased Dutch friend of Dr. van Eeden) only exchanged remarks with Dr. van Eeden for a few minutes he (van Eeden) declared himself much impressed and said: "During a few minutes—though a few minutes only—I felt absolutely as if I were speaking to my friend himself. I spoke Dutch and got immediate and correct answers. The expression of satisfaction and gratification in face and gesture, when we seemed to understand each other, was too true and vivid to be acted. Quite unexpected Dutch words were pronounced, details were given which were far from my mind . . ." (98, p. 82).

Bozzano published a collection of numerous cases of this type (7) and concluded that in some there existed evidence of paranormal knowledge of a foreign language on the part of the speaker. A careful scrutiny of Bozzano's book suggests that some of the mediums or sensitives cited may have exhibited genuine responsive xenoglossy, but the scanty documentation of most of the cases makes impossible a firm conclusion based on his reports.

Wood reported responsive communications in Egyptian from a communicator who claimed to speak the language of ancient Egypt (108; 109). A scholar of ancient Egyptian, A. J. Hulme, testified that this communicator had used that language with grammatical correctness and in appropriate conversational responses (38). Since the case concerns a dead language, we can be certain that the medium, "Rosemary", could not have picked up this language in her childhood. Unfortunately, we do not know how the vowels of ancient Egyptian were sounded and this makes verification of the "Rosemary" Egyptian xenoglossy more difficult, at least in that respect. The evidence developed by Wood (who eventually studied ancient Egyptian himself) tending to show that "Rosemary" really did speak Egyptian seems rather impressive. Unfortunately, Wood was never successful in persuading scholars of Egyptian other than Hulme to take the case seriously. It is not his fault, but nevertheless unfortunate, that the claim of a responsive xenoglossy in this case has not been fully investigated by anyone knowledgeable about ancient Egyptian other than Wood himself and Hulme. Wood (who died in 1963) left behind valuable notebooks and the case may yet receive the further study by experts that, in my opinion, it deserves.

Stevens reported a case—all too casually it seems to me—of a responsive xenoglossy in Karen, the language of a minority people of Burma (83). A man who had been a missionary to the Karens and had learned their language reported that he conversed in Karen with a mediumistic communicator purporting to be Ko San Ye, a person he had known and loved during his days in Burma. (The séance took place in Washington, D.C., and the medium was thought to be completely ignorant of Karen.) The communicator was said to have mispronounced the missionary's name in a manner exactly resembling an error in the pronunciation of his name made by the communicator when living. The missionary claimed that he had conversed in Karen with this communicator through different mediums. Since Karen is a language very little known in the United States, it would certainly not have been picked up by the medium in childhood or casually. One can only regret that this case, if it was not an auditory illusion (a topic I shall come to later), was not documented properly at the time it occurred.

Elínborg Lárusdóttir reported the case of a mediumistic communicator, manifesting through the Icelandic medium Hafsteinn Björnsson, who spoke the Eskimo language of Greenland with a sitter, Professor Svend Fredriksen of Denmark (46). Professor Fredriksen had grown up in Greenland among Eskimo people and knew their language well. But almost no one in Iceland knows this language despite the comparative proximity of Greenland and Iceland. The medium, Hafsteinn Björnsson, had never been to Greenland and he certainly knew no Eskimo language. Unfortunately, only a short conversation took place between the Eskimo communicator and Professor Fredriksen and no tape recordings were made at this séance, which took place in 1966 in Reykjavik.

Xenography

I shall mention briefly here some instances of written communications in foreign languages—xenography. (Richet's case cited on p. 4 belongs strictly to those of xenography rather than xenoglossy.)

The first example (which occurred in 1873 in Brighton, England) is attributed to an infant of less than six months of age, a fact which somewhat diminishes the credibility of the account (97). The reporter of the case deals with this obstacle by saying that the communicating spirit, not the infant itself, held the pencil. Various communications were received through writing during which a pencil was in the hand of the infant. The most remarkable was surely a sentence in Greek, a photograph of which is reproduced in the report.

Von Reuter described a series of remarkable communications in foreign languages for which his mother was the medium (99). The communications were received through a device which for all practical purposes may be considered a type of ouija board. Both he and his mother had a considerable knowledge of European languages, such as German and French, but none whatever of Hungarian, Russian, or Turkish, three languages in which they received intelligible communications. Von Reuter's account of the Turkish communications they received in 1926 is quite detailed. He described how he requested the Turkish-speaking communicator to give the Turkish for various English words, e.g., numbers, calendrical terms, and objects. In about 90 per cent of the instances the communicator promptly furnished the correct word in Turkish. Sometimes the communicator gave short sentences in Turkish which he (the communicator) immediately translated into French or English. Von Reuter listed a considerable number of actual Turkish words and phrases that he says were thus communicated to him. He states that 170 Turkish words were communicated altogether. I looked up twenty-five of the Turkish words in a French–Turkish dictionary and found twenty-four of them (as given by von Reuter) to be either quite correct or satisfactorily close to the spellings and meanings given in the dictionary. (Some allowance may be made for errors in transcribing unfamiliar sounds into written form.) Thus if we accept von Reuter's statement that neither he nor his mother knew any Turkish (they had visited Turkey, but made no effort to learn the language), this case would seem to be one of responsive xenography with paranormal features.

Dumas reported in 1950 two instances of xenography through the mediumship of Mme Berthe Bricout (26). I later became acquainted with Mme Bricout (an amateur medium) and the principal sitter of her séances, M. Jacques Brossy, when I visited them twice in Saint-Etienne, France. I am convinced of their honesty and good faith.

The first of the reported xenographies by Mme Bricout occurred at a séance on January 11, 1930. A communication of a long sentence in Russian was received. (The report reproduces a photograph of the Russian writing.) Neither the medium nor anyone present knew any Russian. But the message, when translated, proved relevant to one of the sitters to whom it had been directed. The sentence itself: "Dear mother, do not cry. I am here and love you", is not at all specific and the importance of the communication for our purposes lies solely in the fact that it was transmitted in Russian.

At a sitting on August 5, 1932, Mme Bricout received a communication in Chinese. This message (also reproduced photographically in the report) was somewhat longer and consisted of several sentences worked into a short paragraph. No one present knew any Chinese. The xenography was submitted to experts in that language, who differed about some details in the translation, but agreed as to most of the meaning. (Dumas' report includes the four somewhat variant translations of the Chinese offered by the different linguists.)

This communication purportedly came from a Chinese discarnate spirit who was attempting to guide the medium's hand to form the Chinese ideograms with which she was totally unfamiliar.

Hope reported the case of a four-year-old English girl who wrote a single word in Greek before she could write any English letters (37). The Greek word written was interpreted by her father as possibly a meaningful message (in the context of the family situation at the time) emanating from his deceased father, the child's grandfather, who was a Greek scholar and used to write to his son in Greek.

Auditory illusions and pseudo-xenoglossies

Wood took detailed notes and made one phonograph record of the apparent Egyptian communications through "Rosemary" (109). This enabled him to avoid an important error which seems to have occurred in another initially impressive report of responsive xenoglossy, that by an English scholar of Chinese, Whymant, who claimed to have conversed with a Chinese communicator (105; 106). According to Whymant, Confucius appeared at séances with the medium, George Valiantine, and provided Whymant with the correct interpretation of certain obscure passages in his writings. Subsequent sittings with George Valiantine which Whymant attended in London failed to reproduce these feats, and a probable explanation occurred to other observers (at these later sittings) for the exchange between Whymant and the purported Chinese communicator (75). It seemed likely to them that an auditory illusion had been built up in the mind of the sitter in the following manner. The ostensible communicator first utters some meaningless syllables which are not English or Chinese, but which the expectant sitter mistakes for Chinese. The sitter then replies appropriately in Chinese according to his assumption of what the communicator said first. The communicator then echoes some or all of what the sitter has said in Chinese, mixed perhaps with some more gibberish. The sitter, now certain that he has heard Chinese, fills in gaps and attributes a sensible reply to the communicator. To this he replies further himself and so the exchange continues. The sitter is talking Chinese; the communicator is echoing Chinese spoken first by the sitter, but with sufficient clarity to confirm the sitter in the illusion that he is conversing with someone in Chinese. When the conversation is slowed down, when it is carefully noted or recorded, and when the sitter himself says little, the poverty of the communications from the medium becomes apparent and the illusion exposed. Fortunately, we can now avoid, or at least detect, errors of this type by the use of tape recorders, which can help us make certain whether the medium introduces a new word in the foreign language before or only after the sitter has done so, and whether his replies are a mere parroting of phrases spoken by the sitter or constitute appropriately adjusted and sensible responses to what the sitter has just said.*

Persons only casually familiar with foreign languages—who have perhaps studied them superficially in high school, but never mastered one—may easily mistake the semblance of a foreign language for the reality. Podmore drew attention to this hazard many years ago (61, vol. 1, p. 261).

Cory published in 1919 a valuable example of pseudo-xenoglossy (15). The subject experienced dissociations in which a secondary personality sometimes spoke and wrote an alleged Spanish. The language contained a good many words evidently derived from Spanish (or Italian) words. But these words (and some others evidently fully invented) were not organized in any grammatical way to communicate an intelligible meaning. The subject herself could not translate the "Spanish" into English. The language spoken amounted only to a kind of Spanish-based gibberish.

West reported the investigation and similar exposure of a case of alleged xenoglossy of African languages, particularly Mende (103). Careful monitoring by an expert in Mende of the language spoken by the mediums (there were two in this case) showed that they were not speaking this language and they were almost certainly not speaking any actual language whatever, but only making unintelligible sounds fashioned vaguely to sound like a language.

In 1962 I studied a similar case of which I hope to publish a full report in the future. The subject when hypnotized and regressed described a life in nineteenth-century Holland and at times seemed to be making an effort to speak Dutch. She herself and others who had heard her evidently genuinely believed that she could speak Dutch. A Dutch-speaking colleague of mine tested her ability to understand and speak Dutch (and also German) during the hypnotic regressed condition and found she could do neither. Her pseudo-xenoglossy included a few tags of commonly known German, but nothing else.

In 1963 I heard of a case of triplets in Norway who were reported to have spoken among themselves when small children a language that was incomprehensible to their parents and other persons and that was thought possibly to have been Finnish. They spoke this strange language up to the age of four. I visited two of the triplets, Tura and Ola Kluge (born

---

* It is perhaps unfair to use this case of apparent Chinese xenoglossy to illustrate the occurrence of an auditory illusion. However, some sitters with Valiantine gathered evidence which strongly suggested fraud on the part of the medium in at least some of his alleged trances (75). But this is not relevant to the question whether the sitter becomes deceived by an auditory illusion, which could occur if the medium tried to produce a xenoglossy either fraudulently or with perfect honesty and in a deep trance.

in 1911) in August, 1963, and talked with them and with one younger and one older person of the village, Hof, where they still lived. It was confirmed that the triplets had spoken to each other when they were small children in a language others did not understand. But the reported identification of the language with Finnish was by no means precise and could not be traced to any Finnish-speaking person. Other suggestions that the language spoken by the triplets was German or English had no greater support.

The triplets spoke Norwegian to other persons without resistance. They were unusually close to each other and used the pronoun "we" instead of "I" when talking. They had no memories of a previous life and no special feeling of affinity for Finland.

I concluded that the Kluge triplets had devised a private language which they found convenient and perhaps amusing for communicating among themselves, but that they had not spoken as children any recognized language other than Norwegian. It seems, incidentally, of some value to discriminate between a private language which has communicative value, if only between two or three persons, and a completely nonsensical "language" which only the inventor understands (76).

Another case of pseudo-xenoglossy studied by my colleagues (notably M. Reşat Bayer and Dr. William Coates) and me was that of a Turkish woman who claimed to remember a previous life which she placed in an unidentified land and thought had occurred several centuries before Christ. She claimed to remember parts of the language spoken in that life and provided some words and short phrases in the unknown language for which she also gave at the same time their Turkish equivalents. A characteristic of the language was invariable placement of the verb at the end of the sentence. This is a feature of Turkish grammar, but also of many other languages. Therefore a terminal position of the verb in the sentence suggests, but does not compel us to believe, that Turkish provided the model for the unidentified language. In any case it has not been possible to trace the words and phrases spoken by the subject to any known ancient or modern language and it seems best to regard her utterances as an invention which she thought harmonious with the ancient previous life she claimed to be recalling.

In 1969 I studied the trances of an American medium of excellent reputation who in the trance condition underwent a marked personality change so that his ordinary personality seemed completely replaced by that of an Indian control called "Great Oak". "Great Oak" spoke English, but at times would also speak what he said was his native language, Chippewa. Recordings of the strange language spoken by "Great Oak" were submitted to experts in the languages of North American Indians, but they failed to identify the language as

Chippewa or any other dialect known to them. I am completely convinced of the medium's sincerity in this case and believe that the language of "Great Oak" is an unconscious fabrication of a pseudo-language. The case is therefore similar to that of Hélène Smith (32) cited earlier.*

Although the first task in the investigation of any apparent xenoglossy is to make quite certain that a true responsive exchange in the language has occurred, the next step is no less important: this is to ascertain that the subject has never normally learned the foreign language spoken. Cases occur in which a person during sleep, illness, or old age simply reverts to a language of childhood. I have already cited examples of this.

Dreifuss reported the case of a patient who, during transient dysphasia with severe migraine attacks, became aphasic for English, but retained (or recovered) a capacity to think and curse in German (23). The patient had grown up in Germany and spoke German until the age of ten when he moved to England, learned English, and discontinued speaking German. His relevant attacks of dysphasia occurred when he was sixteen or seventeen years old. In this case, the patient knew perfectly well that until a few years earlier he had spoken German exclusively, but in other cases with a longer interval since disuse of the original language, the reversion to it may seem surprising until the subject or others around him remember that he spoke or heard the "new" language in childhood.†

To conclude this section on pseudo-xenoglossies and related cases I shall briefly allude to the case of "Patience Worth" (66). Patience Worth was the communicator of an American medium, Mrs. Pearl Curran. She often spoke in an archaic type of English, and although she was not speaking in a language completely foreign to the medium, the linguistic features of the case make it proper to consider it under the heading of xenoglossy, or rather pseudo-xenoglossy, as I believe her archaic language to have been.

---

* Correspondents have often sent me writings or tape recordings of claimed xenoglossy. Nearly all these have occurred in the context of religious "tongue speaking" or domestic experiments with hypnotic regression. A few have been scribblings of children or automatic writings of adults thought to represent a foreign language unknown to the subject. I have examined all these carefully and only found two so far which showed sufficient evidence of an ability to speak or write an actual foreign language. These are the case reported in detail in this book and another still under investigation. Since I can only recognize about half a dozen foreign languages, I have often called in consultants to assist in the possible identification of other languages in order to be as certain as possible that no actual language has remained unrecognized. Despite these disappointments, I remain interested in receiving information about cases of apparent xenoglossy, believing that the potential importance of genuine cases justifies screening many others which may prove unrewarding.

† Charlton investigated the belief commonly held by neurologists that during aphasia the language learned first will be affected less than a language acquired later in life (11). He found that in fact both languages are affected equally, except in rare cases where emotional factors may prompt a greater preservation of one language over another.

An analysis of the vocabulary used by Patience Worth in the long epic poem "The Story of Telka" which she "dictated" to Mrs. Curran shows that 90 per cent of the words used were of Old English origin. This is a far higher proportion of such words than is found in any English writing after the thirteenth century, with the exception of Wycliffe's Bible which was published in the late fourteenth century. Patience Worth's Telka language seems to have been based on southern English rural dialects, although it corresponded exactly to none of them. She could speak and compose in a much more modern English, but she also "talked for hours in the curious language of Telka without once departing from its vocabulary or its idioms" (110, p. 356).

Patience Worth claimed to have lived on earth in the seventeenth century (in England and America), when the standard English contained far fewer words of Old English origin than it did in earlier periods. Telka's language thus contained a much higher percentage of words of Old English origin than were ordinarily used by English persons of the period in which she claimed to have lived. It cannot be completely excluded that some rural persons talked in the seventeenth century as she did, but this seems unlikely. In addition, the language of Telka contains numerous solecisms. All this seems to add up to an archaizing effort not of Mrs. Curran consciously, but of those portions of her subconscious mind which were worked up into the dramatic form of the Patience Worth personality.

Xenoglossies in cases of the reincarnation type

During the course of investigating cases of the reincarnation type I have studied a number of instances in which the subject has been reported to speak words or phrases (or sometimes more) of a language other than that of his parents. I have not yet encountered a case in which I could obtain firm evidence that the subject exhibited a true responsive xenoglossy. I believe most readers, however, will agree that the following examples illustrate an important feature to be looked for and investigated in future cases of this type.

THE CASE OF SWARNLATA MISHRA: In a previously published report on the case of Swarnlata Mishra (86) I mentioned that she sang Bengali songs (while she danced) when she was a small child. Swarnlata was born and grew up in Madhya Pradesh (central India) where her family spoke Hindi, a language related to Bengali (both are Sanskritic languages) but yet quite distinct from it.

Professor P. Pal, who visited Swarnlata's family and studied her case, transcribed three of her songs and later identified two of them as songs of the Bengali poet, Rabindranath Tagore (58). I have learned that these songs were recorded on phonograph records and their reproduction in moving picture films was also permitted. Swarnlata, however, could not have learned these songs from moving pictures. She first performed the Bengali songs and dances when she was between four and five years old up to which age she was under the close surveillance of her family. Her parents had never seen or heard such Bengali songs and dances and knew of no occasion in which Swarnlata could have learned them. They were certain Swarnlata had not been in contact with any Bengali-speaking person from whom she might have learned the songs and dances.

Swarnlata claimed that she had learned the songs and dances during a previous life in Sylhet, a city of Bengal, now in Bangladesh. She said that she had learned them from her friend Madhu, of that previous life.

This is a case of recitative xenoglossy, not one of responsive xenoglossy, since Swarnlata remembered the Bengali songs to sing them, but could not converse in Bengali.*

THE CASE OF BONGKUCH PROMSIN: Bongkuch Promsin was a boy of Nakhon Sawan, Thailand, whose case I have studied extensively and will report in detail later (87). Here I shall merely note that Bongkuch was reported by his family to have used a number of words of Laotian. (I recorded eleven such words altogether.) Bongkuch's family are Thais, but Chamrat Pooh Kio, the deceased person whose life Bongkuch was remembering, was a Laotian. Bongkuch's parents were aware that occasionally Laotian peddlers or other visitors came into their Thai village (and there were other Laotian people settled not far away), but they knew of no opportunity for Bongkuch to have acquired the Laotian words he spoke from such persons.

Here again the subject did not speak Laotian fully, but only showed a preference for certain Laotian words.

THE CASE OF BISHEN CHAND KAPOOR: Bishen Chand Kapoor of Bareilly, India, is the subject of a full case report to be published (87). Of relevance here is the statement by his older brother, Bipan Chand Kapoor, that Bishen Chand could, when he was a child, read Urdu (written in Arabic script) before he had been taught this language. Bishen Chand's father (in his statements about the case to Professor P. Pal) mentioned that Bishen Chand had (as a child) used some Urdu words that he could not have learned in his family. For example, he referred to the women's quarters of a house as "masurate" instead of by the usual word "zenana".† And he used the Urdu word "kopal" for a lock instead of the Hindi word "tala".

The previous personality of this case, Laxmi Narain, was moderately well educated and able to speak Urdu.

---

* Interested readers can find in the second edition of the book in which I reported the case of Swarnlata Mishra (86) transcripts of Swarnlata's Bengali songs and (for two of them) of the original poems by Tagore from which they derived.

† "Zenana" is probably ultimately of Persian origin. It is also found in Urdu, but has been taken into Hindi.

THE CASE OF WIJANAMA ARIYAWANSA: This Sinhalese boy was born on August 28, 1959, in the village of Wehigala, about fifteen miles north of Kandy, Sri Lanka. His parents and all other inhabitants of his village were Buddhists. From the age of about four and a half, Wijanama talked of a previous life in which he claimed to have had circumstances and habits very different from those of his family. For example, the previous family ate meat; there was electricity in the house (not available in Wehigala); water came in a pipe (not from a well or stream); firewood was brought to the house by a vendor; the house was on a street with asphalt pavement; and the previous family worshiped in a house with a well in it and no idols. Wijanama said he had a mother in Kandy and expressed a strong desire to go there and see her. He had a number of habits of eating and dress that are characteristic of Muslims but not practiced by the Sinhalese. From the description of the previous life given by Wijanama and the unusual traits in his behavior it has been reasonable to conjecture that the life he seems to have remembered was that of a schoolboy in a Muslim family of Kandy. Unfortunately, Wijanama did not give sufficient proper names to permit an identification of a corresponding previous personality among Kandyan Muslims. There were no Muslims in the village or surrounding area of Wehigala who could have influenced Wijanama's behavior in the direction of identification with a Muslim.

For the present topic, the most remarkable feature of the case is the habit shown by Wijanama from a very early age of sitting up on his bed at night, crossing his legs, and muttering words in a strange language. After muttering these words for about five minutes, he lay down and went to sleep again. He began this practice when he was about three and a half, that is, before he had actually begun to mention specific details of the previous life. He had continued the habit up to 1970 when I last saw him, at which time he was eleven years old. Wijanama had also sometimes used words that were incomprehensible to his parents during waking hours, but his most abundant use of unfamiliar language came in those five-minute nocturnal periods of posturing with legs crossed on the bed.

In November, 1970, I was able to obtain a tape recording of Wijanama's nocturnal utterances. Mr. T. S. Miskin, a member of the Muslim community of Kandy, listened to the tape recording and identified two of the words as "umma" and "vappa". These are corrupted Tamil words used by Kandyan Muslims for "mother" and "father". On the tape recording one can also hear Wijanama saying "Allaha", the Arabic word for "God". A fourth word "thunga" (to give its best representation with the English alphabet) has not been identified. Wijanama repeated the words several times during the mutterings, which apparently consisted of a kind of call to his (previous) parents and God. Mr. Miskin was particularly impressed by Wijanama's pronunciation of the words which he recognized and he stated that only a Muslim child could have pronounced them so well.

Wijanama also used another word unfamiliar to his parents and which they had never heard used in Wehigala. At mealtimes when asked if he had had enough to eat, Wijanama would reply (if he had had) by saying "podung". This is a Tamil word used by Kandyan Muslims which means "enough" in English. The Kandyan Muslims use the word in exactly the way Wijanama used it, namely to indicate that they have had enough food. The corresponding Sinhalese word is "hari" which is perhaps best translated by the English word "right".

THE CASE OF NAWAL DAW: Nawal Daw was a Lebanese girl (born April 25, 1960) whose case I studied in 1969. She lived in the village of Kabr Shmun. Her parents stated that when very young she showed behavior suggesting memories of a previous life in India. She was, for example, intensely fond of Indian music and showed a preference for Indian styles of dress. But the feature of the case relevant here was Nawal Daw's speaking of a language completely unknown to her parents. At the same time she refused to learn Arabic, which she did not really speak properly until she was five years old.

When she was four years old Nawal's parents took her to a popular tourist center in Lebanon. Some persons dressed in Indian garments were there and Nawal ran over to them with enthusiasm and began to speak her language with them. They replied in their language, and they seemed to be understanding each other. Unfortunately, Nawal's parents did not understand the language (and the Indians did not speak Arabic) so they could not communicate effectively with each other. Nawal did not wish to leave the Indians and eventually her parents were obliged more or less to tear her from them. Afterwards, she became ill and lost weight for a time.

Nawal probably spoke in considerable detail about the previous life she seemed to be remembering, but as she always spoke (until about five) in the language unknown to her parents, they did not understand what she was saying. They tried to make her forget about the previous life and she seems gradually to have done so. She discontinued using the language she spoke earlier and learned Arabic.

Unfortunately, I reached this case too late. In March, 1969, Nawal was nine years old and had ceased to speak the strange language she had spoken up to the age of about five. Her parents had described one of the Indian persons Nawal had talked with at the tourist center (at the age of four) as wearing a turban and a rolled-up beard. From this I inferred that he was a Sikh and therefore that the language Nawal had spoken with him was either Punjabi or Hindi. Miss Rajni Chona (a native of Delhi then resident with her family in Beirut), who could speak both these languages, accompanied me to Kabr Shmun and tried to speak Punjabi and Hindi with Nawal. She gave no signs of understanding either language.

I think it worth emphasizing that Nawal Daw not only spoke a strange language, but refused to learn Arabic, the language of her parents, up to the age of five.

We cannot now know whether Nawal Daw did in fact at one time speak another real language such as Hindi or Punjabi. She may have been speaking only a private language or gibberish. But her case differed in two particulars from that of the Kluge triplets who *did* speak a private language. First, Nawal Daw resisted learning Arabic, but the Kluge triplets learned and spoke Norwegian with other people and only spoke their private language among themselves. And secondly, we have the reports of Nawal Daw's parents that she seemed to engage in a responsive and intelligible exchange with the foreign visitors, evidently from India, whom they encountered at the tourist center.

THE CASE OF KUMKUM VERMA: Kumkum Verma lived in the village of Bahera, Bihar, India. She remembered a previous life as a person of lower caste who lived in the nearby city of Darbhanga. A full report of her case will be published later (87). Of relevance here is the report by Kumkum's father, B. K. Verma, that Kumkum (when a small child) spoke with an accent characteristic of some of the residents of Darbhanga but not of the villagers outside the city. Kumkum also used several phrases characteristic of the city people of Darbhanga but not used in her family. The language spoken in northern Bihar is Maithili (a dialect of Bihari, a language of the Indo-European group). The accent of the lower class people of Darbhanga has been considerably modified by association with Urdu-speaking Muslims of the city.

THE CASE OF VIVIANE SILVINO: The subject of this case was a girl born in São Paulo, Brazil, on March 20, 1963. Senhor Hernani G. Andrade sent me a detailed report of the case in 1970. Subsequently I was able to meet Viviane and her mother in Santos, Brazil, in February, 1972.

Between the ages of one and six Viviane talked about a previous life which she said she had lived in Rome, Italy. She stated a number of details and the names of some friends, but was unable to give the name of the previous family or its address beyond saying that they lived near the Forum. Attempts to trace a family in Rome corresponding to her statements have been unsuccessful.

Of relevance here is the fact that Viviane, during the period when she was talking about the previous life, used about a dozen Italian words and short phrases. Viviane's grandmother made notes at the time of her statements relating to the previous life and of the Italian words she used. Senhor Andrade obtained copies of these notes for me. They provide evidence not only of Viviane's use of Italian words, but of her correct application of them to the occasions when she used them.

Viviane's maternal great-grandfather emigrated from Italy to Brazil and he spoke Italian. Another maternal great-grandparent, who was born in Brazil, had later learned to speak Italian. Both these persons, however, had died before Viviane was born. Her parents and grandparents did not speak Italian or con-sciously know more than a few words and phrases of it. They had to use an Italian–Portuguese dictionary in order to identify correctly and understand some of the Italian words Viviane spoke.

From the information furnished me both in my own interview with Viviane's mother and from the earlier inquiries of Senhor Andrade I am convinced that Viviane had no opportunity to hear Italian spoken at the time she herself used Italian words. I learned, however, that Viviane's mother, who was an amateur spiritualist medium, had on four or five occasions spoken Italian when in a trance. Moreover, she retained conscious knowledge of a short Italian song which she repeated in my presence. She would also have had opportunities for hearing her grandparents speak Italian when she was a child. It is possible, therefore, that she had a considerable, if largely subconscious, knowledge of Italian. This offers the possibility that Viviane somehow, perhaps by telepathy, obtained her know-ledge of a number of Italian words from her mother.

Xenoglossies occurring during hypnotic regression

Claims have occasionally been made that hypnotized and regressed subjects spoke languages unknown to them in their ordinary states of consciousness. The earliest case of this type known to me is that reported
by Denis (22). An amateur "magnetizer" (hypnotist), Prince Galitzin,
in 1862 hypnotized an ignorant and impoverished German woman
in Homburg (Hesse, Germany). To the surprise of the hypnotist and
other persons present, the woman began to speak French very well and
narrated details of a previous life (in the eighteenth century) in which
she was a chatelaine in Brittany who, having found a new lover, got rid
of her husband by throwing him over a cliff. In the hypnotized and
regressed state the subject attributed her present incarnation in circumstances of poverty to punishment for this crime. The report by Denis
states that Galitzin later verified in Brittany the woman's account of this
previous life. Of more importance for our present topic is the investigation by Galitzin of the subject's previous acquaintance with French.
He found that she was quite uneducated and in her normal state knew
only the German dialect she ordinarily spoke. In considering this case
one regrets not having a fuller documentation of the linguistic
features.

Rodney reported the case of a woman in England who, during
hypnosis and ostensibly regressed to a life in late eighteenth-century
France, responded to him in French (72). She answered in French questions
put to her in English. Rodney gave some actual French phrases spoken
by the subject. The range of French seems quite limited, but a definite
responsive exchange was reported. The subject did not understand any
French in her ordinary waking state and claimed never to have learned
it normally. The case had the additional feature that the subject gave
correctly the name (and approximate location) of a street in Paris which
existed at the time of the French Revolution, but not at the time of the
experiments. In this case also, one regrets not having a fuller documentation of the extent of the subject's ability to speak French and of the
evidence that she had not in fact learned French normally.

Xenoglossies of possible telepathic provenance

In considering a case of genuine responsive xenoglossy (such as I believe
the main case of this monograph to be), one of the most important
hypotheses to be considered is that of a telepathic communication of the
foreign language to the subject from some living person who knows the
language. Instances providing evidence of the telepathic communication

of foreign languages are extremely rare, but the following cases seem to me examples that we should take seriously.

In the first example two mediums participated, one of them being Mme Berthe Bricout, whom I have already mentioned in citing her experiences in xenography. The experiment I shall now describe took place in 1932 and was reported by Dumas in 1950 (26). M. Jacques Brossy, who was Mme Bricout's principal sitter, proposed to her control that he communicate a message on some topic or other through Mme Bricout (in French) and at the same time endeavor to have the same or a very similar message communicated through an English medium (choosing one unknown to the French group) and in English. M. Brossy did not suggest a particular topic, leaving that selection to the communicator. He told Mme Bricout's (French) communicator that the English medium should send her script to the Editor of *Light*. Not long afterward, Mme Bricout communicated a message in French which seemed perhaps relevant to this test. Within the same month, an English medium, Elsie Grasser, reported to the Editor of *Light* a message she had received, accompanied by the impression that she should send it to *Light*. Her communication (in English) was less than half the length of the French one received by Mme Bricout. A comparison of the two messages shows not only a similarity of topic, but a quite close resemblance in the ways of handling the subject, including even the use in some places of similar phrases and figures of speech. The messages are not literal translations of each other (which, incidentally, Mme Bricout's control said he could not accomplish), but they show a remarkable correspondence which, considering the temporal coincidence of the occurrence in mediums quite unknown to each other in two countries, goes far beyond chance matching. If this be accepted, and I think anyone with a knowledge of French and English who compares the two scripts will do so, then we have an instance in which someone seems to have impressed the same thoughts on both an English and a French medium at about the same time; each medium then reproduced the message in her own language. Ostensibly, Mme Bricout's control (purportedly a discarnate spirit) thought up the message and then got it into the mind of Mme Bricout, who received it through the working of a planchette. The control then communicated the same message to the English medium, Elsie Grasser, together with the instructions (which she obeyed with apparent reluctance) to send it to the Editor of *Light*.

The case may also be interpreted, however, as one of telepathy between Mme Bricout and Elsie Grasser. Mme Bricout knew no English, but M. Brossy knew English at the time. But even if he had not, we have other evidence that telepathy is supralingual. Such evidence comes from the experiments of Rao who used targets in Telugu in successful experiments with English-speaking subjects (68). Also some of Mrs. Craig Sinclair's experiments (81) showed that meanings or associated ideas can be communicated when the form of the target is not. (The reverse can also occur.) It is therefore conceivable that the ideas in Mme Bricout's mind were somehow telepathically communicated to Elsie Grasser and in her mind transposed into English and then written down without the intermediary of any discarnate spirit or other person.*

A case of xenoglossy reported from Holland showed the apparent paranormal transmission of a foreign language from a living communicator (90). A Dutch spiritualistic circle unexpectedly obtained a communication in English of a few fragmentary phrases and then a (slightly distorted) English two-stanza poem. Two members of the circle had once learned English, but had not kept it up. The others (including the woman who was the presumed medium of the group) knew no English. (Someone in the group seems, however, to have responded in English.) The group learned later that on the night of the sitting at which this communication was received (and at the same time) a fifteen-year-old boy (in a house across the street) had been reading the communicated poem (in English) in a book which he had formerly studied at school.

This case deserves careful study. It is open to several interpretations. Of these, clairvoyance from the medium (reading the boy's book paranormally over his shoulder, so to speak) seems a less probable correct explanation than that the boy, who was dozing at the time, acted as a living communicator and controlled the medium for the period of the very brief and fragmentary English conversation and the transmission of the poem. This second explanation accords with the fact that the communicator interjected a comment "First part" at the end of the first stanza of the poem, and also with the fact that the boy had intensely wished to attend the séance (which he knew about), but had not been permitted to do so.

Relevant to later discussions in this monograph is the fact that the communication was received through a ouija board so it would seem that a telepathically received message induced (in the medium) a motor effect.

Two instances of possible telepathic xenoglossy were reported to me (in 1970) by Thubten Norbu, formerly head of a Tibetan monastery and

---

* Both the telepathic hypothesis and the spirit hypothesis of this case leave many questions unanswered. The case seemed so important to me that many years later I tried to trace Elsie Grasser, but without success. She had never sent her address to the Editor of *Light*. I wanted to ask her what she could remember about her experiences during the communication she had received and whether, for example, she had experienced any French "atmosphere" at the time or had any impressions of actual French words intruding in the communication. Another point of interest was why Elsie Grasser of all possible English mediums was "selected" to participate in this experiment.

later a teacher of Tibetan language, history, and civilization at the University of Indiana in Bloomington. At his home there he had American neighbors with small children. On two occasions these children, aged about two and a half or three years, used quite distinctly Tibetan words in his presence and that of his mother, who was staying with him. One of the children did this with him and one with his mother.

Thubten Norbu was quite certain the words spoken by the American children were Tibetan words. Each child used not more than two or three Tibetan words. The words used were appropriate in the conversation at the time. One was the Tibetan word for "to eat" and another was the Tibetan word for "kitchen". He was impressed by the fact that one of the American children used the "polite" form of a Tibetan word he (the child) pronounced.

The children could not understand Tibetan when it was spoken to them by Thubten Norbu or his mother. Since the words were appropriate for the conversation at the time, one possible explanation of these episodes is that the children reached into the minds of the Tibetan persons, so to speak, and pulled out Tibetan words which were near or at the surface of their minds.

Guirdham reported another instance of minor domestic xenoglossy (35). A mother, an Englishwoman, was running a line from the poem "Lorelei" through her mind. She was thinking of the line in German and not singing it aloud. As she was doing this, her youngest daughter walked into the room and asked her "out of the blue" to sing her a song about a mermaid.* The mother said that so far as she knew the child had not heard the song at any time and knew no German. She herself denied knowing the English words of the German poem.

---

* "Lorelei" by Heinrich Heine recounts the legend of the siren or mermaid whose distracting charms caused shipwrecks at a turn in the River Rhine.

II Case Report

I REPORT the following case because I believe that it provides an example of genuine responsive xenoglossy. I think it almost certain that the medium could not have learned Swedish, the foreign language concerned, by normal means. Yet under hypnosis she underwent a transformation to a male personality which called itself Jensen and which spoke and understood Swedish in an intelligible way.* This personality was not merely reciting meaningless phrases: there was exchange of meaningful phrases with Swedish-speaking persons.

Summary of the experiments and investigation of the case

The experiments with hypnosis during which the Jensen personality emerged were conducted in 1955–56 by a physician whom I shall call K.E. The subject, or medium, of the experiments was his wife and I shall refer to her as T.E.† I heard of the experiments and began investigating the case in 1958. Most of my investigations of the background of the subject and of the linguistic aspects took place in the following six years, but I have continued to consider the case and add whatever additional information I could obtain up to the time of the publication of this report. My investigation included extensive interviews with K.E., T.E., their oldest daughter, and three members of T.E.'s childhood family. I also interviewed three members of K.E.'s family who had lived with or near K.E. and T.E. during part of the 1940's and who, when not

---

* It will be important and helpful for the reader to keep in mind as he reads further that the subject of the experiments is a woman, while the manifesting personality, which called itself Jensen, is male.

† K.E. and T.E. requested that they not be identified publicly in this report. Their stated reason for this request was a wish to avoid any intrusion on their lives from casual inquirers and unauthorized investigators and journalists. They never said anything suggestive of doubts about the authenticity of the case, and their behavior never suggested this to me during my frequent personal visits with them. I have no reason to question their stated reason for wishing to remain anonymous. K.E. read and approved as accurate an earlier draft of this report which did not differ from the final revision in the presentation of any of the main facts of the case. In later revisions I have added only some additional possibly verifying information and some evaluative and interpretive comments based on further consideration of the case. K.E. died on March 21, 1970.

living in the house, had had a close association with T.E. between 1940 and 1956. I also interviewed Dr. John Cordone (pseudonym), who acted as hypnotist for one of the early sessions at which the Jensen personality manifested.

I myself attended one session at which the subject, while under hypnosis, was questioned about her knowledge of Swedish. (I also attended some later sessions at which more conventional mediumistic communications occurred, but which are, for the most part, not relevant to the present case.) I have gathered additional testimony by correspondence from seven other witnesses to various aspects of the case.

I administered the Modern Language Aptitude Test to T.E. and two psychological tests to both K.E. and T.E. I witnessed one of the two polygraph tests for lie detection administered in New York to both K.E. and T.E.

Altogether I spent more than fifty hours in the company of K.E. and T.E., most of this time being occupied with inquiries into the circumstances of the case and the relationships and motives of K.E. and his wife, the subject.

I also interviewed and corresponded with Dr. Nils Sahlin and Mr. Oscar Sunday concerning their roles as Swedish-speaking persons in the experiments. After a review of the four tape-recorded sessions having most material relevant to the study of the case, I decided that verbatim transcripts of these sessions would enable me to make more definite statements about the language spoken by the Swedish personality. Mrs. Eva Hellström then provided me with these transcripts which she and Mr. Rolf Ejvegård annotated.*

Later Mr. W. G. Roll and Dr. Nils Jacobson, who both speak Scandinavian languages, studied the linguistic (and some other) aspects of the case still further and made comments for use in this report.

Relevant history of the subject

The subject T.E. was (at the time of the experiments) a thirty-seven-year-old housewife of Jewish parentage. She was born and grew up in Philadelphia. Her father was born in Odessa, Russia, and emigrated to the United States in 1908, when he was about twenty years old. Her mother was also born in Odessa and emigrated to the United States when she was about eighteen years old. Neither of her parents had ever

---

* The tape recordings of the experimental sessions and the transcripts and notes of the sessions will be loaned to qualified investigators who wish to study the linguistic details of the case. A complete transcript of the Swedish spoken during session seven is given in the Appendix.

been to Scandinavia or knew intimately anyone who could speak any Scandinavian language. They raised their family in a neighborhood of South Philadelphia among English-speaking persons, although many of these were first- and second-generation immigrants from Central and Eastern Europe. In their family they spoke English almost exclusively. Sometimes Polish, Yiddish, and Russian were spoken by the parents in the family, but never any Scandinavian language. In high school the subject had received some instruction in French, but none whatever in any Scandinavian language or any other foreign language. At the high school she attended only French, Spanish, and Latin were taught.

The personality capable of speaking Swedish developed unexpectedly in the course of hypnotic experiments with T.E. She was found to be an excellent hypnotic subject, but had not previously shown any evidence of mediumistic abilities. Subsequent to the experiments reported here, further hypnotic experiments led to the appearance of other communicators of a more conventional mediumistic type.

Summary of sessions at which the Jensen personality communicated

The hypnotist of these experiments (K.E.), a physician in general practice in Philadelphia, had employed hypnosis in his medical practice from time to time for less than two years prior to 1956. He also occasionally engaged in domestic experiments with hypnosis. In the course of these he discovered that his wife, T.E., could enter deep trances readily, and he began more systematic experimentation with her. He attempted age regression with T.E. On one occasion when he was "taking her back", she visualized a scene with water and old people walking into it, seemingly being forced to enter the water and drowning. She felt she was being pushed down into the water, let out a scream, and clutched her head as if she had been hit by a heavy object. A severe head pain persisted and the subject was brought out of hypnosis. Following this session, T.E. complained of headache for two days and kept feeling the top of her head for an imagined lump there. Otherwise she seemed to have no residual effects.

A week later, K.E. again attempted to regress the subject and the same severe head pain with screaming and clutching of her head resulted. The same experience occurred on a third attempt the following week. On a fourth attempt a month later, before the head pain began, the hypnotist* gave the subject the instruction, "You are ten years younger than that". This attempt to bypass the pain seemed to succeed and the subject

---

* The hypnotist for this session only was Dr. John Cordone (pseudonym). For all other sessions, K.E. was the hypnotist.

unexpectedly said, "I am a man". Upon inquiry, he gave his name as "Jensen Jacoby" (pronounced "Yen'sen Yah'-ko-bee") and then described briefly his life as a peasant farmer. During this session (and subsequent ones) Jensen* spoke in a deep, masculine voice. He used broken English and interjected some foreign words which were thought to be in some Scandinavian language. In fact, Jensen did utter two Swedish phrases later identified clearly from the tape recordings. At these earlier sessions, i.e., sessions one through five, no person (other than the subject) able to speak Swedish or any other Scandinavian language was present. At the sixth session and the subsequent two sessions, some person or persons able to speak Swedish and other Scandinavian languages were present. All sessions from the fourth on were tape recorded, with the exception of the eighth, at which detailed notes were taken. T.E. did not hear the tapes at any time during the period of sessions with Jensen. Altogether, eight sessions at which Jensen communicated were held during 1955–56.

At the sixth, seventh, and eighth sessions Jensen communicated almost exclusively in Swedish. (I shall comment further on the language spoken by Jensen in a later section.) Session seven, which is the most important with regard to the evidence of a responsive xenoglossy, and session eight both took place in March, 1956.

Jensen could understand and reply to English, although he replied more quickly if spoken to in Swedish. He himself spoke some English with a rather heavy accent and in a halting manner. He spoke more readily in the Swedish language, and when asked questions in English would often reply in Swedish.

K.E. found that he could suggest to Jensen that he recall himself at different ages and Jensen responded appropriately to these suggestions of age regression and progression. On one occasion, K.E. suggested to Jensen that he recall his existence prior to that of Jensen, but Jensen would not regress behind his "present" life.

Following one session, after the normal personality of T.E. had been restored, she was lying alone resting while the experimenters conferred in another room. She spontaneously relapsed partially into the trance; Jensen again appeared and had to be dismissed once more. Moreover, during the period of these sessions, T.E. seemed to become somewhat tense and much preoccupied with inner thoughts. Her attention to

---

* From this point on in this report I shall refer to the manifesting personality of the hypnotic sessions as Jensen rather than as "Jensen" or "the alleged Jensen", etc. I am also going to use the name Jensen in considering an actual person whose life might correspond with the statements of the communicating personality. This usage will be more convenient, but readers are asked to remember that it does not imply prejudgment of the central question of this investigation, which is: Did a person called Jensen live, die, and subsequently manifest at these sessions? Or alternatively, is the personality Jensen merely a dramatization of aspects of the subject's subconscious mind?

external stimuli became diminished. Although she had complete amnesia for the events of the sessions at which Jensen communicated, these developments nevertheless aroused some concern about a permanent "possession" or other transformation of personality and led to the abandonment of attempts to evoke Jensen. After a period of about two years without further experiments, they were resumed. Jensen, however, was not called for and other communicators have since presented themselves and dominated the mediumship.

The personality of Jensen and the content of his principal communications

The personality of Jensen, even when most fully manifested in the later sessions, usually spoke with some effort and never attained fluency in speaking. Nevertheless, he did engage in sensible verbal exchanges during which he eventually communicated considerable information about himself and the life he led.

Jensen exhibited a "simple" personality harmonious with the peasant life he described for himself. He seemed to have little knowledge of his country beyond his own village and the trading center he visited. He had heard of English sailors landing on the shore and running from their ships. He had heard of Russia and shared the common fear of Russians in Scandinavia. Apart from these scant references to international affairs, Jensen spoke only of the narrow round of life in his village, composed of hard work and simple sensuous diversions.

According to Jensen's account of himself, he lived in a place called Mörby Hagar (or Harger). This seems to have been his name for the place where his house was, evidently a tiny village at most. It seems to have been not far from the residence of Jensen's chief, Hansen. And "Hansen" seems also to have been the name of the chief's place. Some distance away—a day or two by horse—there was a town with a harbor called Haverö. Here Jensen took his produce for sale. Jensen also referred at times to another neighboring community he called Torohaven.

Jensen was a peasant farmer who raised cows, horses, goats, and chickens. His diet included goat's cheese, bread, milk, salmon, and "brännvin" (Scandinavian spirits). He drank mare's milk. Jensen had a wife named Latvia, but no children. His wife made poppy-seed juice and poppy-seed cakes which he drank and ate. He built his own stone house himself. His farm seems to have been a portion of his parents' homestead. He was one of three sons of his parents. He gave his father's name as Hans and his mother's (indistinctly) as Lotte. He said his mother was Norwegian and that she had run away from Norway, but he did not give his father's national origin.

Jensen prayed to Christ, but also worshiped, or at least venerated, a "ruler" called Hansen. The latter may have been a local hero or chief. Several times Jensen described Hansen as "förste man" (first man or chief).

Jensen hunted bears. For diversion, he enjoyed playing games, drinking in the village tavern, and consorting there with women.

In one session Jensen relived an incident occurring when he was sixty-two which culminated in the headache previously noted in T.E. and which may have accounted for it. Engaged in some kind of a fight with enemies, he waded into water (or was pushed into it) and then received a blow on the head which seems to have killed him, but not before inflicting the terrible pain which the subject communicated in the screaming of the earlier sessions when she first experienced this severe headache. Jensen showed an intense dislike of war. He delivered most of his answers to questions in a rather quiet voice with, as mentioned earlier, some signs of effort and hesitation. But when an interpreter touched upon the subject of war, Jensen fairly shouted his disapproval. "War! War! Wars should be abolished." On another occasion, he said, "War takes money." Jensen also showed strong emotion in referring to his hero or chief, Hansen, the speaking of whose name he once accompanied by beating his own chest repeatedly and vigorously with both fists. As he did this he shouted, "Yo Hansen" over and over again. (He might have been shouting "Johansen", a Scandinavian name.)

In session seven, when Jensen's eyes were open, a number of objects and pictures were shown to him which he was asked to identify. Some of the objects were borrowed from the American Swedish Historical Museum in Philadelphia. When shown a model of a Swedish seventeenth-century ship, he immediately called it by the correct name in Swedish: "skuta", possibly with a Norwegian ending, i.e., "skute".

He also recognized and named a Scandinavian wooden container used for measuring grain. When shown a child's bow and arrow, he contemptuously discarded it. But he sighted the arrow in the bow as if completely familiar with its use as a weapon. He correctly named as "seed" in Swedish some poppy seed shown him.

When shown a picture of a wolf, Jensen called this animal by its correct name in Swedish. When shown a sword, he withdrew in revulsion, saying he hated war. He did not recognize or know the uses of modern tools, such as pliers, when these were shown to him.

He preferred to reckon time in "moons" rather than in weeks or years.

The mental state of the Jensen personality

The Jensen personality showed a tendency to sluggish responses. He complained of being tired and sighed deeply rather often. He rarely responded in full sentences, and when he did his sentences were short. He showed a marked tendency to perseveration, that is, to repeat words or phrases more or less automatically. The transcript given in the Appendix provides numerous examples of Jensen repeating a word or phrase almost as if to himself after the interviewers have moved on to some other topic. Jensen seemed also to be preoccupied with a limited number of themes and tended to return to them when not otherwise pulled away. His mental state at times resembled that of a person with an organic brain syndrome such as a delirium (107) or in a state of complete exhaustion (95).

At other times, however, Jensen became much more animated and it would be quite inaccurate to think of the Jensen personality as a mere shell of a person. He showed strong emotion when seeing a picture of a horse, when talking about "förste man Hansen" or "Johansen" (whoever he was), and when talking about war. And the transcript (in the Appendix) does very poor justice to his marvelous representation of a drunk in an inn who is half trying to sing, half refusing to do so!

Where and when the Jensen personality may have lived

Jensen manifesting during the hypnotic sessions did not furnish much specific detail susceptible of verification. Assuming that Jensen lived before, he was obviously not a person of historical significance. I have not been able to trace anyone corresponding to the statements made by the communicating Jensen.

I have not even been able to trace the area in which Jensen claimed to have lived. "Hage" means in Swedish (and Norwegian) an enclosed field or meadows and I have translated "Mörby Hagar", the name Jensen gave to the hamlet where he lived, as "Mörby Meadows". Mr. Ejvegård has pointed out that "Harg" in old Swedish meant "holy place" and the syllable occurs not uncommonly in Swedish as part of old place names.

Places called "Mörby", "Harg", and "Häverö" exist today in Sweden north of Stockholm. Harg is not far from Häverö which is near the east coast. There is also a town called Haverö in the western part of Västernorrland county. It is inland, and on the River Ljungan. I do not think we can definitely identify any of these places with the names Jensen mentioned. I shall, however, offer later some conjectures about the identification of Jensen's Haverö.

I have located no village called Torohaven in Sweden. There is a village called Torhamn in Blekinge, in southern Sweden; since the Swedish word "hamn" is close to the English word "haven" it is possible to surmise that Jensen referred to this place, but one can go no further.

The name "Jacoby" is a name of Jewish people living in Sweden. Jewish people immigrated to Sweden irregularly from the seventeenth century onwards, but were required to become converts to Lutheranism. Jensen spoke in one session of praying, but did not say how. On another occasion he referred noncommittally to Christ and his "claim to save the world". He also spoke of pressures on the community to worship together in one place and his own preference for praying at home.

It has not been possible to identify Jensen's leader or "förste man": "Hansen" or "Johansen". Jensen exhibited a strong attachment to his "ruler" and became angry when the power and importance of this figure were challenged, and, as already mentioned, on one occasion he repeatedly shouted the phrase "Yo Hansen" or "Johansen" in a loud and exultant manner. Jensen's attachment to Hansen verged on worship, giving rise in the minds of some persons who have studied the material to the idea that Hansen was a religious figure of some kind. One might speculate from all these details that Jensen Jacoby had descended from Jewish immigrants to Sweden, but had become attracted to a residue of paganism in the area where he lived and was only partially converted to Christianity. However, Sweden was fully Christianized by 1050 A.D., and it is unlikely that paganism persisted much beyond the twelfth century except in a few isolated pockets.* It seems more probable that Jensen's "förste man Hansen" was a local chief or feudal noble who evoked a kind of religious awe and devotion from nearby peasants.

The names given by Jensen for his father, "Hans", and one brother, "Marty" (Martin), are plausible Swedish names. So is the name of the other brother, if it is taken to be "Fred".† The name Jensen gave clearly

---

* Authorities differ on the duration of the residual covert paganism after the official Christianization of Sweden. Thus Andersson (3) states that "paganism probably lingered on in remote parts of Sweden until well into the twelfth century". But Lauring (47) gives paganism a longer life. Speaking of the time of King Hans of Denmark (1481–1513), Lauring states: "Christianity was no longer a new thing on the farms, but older beliefs had not died out completely. Pilgrimages were still made to holy springs that in some cases still bore such heathen names as Balder's Well and Thor's Spring. Relics of ancient heathen cults were still to be observed at spring and harvest festivals and parish life bore the mark of ancient peasant-settlement beliefs that refused to disappear" (47, p. 124). These remarks could apply equally to southern Sweden, large portions of which were then controlled by Denmark.

† Most of the words used in the analysis of this case are heard distinctly enough on the tapes so that different auditors agree about their identity. Some obscure words can be identified from their contexts. Most other doubtful words have not been considered in the analysis of the case. However, the proper names given by Jensen cannot be identified from their context and sometimes are given indistinctly. For example, Jensen's utterance of his mother's name was heard by one auditor as "Marty", by another as "Lotte". On several occasions the name he gave one of his brothers was heard as "Frère" (French for "brother"), but Mr. Sunday heard this name as "Fred".

and repeatedly for his wife, "Latvia", is not recognized as a Swedish proper name. It is known only as the name of the Baltic country Latvia.

As already mentioned, Jensen recognized and correctly named poppy seed when some was shown to him. He described the making of a juice and an edible cake, apparently from poppy seed. Poppy seed has in fact been treated in these ways. The formal cultivation of poppies in Sweden dates only from recent times. Nevertheless, informal use in Sweden of poppy seeds in medicine and cooking dates back probably at least several centuries and therefore into Jensen's putative time. For example, a seventeenth-century medical herb book describes the use of five or six capsules of *Papaver rhoeas*, boiled in wine and drunk to aid in sleeping. This could well be Jensen's "poppy-seed juice". Another Swedish book describes the (probably old) usage of the mature seeds of *Papaver somniferum* in pastries; these could be Jensen's "poppy-seed cake".* Jensen also seemed to be familiar with flax.

The details of the life described by Jensen are in general entirely consistent with Swedish peasant life before the industrial revolution. A few possible exceptions deserve special discussion.

Jensen seemed to be familiar with potatoes, which were not known in Sweden until the 1720's, when they were introduced by Jonas Alströmer. Jensen referred to "Amerika", a name for the New World that became current in Sweden after the settling of New Sweden in Delaware in 1638. Jensen used the expression "Oslomannen" (meaning "the man from Oslo") correctly. The name Oslo was dropped (and Christiania substituted) after the town was burned in 1624. The city was renamed Oslo in 1925. However, it would still be possible and fitting to refer to someone from the area of Oslo as an "Osloman" after the name of the town had been changed in 1624.

Another possible anachronism occurred in Jensen's reply "hästkrafter" (horsepowers) when he was asked how he went to his trading town. The expression "hästkraft" in Swedish dates, as does "horsepower" in English, from the invention of engines. In England James Watt first used the term in the eighteenth century. Jensen, however, might have used the term facetiously as it often was used in modern times when people said they traveled by "horsepower".

---

* Jensen used words that sounded like "potty seed" or "batty seed', but from the context it appears almost certain that he was referring to poppy seed. When shown some he correctly used a Swedish word "frö" for "seed", although he did not identify the seed as poppy seed.

I am indebted to Dr. Nils Jacobson for information about the use of poppy seed in Sweden.

On the questions discussed above, Dr. Nils G. Sahlin furnished some comments which I print in full:

There were innumerable indications that Jensen was totally unacquainted with modern articles, tools, and exotic fruit. On the other hand, he showed immediate familiarity with articles and things dating back to and before the seventeenth century, many of which had existed in like form for centuries before that. While Jensen apparently understood modern Swedish and Norwegian without difficulty, he had no modern vocabulary, no words for things of exclusively modern date. His usage had a clearly Norwegian flavor, which in my opinion lies closer to the language of the Middle Ages than does Swedish. His apparent familiarity with Norwegian and such straws in the wind as his reference to "Oslomannen" at one point lead to the conclusion that he lived on the west coast [of Sweden] near but probably not in Norway.

With regard to some of the same points, Mr. W. G. Roll furnished the following comments:

If the Jensen personality is not a creation of the subject's imagination, but represents some discarnate entity or trace, what were its times, place, and origin? The Swedish interviewers referred to the personality as "Jens" and I think it can be assumed that the addition of "-en" to this common first name was made by the subject.* I also suspect that, being Jewish herself, the subject is responsible for the surname "Jacoby", or "Jakoby", since it is unlikely that "en bonde" (a peasant farmer) would be a Jew, and for the reference to such Jewish foods as poppy seed. The names Jacob and Jacobsen (or -son) are common Scandinavian names, but a person named "Jacoby" is likely to be Jewish. Jensen said he lived close to Haverö, a town with a market place, water, and boats, and that he ate salmon and mackerel. This would probably place it by the coast. There is a Haverö inland [in Västernorrland county] but it is more likely that Häverö is meant. Häverö is on the east coast, about sixty miles north of Stockholm and twenty miles south of Harg, which may be the "Harge" [Mörby Hagar or Harger] Jens also mentions. I did not find the "Mörby Hagar" Jens talks about, but there is a Mörbylånga [on the island of Öland] in South Sweden.

Jens' chief is "Hansen", who also is said to be his king. If we assume that here, too, "-en" has somehow been added in transmission, we do find a king by that name. King Hans who ruled Denmark and Norway (1481–1513) also inherited the Swedish crown but was able to assert that right only between 1497–1501. However, the peasants may have thought of him as the king, even when he held no power, since Sweden then, and for some years to come, had no king

---

* Mr. Lennart Ekman, an interpreter at session seven, has also suggested that the correct name of the Scandinavian personality ought to be "Jens" and not "Jensen". This personality, however, distinctly uses the word "Jensen" in a number of places when giving his name. I have spelled the name as I think it is best rendered according to the words heard on the tape recordings. As spelled this way "Jensen" is actually a Danish name. "Jönsson" would be the Swedish spelling of the related name in Sweden.

of her own. Jens(en) said there were boats from Hans(en) in Hävfrom Häverö and that, of course, could easily have been the case. However, King Hans, a native of flat Denmark, certainly did not live in the mountains as Jens(en) seems to say, though he may have crossed some in his march against Stockholm in 1497 at the head of his army of Danes and Saxon "lansquenets". When Jensen refers to fighting involving Germans and Russians, could he be thinking of Hans' campaign of which also a Russian attack on Sweden's Finnish possession was part?

There are in fact a number of places in Sweden and Norway called "Havrö" or something close to this. Mrs. Hellström and Mr. Ejvegård are inclined to think Jensen's use of this word unspecific and the word likely to have been applied to any harbor. They state: "Swedish 'ö' = 'island' in English. 'Havr-' can theoretically mean harbor, with the 'v' = 'b'. The word is close to Swedish 'hamn', English 'haven', German 'Hafen', and Old English 'Hæfen'."

Mr. Roll's suggestion that Jensen's chief Hansen may be King Hans of Denmark provides a plausible solution of this problem, all the more so when we read in Lauring (47) that King Hans was also called Johannes, a name extremely close to the name shouted by Jensen when praising his chief. It is important to note also that although King Hans only briefly controlled northern Sweden, large parts of southern Sweden remained under Danish control until 1658. This territory included Bohuslän, the area of present southwestern Sweden south of Oslo and formerly part of Norway.

Mr. Roll's proposal that Jensen's "Haverö" may refer to the Häverö in Stockholm county on the east coast north of Stockholm provides a difficulty in accounting for the Norwegian elements in his language. This feature of the language and the Norwegian origin of Jensen's mother are more easily understood if we locate Jensen, as Dr. Sahlin suggests, in southwestern Sweden. If then King Hans of Denmark is Jensen's "Hansen" he could have come from (beyond) the hills, but these do not really amount to mountains in southern Sweden.

The community of Haverö in Västernorrland county, mentioned above, has a claim to consideration also. The pronunciation of its name comes closer than that of any other proposed place to the way Jensen pronounced the town he mentioned. Haverö also is far enough west in Sweden to have been in an area of the country contested between Sweden and Norway. Four centuries or so ago the Norwegian influence there would still have been strong. Unfortunately, Haverö has a little river traffic, but is not a shipping place of any importance and would not (in all probability) qualify as the place to which a farmer would take his produce for trading, such as Jensen described.

Dr. Jacobson has offered still another suggestion about the location of Jensen's life. A Norwegian friend of his, Miss Inger Teigland, found a small place called Haver in Ostfold, on the east side of Oslofjord, about fifteen kilometers south of Oslo. Haver is traced back to the Middle Ages and its name has probably had its present form since the middle or end of the seventeenth century. The following fact about Haver is of interest in connection with this case. One Peder Hansen Litle (d. 1551) came to Norway from Denmark with the Bishop of Oslo, Hans Mule, for whom he worked. In 1536 Peder Hansen Litle obtained the important fief of Akershus and in 1545 the district of Follo, where the above-mentioned Haver is located, became incorporated in the fief of Akershus. Since Litle was the family name of this overlord, he was almost certainly known simply as Peder Hansen. If Haver dates back to the sixteenth century, then at that time it had a lord called Hansen and might therefore qualify to be the place to which Jensen referred.

Jensen's mention of salmon has some localizing value for the place where he lived since salmon are found only in south Sweden or in the extreme north of the country. They are also found in the Norwegian fjords.

Russia and Sweden fought wars in both the sixteenth and seventeenth centuries, so Jensen's fear of Russia and detestation of war (whether they are related items or not) have slight localizing value for dating his period. Also Jensen's mention of English sailors does not help here much. English ships traded in Swedish waters during these and earlier centuries and some English sailors might have "run from" ships at almost any time.

During session seven the interviewers showed Jensen a model of a seventeenth-century warship which had guns protruding from ports. Jensen recognized this as a ship used in war and indicated that the cannon were for shooting (see Appendix, p. 178). Since naval warships with guns mounted on lower decks and fired through ports did not come into use until the early sixteenth century we may regard Jensen's recognition of this ship model as an indication of the *earliest* period he is likely to have lived, i.e., around 1500, (Jensen's recognition of a potato (see Appendix, pp. 184, 211) actually makes the *earliest* date we can assign him later than the beginning of the sixteenth century and move it up towards the middle of the seventeenth century or even later.) His ignorance of tools and objects developed after the industrial revolution sets a limit to the *latest* period he is likely to have lived, i.e., around 1800.

It is not necessary to believe that Jensen lived all his life in one place. I have found it interesting to consider the possibility that he came to America as a settler in New Sweden. Sweden established a substantial colony on the banks of the Delaware River in the area between the present cities of Philadelphia, Chester, and Wilmington (12; 41; 42; 100). Most of the settlers were peasants (100). This settlement, founded in 1638, continued until 1655 under the sovereignty of Sweden. The colony was then captured by the Dutch, who in turn were replaced in control by the British in 1664. But Swedish settlers identified as such, and the Swedish language, persisted for a hundred years after the colony was no longer under the control of Sweden. Some Swedish immigrants, but in lessening numbers, continued to come to New Sweden in the two decades after 1664.

Names similar to those occurring in the Jensen material were associated with New Sweden. Thus the captain of one ship, the *Grip*, going out to New Sweden, was named Andreas Jöransson (42) and the secretary on another ship was named M. Johansson (41). The mate of the twelfth Swedish expedition to New Sweden (1655–56) was called Jacob Jansson (41). Various settlers were named Jansson (41). In a list of Swedish families in New Sweden in 1693 I found Joranssons and Johansons, but no Jensen. One Syman Jansen was a landowner in the parish of Kraenhoek or Crane Hook (part of the Swedish colony on the Delaware) in 1677–80 (28). Parishioners of the Crane Hook Swedish Lutheran Church in 1675 also included two Jansens, one Janss, and one Jannsen. All these names have no specific reference to New Sweden since obviously these persons all came from old Sweden. They show, however, that names similar to Jensen and Johansen were current in the settlement of New Sweden.

In a map of the Swedish settlements along the Delaware I found Jacobs Ö or Jacques Island and thought this might conceivably be related to the Jacoby mentioned by Jensen.

Several difficult details of the case might be accommodated by supposing that Jensen came out to New Sweden. For one thing, Jensen's mention of America would be more topical, although it is likely that even a simple peasant of sixteenth- or seventeenth-century Sweden would have heard of America. Secondly, the reference to potatoes would perhaps no longer be an anachronism. Potatoes were introduced into Virginia in the late seventeenth century and they were cultivated farther north at the same time or even earlier.* Rising, the Director of New Sweden at the time of its surrender to the Dutch (1655), mentioned potatoes in his description of the colony (71). Incidentally, this surrender of New Sweden to the Dutch might explain a reply Jensen made when asked if he knew about

---

* Jenson's references to "Amerika" occur on two occasions when he is asked where he has seen potatoes. Thus it seems an appropriate association for a life in New Sweden in the late seventeenth century, but potatoes would not have been seen in old Sweden before their introduction there in the 1720s, or at least not ones grown there. The reference to "Amerika" is doubtful, however, since when Jensen seems to be saying this word he may actually be saying "i marken" (in the ground) and on another occasion "från marken" (from the ground), and these phrases would be equally appropriate answers to the question about where he had seen potatoes. See the transcript in the Appendix, pp. 185, 211.

the Dutch. To this question he said: "Dutcherman, they are ruler."*
And finally, poppies were plentiful in the fields of the settlers in New
Sweden and were probably put to some use by them (29).

If Jensen spent some time in New Sweden this might account also for
his seeming to mention different places which he lived at or near, e.g.,
"Haverö", "Torohaven", and "Jacoby". A migrant Jensen might have
lived at or near one of these places in old Sweden and at one or more
others in New Sweden and then have mixed them up somewhat in his
memories.

Jensen might also have seen English sailors in New Sweden, especially
during the years 1664–74 when Holland and England struggled over their
colonies in North America which included New Sweden. English ships
were probing the Swedish and Dutch colonies for years before the
English finally ousted the Dutch in the area. We might even conjecture
that Jensen learned English in New Sweden after the English conquest
in the late seventeenth century.

The linguistic details (to be discussed in the next sections) contribute
some information relevant to the location of Jensen's life in time and
place. The language spoken by Jensen contained a strong admixture of
Norwegian in the Swedish. This blend could be due to (a) location of
Jensen's residence near the Swedish border with Norway, or even perhaps
within what is now Norway; or (b) Jensen's having a mother who came
from Norway and who would presumably have spoken much Norwegian
to him. It is also possible that (as Dr. Sahlin suggested) the Norwegian
elements in Jensen's language indicate an earlier period for his life than
seems likely from other evidence—namely, a period before the Scandinavian languages had fully differentiated from their common predecessor
Old Norse. This separation mainly took place between the tenth and
thirteenth centuries.

To sum up the facts considered in this section, I have been unable to
make any definite identification of person, place, or time for the life of
Jensen. With regard to time, Jensen's ignorance of modern tools and
expressions makes it out of the question that he lived after 1800. His
speaking a definitely modern Swedish makes it improbable that he lived
earlier than 1400 at the other extreme. A placement in the seventeenth
century seems most reasonable and accords with the largest number of
details. With regard to place, the facts seem most harmonious with the
supposition that Jensen was born and lived at first in southwestern
Sweden near the Norwegian border, perhaps in the area of the present
province of Bohuslän not far from the sea. (Or he may have lived in

---

* I have wondered, however, if what sounds like "Dutcherman" might have been intended
as "Deutsche Männer" with reference to German traders and raiders in the Baltic Sea.

southeastern Norway near Sweden.) If we add the further conjecture that Jensen came to New Sweden in the middle or latter part of the seventeenth century we can account harmoniously for some additional items. Such a life is consistent with all the details of the case and inconsistent with none. I do not claim that no other location of the time or place would fit the facts, but I do not know of any other that fits them so well.

The language spoken by the Jensen personality

The identification of the language

With regard to the identification of the language spoken by Jensen, I reprint statements from three Swedish-speaking persons who conversed with him during two different sessions at which he communicated.

I testify that Mrs. T.E. during a hypnotic trance in 1956, when manifesting a personality called Jensen, spoke an early form of Swedish with me.

Most remarkable to me was the medium's pronunciation of the words she used, whether ours or her own. She did not speak her Scandinavian as an American would. She had absolutely no difficulty with the umlaut sounds or other peculiarly Scandinavian sounds and accents. By and large she used the correct articles (attached to the noun in Scandinavian) and correct inflectional endings. Having taught Swedish, I know how difficult it is for an American even to repeat after the teacher the correct endings. She even made the proper elisions, such as "ja" (I) for "jag".

I was especially on the lookout for the medium's use of the very frequent English–Swedish cognates. But even when she used the word "lax" (salmon), she did not say "lochs", which would have been expected from a Jewish person; she said clearly "lax" as it is said in Scandinavian. Most convincing (and here the word was *not* given before she said it) was her identification of some poppy seeds. She was asked what it was and called it "frö"—not the cognate "säd" (seed) which really means grain in Scandinavian. She did not know what kind of "frö", had apparently never seen it before, but "frö" it was.

She did not use any German words, hence did not lean on any Yiddish she might know.

(*signed*) NILS G. SAHLIN

As a second interpreter here at this session [number seven], I have to say that the person talked Swedish so that I could understand it, and it was very evident that the language in question was Swedish with a little Norwegian in it.

(*signed*) LENNART EKMAN

I testify that Mrs. T.E., during a hypnotic trance when manifesting a personality called Jensen, spoke an early form of Swedish with me. This had considerable Norwegian and some Danish in it. When Jensen spoke I recognized his accent and vocabulary as somewhat resembling those of Norwegian. Accordingly, I changed my language and most of the time spoke Norwegian with him. I asked Jensen if he could say the word "seven" in Swedish. I said it plainly in Norwegian, and several times over. Jensen finally answered and said the word "seven" correctly. Only a native Swede can pronounce the word "seven" correctly. All other nationalities have to practice a great deal to learn it.

Swedish is my native language. I can also speak Norwegian. I had some difficulty in understanding the language Jensen spoke, and I needed help to translate my notes correctly.

(*signed*) OSCAR SUNDAY

To the foregoing testimony I can add that of Mrs. Hellström and Mr. Ejvegård who, from their study of copies of the original tape recordings (sent from the University of Virginia to Stockholm), have concluded that the Jensen personality exhibited a capacity to speak Swedish.

The period of the language

The Swedish-speaking persons who conversed with Jensen or examined tape recordings testify that he spoke in general a modern Swedish with considerable admixture of Norwegian. His lack of familiarity with modern names probably requires a dating earlier than 1800, as already mentioned. The inclusion of Norwegian words might be regarded as evidence of Jensen's having lived before the eighteenth century at a time when Swedish and Norwegian were closer linguistically than they were later. But the Norwegian admixture is more likely due to Jensen's having lived near Norway and/or to his having had a Norwegian mother.

With regard to the period of the language spoken by Jensen, Mr. Sunday stated: "The words used by Jensen were those of an early type, that of the Union period (1397–1523) provincial dialect."

Mr. Ekman commented:

The subject answered in a dialect that seemed to me sometimes more Norwegian than Swedish. Perhaps this impression of mine can be derived from the fact that the subject's choice of words appeared to be from about three hundred years ago. The opinion regarding the time period of Jensen's life—about three hundred years ago—is based mainly on the impression I got when talking to the subject and when showing her various objects of different age and geographical usage.

Evidence of a sensible conversation in Swedish

Of particular importance in cases of this kind is the evidence that the subject actually conversed responsively and sensibly with other persons in the foreign language and did not merely repeat material previously learned or picked up from the linguists as he went along. This is the crucial distinction between recitative xenoglossy and responsive xenoglossy already mentioned. In this connection we should notice the occurrence in the interviews of items of the following types:

1. Words and phrases first used by the subject.
2. Appropriate changes in the words or phrases repeated by the subject if he was applying them to himself; for example, appropriately changing "Did you hunt?" to "Did I hunt?" if he was checking what the interviewer had said.
3. Sensible replies to questions showing that they had been at least partially understood.

With regard to this last question, Dr. Sahlin provided the following statement:

I firmly believe that Jensen's responses, though most of them were in single words, indicated that he understood, for the most part, both Swedish and Norwegian. His answers were never ridiculous or nonsensical as they may well be even to leading questions, if the language is not understood. During the conversation I had with him, Jensen used a vocabulary of well over a hundred Swedish words. It is quite certain that some of these Jensen introduced into the conversation for the first time himself, although others he repeated (often with appropriate modifications) after I had first spoken them. Jensen did not speak any long sentences. He did, however, express some phrases such as the following: "Ja' ä' trött" (I am tired), and "Jensen har inga vänner" (Jensen has no friends).

The following is a partial list of words and expressions in Scandinavian (mostly Swedish) used by Jensen in session seven with obvious comprehension and sensible responses. Many were, of course, inevitably suggested or first used by the interlocutors (Dr. Sahlin and Mr. Ekman), but some were undeniably used by Jensen for the first time. With the list is the English translation of the word or phrase and, in most instances, a brief comment by Dr. Sahlin.

Scandinavian	English	Comment
jaa då, ja, ja	Why, of course	Typical stressed affirmative
en bonde	a farmer	Pronunciation not clear
ja-a	yes	Colloquial lengthening of "ja"
min vän	my friend	Spontaneous remark
i huset	in the house	Correct article appended
i Hansen	in Hansen	Place name
salt	salt	Obvious cognate, but correctly pronounced
ett stort by	a large town	Wrong gender, he should have said "en stor by". "By" is Norwegian for town, not Swedish

Scandinavian	English	Comment
Ja' ä' trött	I am tired	Spontaneous. One of the few full phrases used
Ja' kör	I drive	Pronounced "chur" as in "chur(ch)", but long
nej, ne-ej, nej!	no	Long when hesitating, as it should be
kornet	the grain	Correct article
Ja' sover	I am sleeping	Verb not previously mentioned
vin	wine	Correctly pronounced as "veen"
inga pengar	no money	Refusing invitation to go to bar to drink. "Pengar" previously used; "inga" spontaneous*
brännvin	brandy	Grimaced (properly), cleared his throat when he "drank"
stort glas	big glass	Suggested in question
hästen	the horse	
en kirk or körk	church	Indecisive. Norwegian dialect would be "kirke", pronounced "churke", but very doubtful
norsk	Norwegian	
ett lite'	a little	Not correct usage, but passable
Oslomannen	the man from Oslo	Pre-1624 usage? Oslo became Christiania at that date. See earlier comments on Oslo on p. 31
Ja' förstår Dem icke	I don't understand you	Good phrase, spontaneous, with Norwegian flavor
laxen	the salmon	Correct article attached, but probably repeated†
makrill	mackerel	Obvious cognate, but correctly used
timglas	hourglass	Probably suggested, but immediately recognized when shown the object
klädren (old Swedish)	clothes	Slightly irregular form‡
krige' (for kriget)	(the) war	When shown a sabre
ett djur	an animal	Spontaneous. Pronounced "yur"

---

* However, Jensen had previously spoken the ungrammatical phrase "nej pengar" and then heard the interpreter say "inga pengar" before he himself later spoke the correct phrase. See Appendix for details.

† Careful study of the transcripts shows that in fact Jensen was the first speaker to use the word "laxen". See the transcript in the Appendix. The word did not occur in sessions before session seven.

‡ Other auditors have not heard the "d" in Jensen's pronunciation of this word, which seems closer to Norwegian "klærne". (See the transcript in the Appendix, p. 140.)

Scandinavian	English	Comment
björnjakter	bear hunts	Spontaneous
O, ja, bra!	Oh, yes, fine!	Probably spontaneous
sticker	wood sticks or torch	Norwegian; used for illumination by Jensen who knew nothing of candles
brannte	burned	Vague form in connection with burning; Swedish is "brann". Jensen may have said "brand", putting an "e" at the end of the word as he often did
lur	birch horn	Did not recognize article shown, but amused; tried to blow it
vannet	the water	Norwegian
fjället	the mountain	Used correctly*
kagge	small keg†	
förste man Hansen	chief Hansen	

On the question of a sensible conversation, Mr. Ekman made the following statement:

I had the impression during the session, and I still feel (1962), that I received intelligible answers to my questions to the subject. The questions and answers were in Swedish. I do not recall that the subject ever asked any questions. The conversation was one-sided. Although the subject at times repeated some of my words, I am of the opinion that she appropriately selected her own words in her replies. I believe that the subject introduced many words and used them properly.

On the same question, Mr. Sunday stated:

I testify that the personality Jensen seemed to understand Swedish and Norwegian and to reply sensibly with words of his own to what I was saying. He replied promptly and seemed to have no difficulty in finding words to say what he wanted. He definitely used some words before I had myself used them in talking with him. The following English translation of a portion of the notes I took while

---

* Dr. Jacobson commented on Jensen's use of the word "fjället". It suggests a Norwegian location, for the word means a *high* mountain, not just an ordinary one. Hills in the south or southwest of Sweden would not be called "fjäll", although those in Norway and in the north of Sweden would. The only exception known to him is "Kroppefjäll" which is in western Sweden near the Norwegian border.

† Several of the words mentioned above by Dr. Sahlin are not heard on the recording transcribed in the Appendix. "Timglas", "kagge", and "lur" are among these. I believe Jensen must have spoken these words during a period when, judging by an interruption in the recording, the tape recorder was not recording, although the interview continued.

conversing with Jensen illustrates the basis for my impression that Jensen introduced words before I spoke them:*

I:	Describe how you spend the day.
Jensen:	We awaken in the house, then we have breakfast,† consisting of goat's cheese, bread, and milk.
I:	What do you do after that?
Jensen:	We start working.
I:	Tell us about the animals on the farm.
Jensen:	We have cows, chickens, and rabbits.
I:	Do you see anybody now?
Jensen:	Yes, I see a drunken man? [Was Jensen's father a drunkard?]

The hypnotist then instructed Jensen to "advance" in age and he was supposedly sixteen years old when the following exchange occurred:

I:	Jensen, where are you now?
Jensen:	We are on a visit to Torohaven.
I:	Who is with you?
Jensen:	Latvia, my wife! [This suggests that Jensen married very young, but the age may not have been fixed where the hypnotist thought it was.]
I:	Do you have many relatives?
Jensen:	Only Latvia, we have no children.
I:	Are you the only child?
Jensen:	I have two brothers.

*   *   *   *

I:	Jensen, let us go to the inn and have a drink.
Jensen:	But I have no money.

---

* I remind readers at this point that the session at which Mr. Sunday acted as interpreter was not tape recorded. At the time, Mr. Sunday made detailed notes in Norwegian of the exchange between himself and the Jensen personality. These he afterwards translated into English and I have reproduced a portion of this translation. However, since I do not have a verbatim transcription of this session, I do not cite this quotation as compelling evidence of responsive xenoglossy. The case for this rests mostly on the tape recordings and transcripts of the earlier sessions, chiefly the sixth and seventh sessions. Readers will notice also that in this extract Jensen seems to show greater fluency and uses more whole sentences than he does in session seven transcribed in the Appendix. Since session eight was not tape recorded we cannot say whether Jensen really did attain more fluency at this later session or whether the notes made afterwards only gave an appearance of greater fluency.

† A seemingly implausible order of events in starting the day. Most farmers even today and certainly in southern Sweden several hundred years ago would begin the day by feeding the stock and then having their own breakfasts. Jensen, however, was ostensibly regressed to age ten years in his life when he gave these responses. The children might have been given breakfast before working on the farm.

Dr. Jacobson furnished the following statement:

I have carefully listened to the tape of the seventh session with the Jensen personality and also read the transcripts. The subject does clearly show a considerable knowledge of Scandinavian languages in this interview. She seems able to understand and answer appropriately even rather complicated questions in Swedish, and even if she is often not able to give an answer, it seems clear that in most cases she does understand the question. Her answers contain a number of clearly Swedish words and a few short phrases with good pronunciation. In many cases, however, it is difficult to hear if the answer is a Swedish or a Norwegian word, and in other cases it is clearly Norwegian. If the subject had learned Swedish, her teacher must have also known and spoken Norwegian. Otherwise it seems impossible to explain the considerable mixture of Norwegian words in her speech.

To give readers further evidence of appropriate responses made by Jensen in Swedish to questions asked him in Swedish or English, some additional examples are listed below. Several of these examples occurred in session six and will therefore not be found in the transcript of session seven in the Appendix.

Further examples of appropriate responses by the Jensen personality

Questions spoken in Swedish	Response of subject in Swedish (with English translation)
What else do you eat besides salmon?	Makrill (mackerel)
Which animals do you like?	Björnjakter (pl. bear hunts)
What do you use for light in the house?	En brand (literally: a fire, but here meaning a torch)*
Where do you get water?	I fjället (on the mountain)
Where do you live?	I huset (in the house)
What have you to give me?	Kornet (grain)
How do you travel about?	Hästkrafte (horsepower)
What do you say to traders?	Jag förstår Dem icke (I do not understand you). A response made several times when Jensen did not understand the question put to him by the interpreter
How do you make clothes from skins?	Jag tørrer dem (I dry them). "Tørrer" is the Norwegian cognate of Swedish "torkar"
What kind of fish is this?	Älvfisk (river fish)
Can you make one like it?	Nej. Det är icke möjligt (No. That is not possible)

---

* Ward states that in New Sweden: "For lighting ... splints of resinous pine about three feet long were stuck into crevices ... and ignited" (100). Dr. Jacobson has learned and informed me that such pine torches were also used in (old) Sweden at the same period.

Questions spoken in Swedish	Response of subject in Swedish (with English translation)
See the children playing in the snow (Jensen with eyes open was looking at a picture)	Dom fryser (they feel cold)
Why have you no money?	Fattig (poor)
Who lives in the house with you?	Latvia (name of his wife)

Questions spoken in English	Response of subject in Swedish (with English translation)
What will you have to drink?	Brännvin (brandy)
Are you a big man or a little man?	Kort (short)
How do you ask for water?	Vannet (water)*
What do you do with this flax?	Klærne (clothes) (The question had also been put in Swedish before Jensen replied. "Klærne" is Norwegian)
What do you call the little boy and girl? (Asked as Jensen, with eyes open, was looking at a picture of children)	Børne (correct word for child in Danish or Norwegian without the final "e" given here, as often, by Jensen)

Familiarity with previous cases of this kind and the sources of error in investigating them led me to consider that the subject might have used appropriately in a later session phrases picked up in an earlier one. Such use might have given rise to an illusion of responsive xenoglossy when one had not occurred. A criticism of Richet's case (49) developed along this line. It was suggested that his subject had memorized a few phrases of rather wide applicability which she then applied to occasions when they happened (more or less accidentally) to fit the circumstances and therefore seemed like appropriate responses. Most of the material produced by Richet's subject was a xenography consisting of phrases written down as if from memory (69). She exchanged only a few Greek phrases with investigators, in comparison to the rather large number she wrote as if copying them. But these few phrases were disposed of, or at least challenged, by the critics of the case as offering only an appearance of meaningfulness.

Returning to the present case, there are then two aspects of the xenoglossy to be scrutinized carefully. First, we must be certain that throughout the sessions the subject introduced words and phrases for the first time and did not merely echo, more or less appropriately, phrases picked up in earlier sessions or earlier parts of the same session. Secondly,

---

* Jensen gave the Norwegian word for "water" instead of the Swedish "vatten". But "vannet" is also heard in southern Sweden (Skåne).

we must have assurances that the subject showed a reasonable number and range of new words and phrases. We must be sure she was not merely calling on a small stock of phrases, what someone has called the "small change" we all have of foreign languages, which is applied at random without actually understanding what is being said, but with a spurious appearance of engaging in a sensible conversation.

To settle these questions I arranged for complete transcripts of sessions four to seven to be made and asked Mrs. Hellström and Mr. Ejvegård in Stockholm to study thoroughly the transcripts and tape recordings of these sessions. There was no need to make transcripts of sessions one to three since they were introductory and no Swedish was spoken during them. From this study, Mrs. Hellström and Mr. Ejvegård concluded that the Jensen personality did exhibit a responsive xenoglossy; that is, the Jensen personality engaged in an appropriate, meaningful exchange in Swedish with the Swedish-speaking interviewers, Dr. Sahlin and Mr. Ekman, in session seven. In addition, Mr. Ejvegård made a summary of the phrases spoken by Jensen in this session and divided them as follows:

Incomprehensible words	38
Repetitions	34
Independent responses*	21
Inappropriate responses	21
Appropriate responses	56
Not an answer, but an appropriate remark	15

In the above categorization, Mr. Ejvegård did not include "ja" and "nej", simple affirmative or negative responses which were sometimes quite appropriate. The meaning and appropriateness of a number of the words and phrases were difficult to categorize.

Mr. Roll, who understands Scandinavian languages, studied the tape recording of session seven and has furnished the following comments:

I have been asked for my comments on the Jensen case of apparent xenoglossy of Norwegian and/or Swedish since I understand the languages. My remarks refer to the tape from the seventh interview with the subject and are mainly concerned with the question whether she knows Scandinavian, and not how such knowledge was obtained.

---

* These "independent responses" were utterances made by Jensen that the preceding remark or question by the interviewer apparently stimulated. Jensen's utterance was related to the question, but not an appropriate answer to the question itself. Nor was the response entirely inappropriate. So it seemed best to Mr. Ejvegård to categorize these utterances separately.

The interview consists of questions, mostly in Swedish, and the subject's replies. In assessing the latter I exclude responses which might have been repetitions of one or more words from preceding questions, as well as meaningless, though Scandinavian-sounding, utterances which were somewhat like words which might make sensible replies. It is possible, of course, that these utterances represent archaic usage or dialect. But I assume that such features would have been detected by the interviewer or the other language experts who analyzed the tapes.

Another class of responses I disregard are words which might have been English coated with a Scandinavian accent: "makrill" (mackerel) and "sten" (stone) fall into this category. Similarly, a few of the questions put to the subject in Swedish, to which sensible replies were given, might be understood by a person who knows only English. This may be the case, for instance, with the questions, "vill (will) du (you) ha (have) det (this) här (here) svärdet (sword)?" and "var (was) det (it) starkt (strong) nog (enough)?" I assume that the only language the subject knows normally is English. If she is familiar with others, say German or Yiddish,* this might increase her ability to make up "Scandinavian" words and understand questions in Scandinavian languages.

When responses that fall into these classes are discounted, out of a total of about sixty, thirty-one intelligible words remain which are appropriate to the context of the interview. Some of them are used in grammatically complete sentences. Her vocabulary, however, is a mixture of Norwegian and Swedish, with the pronunciation on the Norwegian side.

These words were not learned in the course of the interview. They were not converted English terms, nor do I think they were random mumblings which by chance occasionally matched a Scandinavian word: the subject said comparatively little, the greater part of the tape consisting of questions and admonitions to her to get the conversation going. I conclude therefore that this subject knew at least thirty-one Scandinavian words at the time this tape was recorded and, what is more, knew how to pronounce them with a Scandinavian accent in which I found no trace of English. Since the particular questions asked during this session probably did not exhaust her vocabulary, it is likely to contain more words than those I heard.

The foregoing statements, in my opinion, provide ample evidence of a responsive exchange in Swedish between the Jensen personality and the persons with whom the subject was speaking.

To answer fully the question of possible acquisition of Swedish in early experimental sessions, I carefully studied the transcripts of sessions four to seven inclusive. It will be recalled that sessions one to three were exploratory sessions at which only the closing scene of Jensen's life (in

---

* As mentioned earlier, the subject had some exposure to Yiddish as a child when her parents sometimes spoke it. Yiddish, a language spoken by Jews in eastern Europe and America, is derived from fourteenth-century German into which elements from Hebrew, Polish, French, and (more recently) English have been blended. No other auditor of the recordings has suggested that Yiddish could have contributed to Jensen's Swedish and Dr. Sahlin (see above) specifically denied that it did.

which he was hit on the head) was revived. There was no Swedish spoken at these sessions. Transcripts were made of the next four sessions. At session four Jensen himself spoke two full Swedish phrases, but no one else did, there being no one else present at this or the next session who could speak Swedish with him. At session five Jensen spoke no Swedish, but simply reviewed and gave further information in English about his life and attitudes. In sessions six and seven, Swedish-speaking persons were present, and in these sessions, particularly the seventh, there was a considerable exchange of Swedish between Jensen and his interviewers. (Session eight, which was not tape recorded, will not be considered here since if Jensen learned Swedish from his interviewers he must have done so in sessions six and seven.) I therefore went through the transcripts of sessions four through seven and noted whenever Jensen spoke whether what he said someone else had said before him.*

In this analysis, I did not count (*a*) doubtful words; (*b*) words initially mispronounced by Jensen, correctly repeated by an interviewer and then correctly pronounced by Jensen; or (*c*) English cognates, e.g., "en körk" for "a church" (Scottish: "kirk"), "makrill" for "mackerel", and "trettio" for "thirty". These rules led to the discarding of many distinctly Scandinavian words undoubtedly used appropriately by Jensen. On this basis, however, Jensen introduced first into the conversation sixty words not previously used by his interviewers. Jensen's functional vocabulary in these sessions was considerably larger and is reckoned by Dr. Sahlin to have been more than a hundred in session seven in which he participated.†

---

* A small number of short gaps occur in the tape recordings. Sometimes voices in the background can be heard talking. In recording these sessions a microphone was moved around somewhat according to who was speaking at the time. Occasionally the microphone was not in front of the person talking. Although K.E. was certain that the Swedish-speaking interviewers did not talk Swedish to themselves in the presence of T.E. or Jensen, they did speak some Swedish to Jensen that was not recorded. Probably a portion of what Jensen said was similarly missed. The total amount of Swedish not recorded is small, and I believe that it can be disregarded in studying the case. Its only relevance in any case would be to the consideration of who said what first. Jensen's utterances of Swedish words not used before by the interviewers are too numerous and too appropriate to be accounted for by the hypothesis that they were spoken to him *sotto voce* in unrecorded passages, for gaps in which this might have occurred are too few and brief.

† The discrepancy between the counts of different students of the transcripts and tapes requires a brief explanation. Mr. Ejvegård included cognates in his counts of session seven and chiefly concerned himself with the responsive appropriateness of Jensen's utterances. Dr. Sahlin's allowance to Jensen of a vocabulary of "well over a hundred words" also includes Jensen's entire demonstrated vocabulary with cognates in session seven. Mr. Roll and I excluded cognates in our counts, although this sometimes proved a difficult task. Thus, in addition to the examples mentioned, "kornet" (grain) was rejected, but "brännvin" (brandy) was accepted. The above figure of sixty words for all four sessions includes the thirty-one words noted by Mr. Roll in session seven and another twenty-nine words which I counted in sessions four, five, and six. Words not acceptable to both Mr. Roll and myself were not included in the final count of words for session seven.

The Swedish accent of the Jensen personality

I have quoted above the testimony of Dr. Sahlin and Mr. Sunday to the excellence of the Swedish accent of the Jensen personality. Although having only copies of the original tapes to study, Mrs. Hellström and Mr. Ejvegård likewise confirmed the exhibition by Jensen of "a very good Swedish accent in some places", although in other places Jensen's accent had, in their opinion, a more American quality. Mr. Roll (who studied a tape recording of session seven) also commented on the excellence of the Swedish accent.

Dialect forms used by the Jensen personality

Dr. Folke Hedblom examined all the available tape recordings of the Jensen xenoglossy with a view to possible recognition of a specific dialect spoken by Jensen. In his opinion the Swedish spoken by the Jensen personality could not be identified with any definite Swedish dialect such as those of the extreme north or south (Skåne). It suggests rather a middle Swedish.

As already mentioned, Jensen's Swedish contained a number of Norwegian words and his accent sometimes went over to the Norwegian side when he used words that are cognates in the two languages. (But he did not seem to understand Norwegian as well as Swedish when it was spoken to him.) At times also Jensen used other dialect forms of which one good example is his use of "potäter" for "potatis".

Jensen's Swedish grammar was generally good, but not impeccable. From time to time he attached an article of the wrong gender to a noun. And he committed the solecism of saying "nej pengar" instead of "inga pengar" when he wanted to say he had "no money". This error is equivalent to a German saying "nein Geld" instead of "kein Geld".

The Jensen personality also had the habit of often adding a vowel sound at the end of many words with a terminal consonant. But Mr. Ejvegård does not think this in any way distinctive since a great many native speakers of Swedish add, or seem to add, a vowel sound at the end of words. Moreover, the definite article in Swedish consists most often of "-et" placed at the end of the noun. In many Swedish dialects the final "t" of this suffix is not pronounced. Thus Jensen's sounding of "Brännvine" could be a dialect way of saying "Brännvin" with a superfluous vowel sound added at the end and it could also be a dialect way of saying "Brännvinet" without pronunciation of the final consonant. In some instances it has been difficult to decide whether Jensen was or was not intending to add the article to the noun.

The anomalies in Jensen's Swedish led Dr. William Coates to suggest that perhaps he was not a native speaker of the language. Indeed Jensen himself said that his mother came from Norway and if his father had the name "Jacoby" he may have come from central Europe and settled in Sweden. Jensen thus may have had a mixed linguistic background.

The subject's knowledge of Swedish and other foreign languages when in the waking or the hypnotic state

To check on the subject's knowledge of Scandinavian languages, she was asked three times when in deep hypnotic trance, but not manifesting the Jensen personality, whether she had ever studied or learned any Scandinavian language. K.E. was the hypnotist for these occasions. I was present myself on one of them. Each time T.E. replied firmly in the negative. On two of these occasions she was in a deep hypnotic trance, but not regressed. On the third, she was regressed through the years of her early childhood. In response to further questions, she could recall no exposure to any book containing Scandinavian words. She said that she had once read a travelogue or pamphlet about travel in Norway. This pamphlet contained no Scandinavian words other than place names.

On one of the above occasions (in 1959), when the subject was deeply hypnotized but not manifesting the Jensen personality, Dr. Sahlin asked her if she understood some words which he pronounced to her in Swedish. She understood nothing of the Swedish he spoke. He then asked her to give the Swedish translation of several English words with the Swedish words for which Jensen had previously shown familiarity. She was unable to do this. She was equally unable to understand Swedish words spoken to her in her ordinary waking state.

I have already mentioned the fact that the subject's parents knew and did sometimes speak in their home some of the languages of Eastern Europe, especially Polish. If, therefore, the subject had learned as a child any language other than English, we would expect this language to be Polish. On one occasion when the subject was hypnotized, but not manifesting the Jensen personality, T.E.'s mother (Mrs. G.F.) spoke Polish to her, but she did not understand a word.*

---

* Perhaps it would have been more satisfactory if the interviewers had investigated T.E.'s abilities to speak Swedish and Polish not only when she was deeply hypnotized, but also when she was regressed to an earlier age while hypnotized. Ås has published an instructive report of the case of a man who had learned the Finnish dialect of Swedish when a child, but subsequently had forgotten it in his normal waking state (4). Under hypnosis and regressed to his early childhood (age five), however, he recovered more of the language of his childhood than he could demonstrate in the normal waking state. He did not, however, demonstrate anything like the command of the language of his childhood that Jensen showed of Swedish. He showed no improvement with hypnotic regression for 52 per cent of the items tested.

T.E. studied French for four years in high school and later maintained some interest in this language in the study of which she sometimes assisted her daughter when she in turn studied French in high school. T.E. stated that she had enjoyed French in school and had performed well in it, so that her teacher used to call on her for reading in classes more often than she asked other students to read.

I obtained a transcript of T.E.'s record at the South Philadelphia High School for the years 1932–36. This showed that she had performed above average for her class in which she ranked in the first quartile. In a test of intelligence she was found to have an I.Q. of 102. The transcript gave details of her performances in different subjects. She did very well in French in her first year, with an average grade of 90 for that year. However, thereafter her performance fell off successively each year, and in her fourth year she obtained a barely passing grade of 73. Her average grade in French for the four years was 79·7. I cannot say what degree of excellence this represents by national standards of skill in learning French. But within T.E.'s own range of skills, her performance in French did not exceed most of her performances in other subjects; her average grade on all subjects for the four years amounted to 80·6. It would seem then, that when strongly motivated, as in her first year of high school, T.E. could perform well in learning French. But as time went on, her performance declined markedly. In a discussion of this, T.E. acknowledged that her interest in studies had diminished considerably after her first year at high school. Her grade in French in her last year of school became quite poor and, perhaps reflecting her basic aptitude rather than her best performance when fully motivated, this grade seems consonant with a more formal test of her aptitude, which I shall describe shortly. However, since T.E. had studied French with pleasure and some success for four years, it might be supposed that she would have a considerable command of this language if she had great powers of retention for foreign languages. Since I can myself speak French I asked T.E. (in the spring of 1962) to read and translate two paragraphs of intermediate French. She performed these tasks poorly. Her pronunciation of the French "r" was excellent, but the rest of her French accent in reading was quite American. And her translation missed much of the sense of the passage before her.

A test of the subject's aptitude for modern languages

The Modern Language Aptitude Test devised by Carroll and Sapon (10) measures the ability to learn a modern language easily. It consists of five parts which I shall briefly describe. Part I requires the subject to learn numbers in a new language. The subject hears the new numbers on a tape recording and, after brief instruction, is tested on his remembrance of the numbers in the new language. Part II tests the capacity to associate sounds with their symbols in phonetic script. It therefore seems to measure sound-symbol association ability. It may also test memory for speech sounds. It tends to correlate highly with the capacity for mimicking sounds of speech and combinations of sounds in foreign languages. Part III tests the ability of the subject to identify a word from a misspelled representation of it and hints as to its meaning. To some extent it measures the same ability for sound-symbol association that Part II measures. Part IV measures sensitivity to grammatical structure by requiring the subject to identify the grammatical function of words in sentences beginning with simple phrases and gradually reaching complex sentences. Part V consists of brief instruction in a forty-word vocabulary of Kurdish followed by a test of the ability to associate the English meanings with the Kurdish words just learned.

Comparisons have shown that the Modern Language Aptitude Test predicts more accurately than conventional intelligence tests which students will perform well in modern language courses. The test therefore seems accurately to measure aptitudes used in the acquisition of language, which aptitudes are not measured, or at least not measured so well, by intelligence tests. The Modern Language Aptitude Test does not predict whether a person can or cannot learn a foreign language. It only predicts whether he can do so more or less easily. Obviously a person with high aptitude and low motivation to learn a foreign language may learn one less readily than a person with low aptitude and high motivation. But, in general, the test has proved valid in predicting success in language courses. It has found application in selecting persons for special training in languages, e.g., members of the armed services or diplomatic corps.

The developers of the Modern Language Aptitude Test believe that aptitude for languages changes little with age and therefore that the test measures capacities which remain rather constant throughout a person's life. This point is relevant in considering the application of the test to the subject of this case six years after her demonstration of a knowledge of Swedish.

The Modern Language Aptitude Test seemed worth applying in the present case for the additional evidence it could contribute to the possibility that T.E. had learned Swedish by normal means. A high score by T.E. on the test would increase the possibility that she might have acquired her knowledge of Swedish with little effort, perhaps when she was a child. On the other hand, a low score by T.E. would indicate that she would have had to work hard to acquire command of the language. Accordingly, I administered the test to her in June, 1962. She achieved a very low score on the test and ranked in the 5th percentile of female first-year college students, the group matching her own educational level. She scored particularly low on Part III, the instructions for which she afterwards said she did not adequately understand. However, her score was significantly low on the other sub-tests and if we discard her results on Part III and recalculate her score using only the other four parts, the revised score leaves her still only in the 5th percentile of her group.

At the time of taking the test, T.E. experienced some initial anxiety, since despite my preliminary explanations she misunderstood the test as in some way appraising her for psychopathology. She said that once she got into the test and saw what it was her anxiety ceased. A comparison of her scores on the sub-tests indicates that if anxiety contributed to her low score, it must have done so evenly throughout and not only initially when she consciously experienced anxiety; for her scores in later parts of the test were no better and were in fact somewhat lower than those in the first two parts of the test.

I considered and inquired about the subject's motivation for performing well in the Modern Language Aptitude Test. At the time of taking the test, T.E. seemed to be working assiduously and with interest at the tasks of the test. In response to questions asked in her waking state and later when she was deeply hypnotized, she twice asserted that she had tried to do as well as she could in the test.

I interpret the low score achieved by T.E. on the Modern Language Aptitude Test as additional evidence worth noting that she is unlikely to have acquired her knowledge of Swedish casually and effortlessly by normal means.*

Investigations into the subject's opportunities and motives for learning Swedish by normal means

Since I believe I have established that in the present case a responsive xenoglossy with a vocabulary of more than a hundred words used in sensible conversation did occur, we must next try to account for the subject's acquisition of this degree of familiarity with Swedish.

The subject herself was quite certain that she never had any exposure to any Scandinavian language, much less enough to acquire a speaking familiarity with Swedish. She recalled that some years earlier she had observed a series of television plays dealing with the life in America of

---

* On reading this passage, Dr. William Coates pointed out that *no* adult learns a foreign language "casually and effortlessly". To do so invariably requires much effort and practice, something I know from my own studies of languages in adulthood.

immigrants from Sweden. Although the dialogue of these plays was in English, occasionally one of the characters would use a word or phrase of Swedish. Apart from this, she could not recall ever having heard any Scandinavian language prior to the sessions here described. She had never seen a moving picture film made in Scandinavia. K.E. and T.E. had never had a servant from Scandinavia. All their servants had been Negroes with one exception, an Irish-American girl. T.E. provided the following statement on this aspect of the case.

I, T.E., hereby certify that to the best of my knowledge I have never acquired any understanding of a Scandinavian language or the capacity to speak one.

I have never had more than casual contacts with persons from Scandinavia, either in our home or at school when I was a child, or elsewhere. I have not read any books written in Scandinavian languages.

In our family when I was a child English was the language chiefly spoken, but my parents did sometimes speak Polish, Russian, and Yiddish. They never spoke any Scandinavian language.

I have never visited the American Swedish Historical Museum in South Philadelphia or other museums or exhibits from which I could have learned details of Swedish life or the Swedish or other Scandinavian language.

(*signed*) T—— E——

In the course of inquiries into this case, I interviewed T.E., her mother, her older sister, and her older brother with regard to the present question. It seemed possible that T.E. might have learned Swedish when she was extremely young and then forgotten that she had learned it, but remained capable of speaking it later. The cases reported by Monboddo (51), Coleridge (13), Goethe (27), and Freeborn (34) illustrate the persistence over many years of submerged passages in foreign languages learned during youth and childhood. And the case reported by Dreifuss (23) showed that an ability to speak intelligibly (not merely to recite) a foreign language may remain dormant and emerge later in life. In the cases reported by Monboddo, Coleridge, Goethe, and Freeborn, the subjects did not achieve more than a recitative xenoglossy and, in all four cases, the fact of their having earlier known the languages was known either to themselves later or to other persons who remembered that they had learned the languages even when the subjects themselves had forgotten this fact. It would seem extremely unlikely, if not absolutely impossible, that a small child could learn enough of a foreign language to be able later to converse intelligibly in it without any awareness on the part of his or her mother that the child had learned such a language. Ignorance on the part of the mother of such linguistic training would surely only occur if child and mother had been separated when the child was young and this did not occur in the present case. The subject's mother signed the following statement bearing on this question:

I, G.F., hereby certify that to the best of my knowledge my daughter, T.E., has never acquired any understanding of a Scandinavian language or the capacity to speak one.

She has never had more than casual contact with persons from Scandinavia, either in our home or at school when she was a child, or elsewhere. She has not read any books written in Scandinavian languages.

In our family when she was a child English was the language chiefly spoken, but my husband and I did sometimes speak Polish, Yiddish, and Russian. We never spoke any Scandinavian language.

My daughter, to my knowledge, has never visited the American Swedish Historical Museum in South Philadelphia or other museums or exhibits from which she could have learned details of Swedish life or the Swedish or other Scandinavian language.

Since I know that my daughter was never for long periods out of our home without our knowing where she was and what she was doing as a child, I am quite certain that she could not have had sufficient contact with a Scandinavian-speaking person to have acquired from such a person knowledge of any Scandinavian language so that she could speak or understand it.

(*signed*)   G—— F——

Mrs. G.F. included the reference to "casual contact with persons from Scandinavia" because she did recall somewhat vaguely that a man who came from Norway had lived in the neighborhood at one time when T.E. was a child. The family would see him on the street from time to time. They knew nothing more about him than that he was Norwegian and he never entered their house. She could recall acquaintance with no other Scandinavians.

Not satisfied with the foregoing testimony, I interviewed also Mrs. F.C., the sister of T.E. who was eight years older than she. When children, Mrs. F.C. and T.E. shared a bedroom and indeed most of their activities from the time T.E. was born until she (T.E.) married. As is common in American families of Jewish origin from central or eastern Europe, the younger children were kept under extremely close surveillance by the parents and older children. Although the family lived in a large city, their social environment was a constricted one. All the friends and acquaintances of the children were known to others of the family and were mostly of the same stock and religion. The children did not have keys to the house; they could not go out without their mother's knowing where they were going and what they were doing. Vacations were taken *en famille* at Atlantic City, New Jersey. Mrs. F.C. recalled one summer when she went on a vacation to a camp for two weeks. That summer T.E. went with her mother alone to Atlantic City. Mrs. F.C. cited this occasion as the only time she could recall a separation from

T.E. prior to T.E.'s marriage at nineteen. Mrs. F.C. married later. The children lived their lives between home, school, neighborhood homes of friends, corner stores, and the moving picture theater of the neighborhood. The latter showed moving pictures from Hollywood and some Jewish films, but never any foreign ones. T.E. could not go outside the neighborhood without being accompanied by her mother or sister until she was in high school, nor had she ridden a street car alone until that time. Mrs. F.C. confirmed the testimony of T.E. about the absence in the neighborhood and in her schools of anyone who could speak a Scandinavian language. She did not mention the Norwegian person referred to by Mrs. G.F.

I then covered the same ground with the subject's brother, Mr. M.F., who was four years older than T.E. His testimony corroborated in all respects that of T.E. and their sister, Mrs. F.C. He also could recall no Scandinavian persons in the neighborhood of their childhood home. And he fully confirmed the opinion of Mrs. F.C. that T.E. could not have strayed away from their home into some other one without their knowing about this.

Formal statements similar to those signed by Mrs. G.F. were also signed by Mrs. F.C. and by Mr. M.F. The wording of these statements is similar to that of the statement signed by Mrs. G.F. and they are accordingly omitted from this report to conserve space.

It may be thought that T.E. could have learned Swedish secretly after her marriage and concealed this fact from her husband in preparation for a hoax or to please him. Even if we ignore T.E.'s reputation for integrity, this would have been virtually impossible. T.E. lived with her mother and sister until her marriage at the age of nineteen. She and her husband (K.E.) were unusually closely attached. They rarely spent time apart. Her husband was a physician and she assisted him in his office which was located in their home. While these arrangements were not designed for control, they did in fact provide this and made it most unlikely that T.E. could have absented herself unaccountably for the purpose of learning Swedish covertly. She might have secretly learned Swedish from a book, but could hardly have mastered the accent so perfectly without much conversing with an instructor. On the possibility of his wife's having learned Swedish since their marriage, K.E. made the following statement:

My wife and I have lived closely together since our marriage, prior to which she lived in the home of her parents. My wife assists me in my office which is in our home. We have been separated very rarely and (with the exception of one occasion lasting two months) for brief periods only. I trust implicitly her statement that she has never learned Swedish, but even if I did not, I think it absolutely out of the question that she could have learned this language since our marriage without my having been aware of her absences from our home to converse with an instructor.

(signed)   K—— E——, M.D.

Notwithstanding the confident assurances of members of her biological and marital families that T.E. could not have learned Swedish without their awareness, I think it important to present to readers two pieces of information they will need in order to evaluate all the possibilities for her previous normal acquisition of a knowledge of Swedish.

The first such circumstance is the fact that during World War II, K.E. was stationed in the armed services during 1943–46 in several other cities of the eastern United States while his wife remained in Philadelphia. During this time, T.E. lived with K.E.'s mother, who was deceased at the time of my investigation of the case. During most of these years, K.E. returned from Washington to his home in Philadelphia once or twice a week. Once he was away continuously for two months. During most of the years in question, however, his nephew and niece either lived in the house with T.E. and her mother-in-law or in Philadelphia and were in extremely close contact with her. T.E.'s sister-in-law (K.E.'s sister) also lived near her and during the same years she was in close, almost daily contact with her. Although K.E.'s sister, nephew, and niece did not consciously monitor T.E.'s movements and their observations of her include some gaps, they did testify to me that they had never noticed unexpected absences of T.E. from her home or other abnormal behavior during this period. They believed she was entirely occupied with her domestic duties, her parental responsibilities, and her attention to her husband's business affairs.

At a later period (1947–50) T.E. and her husband were somewhat separated when she ran a hospital which they owned in another city (in New Jersey) while her husband worked partly in that hospital and partly at his practice in Philadelphia. During this period, they were often separated at night if, for example, K.E. remained in Philadelphia while T.E. slept at the hospital. K.E. testified that he never found his wife unexpectedly absent when he arrived at the hospital. Nor did he ever observe the disappearance of any money from their bank accounts.

I also interviewed the oldest daughter of the family, later Mrs. K.L., who was born July 17, 1941. Mrs. K.L. could not remember the time of her father's absence from the family when he was in the armed services. She did, however, remember the period of the later separation of the family while her parents ran the hospital in New Jersey and continued K.E.'s practice in Philadelphia. During the winters of this period K.L. remained in Philadelphia at school while T.E. spent most of her time in

New Jersey. But during the summers, K.L. was in New Jersey with her mother. Neither at these times nor any other did she observe unexpected absences of her mother. Although her mother was busy much of the time working in the hospital, the family saw her regularly and also whenever they needed her at other times.

I obtained the testimony of a female employee who had worked in K.E.'s office (and also at the hospital in New Jersey) during the years 1945–50. This woman was very closely associated with T.E. (who was administrator of her husband's hospital) during these years, sometimes even sleeping in the same room with her. She continued to have a close association with the family afterwards. As far as she knew, neither K.E. nor T.E. had any Scandinavian friends, acquaintances, or patients. She never observed any "spells", trances, unusual behavior, or unexplained absences on the part of T.E., either during the five years of their particularly close association or later.

Similar answers to similar questions came from a second employee of K.E. at the hospital in New Jersey during the years 1947–50. This informant worked as charge nurse and then superintendent of nurses at the hospital from October 1947 to April 1950 when the hospital was sold and T.E. returned to Philadelphia. She had an unusually close relationship with T.E., working with her every day and often sleeping in her apartment in the hospital She emphasized that T.E. was extremely busy at this time, working long hours in the hospital and also looking after her children. She never noted any unusual absences or abnormal behavior, e.g. spells or trances, on the part of T.E. She did report that a Scandinavian masseuse was briefly employed at the hospital for four weeks in 1947. The masseuse left the hospital to return to Europe. T.E. had forgotten about the existence of this Scandinavian masseuse until this informant mentioned her, and could furnish no further details about her association with the hospital or herself.

The testimony of these two employees to a considerable extent fills the gaps in the observations of T.E. by her husband (K.E.) during the period 1947–50. Nevertheless, it is conceivable that during this period, or the earlier period of 1943–46 when K.E. was in the armed services, T.E. had herself secretly tutored in Swedish for the purpose of later presenting herself as a case of xenoglossy. Since the observation of her movements by other persons was less complete than it was before 1943 or after 1950, we have to fall back on our assessment of T.E.'s honesty to evaluate the possibility that she learned Swedish during some of these years and concealed the fact. I myself accept as true her statement that she did not do so then or at any other time.

The second noteworthy circumstance is the occurrence in T.E. during the years 1960–61 of at least two episodes of involuntary trance. I have already mentioned that since the Jensen experiments were discontinued in 1956, T.E. developed a more conventional mediumship with a control and various communicators whose status does not concern us here. Some of these communicators delivered messages about scientific investigations in biology. On two occasions it was possible to trace these messages to sources earlier than their delivery by the subject in the mediumistic trances. Once notes closely resembling one of the "scientific messages" were found scribbled in a notebook T.E. carried in her purse. And once a book she had borrowed from a public library was found to contain passages which were repeated almost verbatim in a message delivered during a trance. When T.E. was told about the existence of the messages in her notebook and of the passages in the library book, she became extremely anxious and frightened. I was present during this scene. She insisted she had absolutely no recollection of having read the book in question or of having written the messages in her notebook (although she recognized her own handwriting) and concluded that she must have made these entries during an involuntary trance for which she was afterwards amnesic. Her fright included concern over insanity if the trances got out of control or of injuring herself during a trance. However, there is absolutely no evidence that T.E. ever had any trance at all (including any involuntary ones) before the first Jensen hypnotic regression. I asked most of the witnesses whom I interrogated about her opportunities for learning Swedish if they had observed any odd behavior or trance-like actions on her part at any time, apart from the induced trances under hypnosis. None had observed any such unusual behavior. Nevertheless, the foregoing observations of involuntary trances raise the possibility that T.E. may have learned Swedish in an involuntary trance state and become amnesic for having done so. I think this extremely improbable, but I want others to form their own opinions on the matter.

Some readers may question also why I attribute the origin of the messages found in T.E.'s notebook to involuntary trances rather than to deceptive planning for a "communication". Apart from my reliance on T.E.'s honesty and her contention of complete amnesia for having written the messages, I obtained other evidence that, in 1960–61, she had dissociated states bordering on involuntary trances in which messages or preparations for the giving of messages occurred. On one such occasion T.E. had an extremely vivid dream containing a message on biological investigations similar in type to those communicated during her trances. On the day following this dream she had a strong compulsion to tell her family the dream, something unusual for her, and delivered the content of the dream with great pressure of speech. On another occasion, K.E. observed her arise from bed during the night and walk around their bedroom in a somnambulistic state. While in this condition she started leafing through a book as if reading it, made writing motions with her hand, and while doing all this muttered the name of one of the communicators of her regular trances who gave out "scientific messages". It would seem, therefore, that whatever the origin of these later communicators may be, they gained some control over T.E. at times other than those of the "official" trances induced when she wished them. I repeat, however, that to the best of my knowledge (and that of the informants I interviewed) T.E. never had any trances, either voluntary or involuntary, prior to the original hypnotic sessions just before those at which the Jensen personality manifested.

Observations of the relationship between the subject and her husband with regard to motives for fraud

I had numerous opportunities to observe the behavior of K.E. and his wife both when alone and together. In my opinion, K.E. and T.E. showed in public the behavior of people who are happily married and love each other. I noted, however, that K.E. adopted an authoritative tone toward his wife and family. He was definitely the dominant partner in the marriage. T.E. seemed to prefer this kind of relationship and showed no overt resentment of her husband's authority. Her devotion to him, sometimes verging on subservience, seemed to exceed that of most American wives for their husbands, although perhaps not that of many Jewish-American wives. But this devotion, which both K.E. and T.E. acknowledged, raises the question of whether T.E. might have learned Swedish not for the purpose of hoaxing the public, but in order to please her husband, as, for example, one of Pavlov's assistants once faked some results for his employer (112). The responsive xenoglossy occurred in 1956. K.E. had been experimenting with hypnosis for more than a year before this. He took the initiative in these experiments and T.E. did not urge herself as a subject for them. Prior to 1954 she would not have known that she might become her husband's hypnotic subject since he had shown no interest in studying or using hypnosis up to that time. This hypothesis therefore almost requires that she learned Swedish during the years 1954–56. But these were years when the family was together and K.E. had ample opportunity to observe the whereabouts and activities of his wife almost continuously.

Observations and inquiries concerning the motives and integrity of the subject's husband with regard to fraud

As relevant to the hypothesis that K.E. worked up the case fraudulently, with T.E. as a willing (or involuntary) accomplice, the following points deserve attention.

First, K.E. took up hypnosis in 1954. Initially he was rather skeptical about hypnosis, but wanted to discover if he could use it to benefit his patients. The Jensen experiments did not take place until more than a year later, i.e., in 1955–56. After that, K.E. lost interest in experiments of this type and made no move to report the case until the time I first interested myself in it in 1958. From then until his death, K.E. was generally reluctant to have the case published. His attitude toward its publication actually vacillated. At one time he was enthusiastic and even wished to be a co-author. Usually, however, he seemed to me either indifferent or actually opposed to publication of the case for the reasons stated earlier. He remained opposed to publication for the several years preceding his death. He never sought any publicity for the case. His attitude and behavior toward it did not seem at all typical of someone eager to exploit a fraud.

Secondly, I made five independent inquiries as to K.E.'s standing as a practitioner of medicine in Philadelphia and in the medical societies of that area to which he belonged. Two inquiries went to past and present officials of the Philadelphia County Medical Society and one inquiry to an officer of the Philadelphia Society of Clinical Hypnosis. K.E. was a member in good standing of both these societies. I initiated two other inquiries through friends of mine, one a colleague professor of psychiatry in Philadelphia and the other a former hospital administrator in Philadelphia. Nothing adverse to K.E.'s integrity or his position as an ethical practitioner of medicine came from any of these inquiries.

Psychological tests for motives or evidences of fraud

In my interviews with the various people who belong to the families of K.E. or T.E., or other persons who knew them, I never uncovered the least hint of suspicion on the part of any of these people that either T.E. or K.E. had contrived a fraud in the present case. Nevertheless, since it remained possible that they had combined in a fraud, a further exploration of their motives and integrity seemed justified by the apparent importance of the case. Accordingly, three different tests were administered to each of them.

THE WORD ASSOCIATION TEST: Since the early experiments of Jung and Riklin (43) the word association test has been used for the detection of topics of special (emotional) significance for a subject. Jung called such emotionally charged topics complexes. Subjects show delayed response times and unusual response words to stimulus words which are associated in their minds with events of special importance to them. The delayed response time and the unusual response are considered indicative of an interference with mental functioning by the emotion which the stimulus word arouses through its association with past events of special significance for the subject. The stimulus word evokes a slight, but identifiable emotion of the quality associated with the original significant events. These features of the word association test led to its use as a means for detecting deception. Although a subject may consciously wish to conceal some act or event of which he has knowledge, he cannot (or cannot readily) control the emotional responses which stimulus words related to the event evoke. Consequently, delayed response times and unusual response words provide evidence of the emotional "charge" on the memory of an event to which the stimulus words are related. This brief and simplified account of the use of the test in the detection of deception does not do justice to its complexity and to the practical difficulties which may interfere with its successful application to a particular case. Investigators of the use of the word association test in detecting deception have differed in the confidence they placed in the test (16; 17). Nevertheless, an application of the test in the present case seemed justified in the hope that if positive results were obtained they would indicate the need for additional investigations. Accordingly, I administered word association tests in December, 1962, to both K.E. and T.E. independently.

One hundred and five words were used as stimuli in the test. Of these, eightynine were words used in the test as usually given in the Department of Psychiatry of the University of Virginia. Sixteen other words related to the present case were mixed with the standard words, one of these occurring in the list every four to six words. These special words and their relation to the case are listed later.

K.E. showed a slightly greater mean reaction time to the words related to the case (2·6 seconds) than to the standard words (2·4 seconds). T.E. showed a greater difference between the mean reaction time to the words related to the case (4·2 seconds) and the mean reaction time to the standard words (3·4 seconds). A t test of significance applied to the differences between the mean reaction times showed that the difference between the means was not significant in either the test responses of K.E. ($P = 0·40$) or those of T.E. ($P = 0·25$) (30).

Of interest nevertheless is why T.E. showed a greater mean reaction time to the words related to the case than to the standard words. Before considering this and other inferences from her test responses, I shall give in Table 1 below the stimulus words related to the case, T.E.'s reaction time to them, the response words, and some notes explaining the selection of the words for use in this test. The words were selected to give a representative sampling of important details of the case.

Study of this table shows that nearly all of the reaction times which exceeded the mean reaction time for the standard words (3·4 seconds) occurred in response to stimulus words which were proper nouns, e.g., "Sweden", "Norway", "Latvia", "Russian", "Marty", and "Johansen". Two prolonged reactions occurred to common nouns, namely "hypnosis" and "poppy seed".

Studies of word association tests have shown that unfamiliar words, e.g., proper nouns, may produce a prolonged reaction time because of the comparative lack of common associations to unfamiliar words in contrast to the more abundant associations we all have to many common nouns, e.g., "salmon", "war", and "brandy". If the difference between mean reaction time to words related to the case and to the standard words had been significant, it would have been necessary

Table 1

Results of the Word Association Test

Stimulus Word	Relation of Word to Case	Reaction Time (seconds)	Response Word
peasant	Jensen was a peasant. The word "farm" occurred as a standard word in the test, with a response time of 4·0 seconds	3·4	farmer
poppy seed	Eaten by Jensen	10·4	polly seed ("I don't know what that is")
Sweden	Country where Jensen lived	3·8	Europe
juice	Jensen's wife made a juice from poppy seed	1·6	drink
Johansen	Name shouted by Jensen in referring to his "chief"	8·0	Jensen
hypnosis		3·8	trance
salmon	Food eaten by Jensen	3·0	fish
Latvia	Jensen's wife	5·4	Europe
Norway	Home of Jensen's mother	4·2	Europe
war	Jensen hated war	3·0	waste
brandy	Jensen enjoyed brandy	2·6	bitter
Marty	Name of one of Jensen's brothers	5·0	boy
headache	Jensen died apparently of a blow on the head	3·2	pain
Russian	Jensen was afraid of Russians	4·6	Europe
Jensen		3·0	name
moon	Jensen measured time in moons	2·2	sun

to test this hypothesis in the present case by administering the same group of standard and special words to a control group of subjects for the purpose of ascertaining whether they also showed a prolonged reaction time to the unfamiliar words. In view of the lack of a significant difference between T.E.'s mean reaction times to the two groups of words I judged this step unnecessary.

I interpret the results of the test as providing no evidence that the aspects of the case touched upon in it were significantly connected in the minds of either T.E. or K.E. with other topics of emotional importance to them. Such a topic would be fraudulent contrivance of the case, so a secondary inference of the test results is that they provide no evidence of fraud on the part of either K.E. or T.E.

I may make one other inference from the results of the word association test administered to T.E. It gave some evidence that the Jensen personality was deeply "buried" beneath T.E.'s current personality, if indeed it formed a component of that personality. For example, although T.E. showed a delayed reaction time to the word "Johansen", a figure charged with emotional significance for Jensen, she did not show abnormal responses to two other words, "war" and "headache", which were of great emotional significance to him. Also Jensen drank brandy with the utmost relish, but T.E.'s response to this word was "bitter". On the other hand, Jensen was strongly opposed to war and T.E.'s response word to "war" was "waste".

THE MINNESOTA MULTIPHASIC PERSONALITY INVENTORY: This test consists of 566 statements related to symptoms, attitudes, and personal relationships and the subject is asked to state whether they are true or false with regard to himself (19; 102). The test has been standardized by repeated use on many subjects in a wide variety of institutions. Comparisons of the results of the test in different populations of healthy and mentally ill people permit inferences to be drawn about the membership of a subject taking the test in a population liable to particular kinds of mental illness or showing particular personality traits. Probabilities of such membership, not certainties, are inferred. The test is evaluated according to a number of scales the scores of which, if falling outside the range for normal persons, indicate the subject's tendency to abnormalities of feeling or behavior in the area of the scales, e.g., hypochondriasis, hysteria, depression, in which deviations occur. The test evaluates the subject's conscious responses to the statements which he checks as being true or false with regard to himself. Unconscious factors may influence the subject's interpretation of the statements, especially those which include qualifying adjectives and adverbs. The test includes some statements designed to detect attempts at deception or misrepresentation as well as inconsistency of responses.

I administered this test to K.E. and T.E. independently in December, 1962, and Dr. Burke Smith evaluated the responses. T.E.'s responses were within normal limits on all scales. K.E.'s responses showed slightly greater but unimportant deviations from the normal range of responses. By "unimportant" I mean irrelevant to the hypothesis of fraud. There was no evidence of conscious or unconscious deception in answering the test questions in the responses of either K.E. or T.E.

POLYGRAPH TEST FOR LIE DETECTION: The polygraph test for lie detection employs principles similar to those of the word association test used for the same purpose. In the polygraph test, however, the emotional response of the subject to the test questions is indicated by changes in physiological functions, e.g., skin conductivity, respiration, heart rate, and blood pressure. The investigator observes changes in these functions during the asking of questions related to the topic under investigation. A subject may verbally deny some event of which he has knowledge, but cannot usually control the physical changes which accompany (strictly speaking are a part of) his emotion as he attempts to conceal the truth (39).

Although the polygraph test for lie detection has many enthusiastic advocates of its usefulness in detecting deception, I must draw attention to its important limitations.

The test does not expose deception directly. It only shows physiological (emotional) responses to particular questions. The usefulness of the test depends first on the care with which questions are phrased to elicit relevant and specific responses; and secondly, upon the experience and competence of the person administering the test both in handling the subject and in interpreting the indications of physiological change he observes in the record.

W. G. Roll reported a poltergeist case in which the ostensible agent (a teenage boy) was observed (through a one-way viewing window) throwing objects allegedly thrown by the poltergeist; yet subjected to a polygraph test for lie detection, this boy gave no evidence on the test of deception with regard to his denials of having done what he in fact had been observed doing (73). Dearman and Smith studied a case of the opposite kind in which a "false positive" interpretation of polygraph test results occurred (20). A young bank employee, to whom a polygraph test was administered, showed evidence of emotional reactions to questions related to the theft of money from the bank where he worked. The first polygraph examiner offered an interpretation of "guilty". On confrontation with the evidence of the polygraph test the subject actually signed a confession of theft, although consciously he knew he had not stolen money from the bank. A careful inquiry showed that he had not in fact done so; and no money was missing. Then a review of the first interrogation and polygraph record and a careful retesting using more specifically worded questions showed that the subject had responded emotionally to questions which (through their too general wording) aroused guilt he felt toward his mother, which guilt was responsible for the detected but originally misinterpreted emotional responses to the questions.

Weinstein *et al.* (101) have shown that hypnotized subjects may mislead a polygraph operator trying to detect lies so that he draws false conclusions in both directions. Thus subjects instructed under hypnosis could successfully conceal from the polygraph operator an actual guilt or could give physiological indications to him of "crimes" which they had not in fact committed.

In view of such limitations, I approached the use of a polygraph test for lie detection in the present case with the understanding that the results would not be regarded as conclusive either way, although contributing to the total amount of evidence bearing on the question of fraud.

The polygraph test was administered twice to both K.E. and T.E. by Mr. Richard O. Arther in his office in New York City on January 10 and February 3, 1963. I was present on the first occasion. The following "key questions" were asked of T.E.:

1. In your ordinary state of consciousness, did you ever know how to speak any Scandinavian language?
2. In your ordinary state of consciousness, did you ever have the ability to speak any Swedish?
3. Do you recall ever learning any Scandinavian language?
4. Do you recall ever being taught a Scandinavian language?

5. Before you met those Swedish interpreters around five years ago, in your presence did you ever hear anyone talk a Scandinavian language?
6. Before you met those Swedish interpreters around five years ago, did anyone ever talk to you in a Scandinavian language?

To all these questions T.E. answered "No". Mr. Arther interpreted the physiological responses during the test as indicating that she was telling the truth.

Similar "key questions" were put to K.E. with appropriate phrasing to inquire about his knowledge of his wife's ability to speak Swedish or of her ever having heard it. He answered "No" to all six questions and Mr. Arther interpreted his physiological responses as indicating that he also was telling the truth.

III Discussion

The possibility of fraud

IN the course of my investigation of this case, which extended over many years, I became acquainted with the subject, her husband, and other members of her family as well as with the two principal Swedish-speaking linguists who testified about their conversations with the Jensen personality. Whatever other explanations may prove best, I have satisfied myself that I cannot explain this case on the basis of fraud.

It seems most improbable that T.E. learned Swedish in adulthood and concealed this fact from others, including K.E. I have already cited K.E.'s opinion that this was virtually impossible, both from lack of opportunity and from his knowledge of his wife's integrity. Nothing in the subject's behavior had ever given him the slightest suspicion of dishonesty which could make plausible the suggestion that she had perpetrated a hoax. Such behavior would be quite out of harmony with other aspects of her character which showed an exceedingly strong sense of responsibility to others.

But let us consider the possibility of fraud further. The excellence of the Swedish accent in at least some places requires that T.E. had considerable experience in speaking and improving her accent with a Swedish-speaking person. Phonograph records would hardly suffice. In the first place, they do not provide the sort of correction to accent and grammar which conversation with a tutor alone can offer. Secondly, their vocabulary is designed for tourists and better suited to help people find their way through the customs house than a peasant's farmhouse. Thirdly, in this case one would have to imagine records that instructed in Swedish with a fair mixture of Norwegian words worked into the language in a natural manner. So far as I know, commercially available phonograph records for home study of languages always provide the language to be learned in pure form and would never mix in words from a neighboring country. (Swedish and Norwegian have drifted sufficiently apart during the past seven or eight hundred years so that, although they are still close, they are also distinct languages.) Fourthly, where and when would T.E. have found an opportunity to study with phonograph records? Certainly not in her childhood home if we accept the testimony of her older sister as to circumstances there. And opportunities would have arisen with little more frequency after her marriage. It would have been possible, but extremely difficult for her to have played Swedish phonograph records in her home after her marriage. She was in her husband's office during the day and with either her husband or her children at nearly all other times. It seems clear that if she learned Swedish from phonograph records, she must have used them away from her home rather than in her home either before or after her marriage. Yet she was never reported to be unexpectedly absent by any of my informants.

For reasons already mentioned, it is most unlikely that phonograph records would have sufficed for the task at hand. Learning a language (with a good accent) as well as Jensen knew Swedish really demands a tutor and the opportunity to converse with him. In the present case this would have required secret visits to the tutor, and these would have entailed absences and expenditures to be explained to K.E. Only during 1943–46 or 1947–50, when K.E. was away for several days a week and came home only one or two nights a week, could T.E. easily have slipped away from her home for interviews with a tutor. All things considered, her husband's absences provided the best and perhaps the only occasions for a secret learning of Swedish. But then what could she have had in mind if she had done this? Certainly she must have been prepared for a long wait before an occasion arose for her to use her Swedish. She did not push herself forward as a candidate for age regression. The occasion when it did come, six or more years later, occurred accidentally as far as she was concerned. She had not previously been hypnotized and only the fact that she proved to be an excellent subject led to the further experiments in age regression with her. Regressions during the "present life" were attempted first and the regression to the Jensen personality was an originally unexpected development from her excellence in age regression in the present life. She did not volunteer for regression to another personality.

Finally, I should mention the thorough examination of T.E. under hypnosis when not manifesting the personality of Jensen. She gave every indication of being fully under the influence of the hypnotist when she was in deep hypnosis. I think it extremely unlikely that she could have concealed from him the correct answers to questions asked her in the deeply hypnotized state about her (conscious) knowledge of Swedish or her recollection of any previous exposure to the Swedish language or other Scandinavian languages. In my opinion, any subject deeply enough hypnotized to undergo a personality transformation of the kind here described can also be deeply enough hypnotized to make extremely unlikely the concealment of evidence bearing on fraud. In answer to this, it may be supposed that the subject never was hypnotized at all, but was merely simulating hypnosis. This seems most unlikely, especially since hypnotic trances of this subject were observed by other witnesses, including myself, who have considerable familiarity with hypnotism. One session (number four) was entirely conducted by another hypnotist, Dr. John Cordone, who testified to his conviction that the subject had been deeply hypnotized. Yet I will not deny that experts in hypnosis may be unable to distinguish subjects actually hypnotized from those simulating hypnosis. Orne demonstrated this difficulty very clearly in his experiments which showed that sometimes even experts cannot distinguish real from simulated hypnosis (53). It is also conceivable that prior suggestions administered during hypnosis prepared T.E. to conceal the truth when hypnotized later as the experiments of Weinstein *et al*. have indicated may be possible (101).

The foregoing discussion of fraud may take insufficient account of the possibility that T.E. and her husband, K.E., *joined* in a fraud. This possibility provided one motive for administering to both of them the various psychological tests that I thought might help to uncover a fraud if it had occurred. And I have previously described my inquiries in Philadelphia into the reputation of K.E. in the medical community. In addition, I myself actually spent more time interviewing K.E. than in talking with his wife. I never detected the slightest hint of any hoaxing on his part or any motive to do so. To the time of his death he had gained no remuneration or other public reward for the case which has, up to the publication of this book, remained known to only a small circle of friends and parapsychologists.

Cryptomnesia

I shall discuss next cryptomnesia, another possible normal explanation of the case. As already mentioned, it is conceivable that T.E. learned Swedish as a small child and then forgot that she had done so, but preserved her capacity to speak it in altered states of consciousness. I have already said why I do not believe this could have happened without the awareness of her mother, her older sister, or her older brother. And if the subject did have such a subconscious knowledge of Swedish, one would have expected it to manifest when called for in the ordinary deep hypnotic state and not only during the personation of Jensen. For Jensen was a personality who differed not only in sex, but in a number of his attitudes from the personality of the waking subject. Jensen did not have the personality of a small child, such as might have been expected if the language were part of the revival of childhood years. He acted like a grown man, and not at all like a small girl. His attitude toward adult women was that of a rather lascivious male peasant, quite different from what we observe in a small girl or another adult woman. We have as yet no reliable way of quantifying such differences between personalities, but they remain nevertheless impressive and important. Any explanation of the xenoglossy should also account for the expression of the language through a different and distinctive personality.

Even if we set aside the possibility that T.E. acquired her knowledge of Swedish in early childhood, say, before her marriage, we must still consider the possibility that she learned Swedish in adulthood during involuntary trances prior to the first Jensen experiments. T.E.'s sister, Mrs. F.C., and her husband, K.E., had no knowledge whatever of her ever having had such trances prior to 1961. Since it is certain (on the testimony of K.E.) that she was never put into a hypnotic trance before 1955, a question of the first agency for such involuntary trances arises. If they did occur for the express purpose of her learning Swedish, what was the agency of induction? I have already mentioned that T.E. was strongly attached to her husband (the hypnotist) and was so before the experiments began. One could conceive that a wish to please him by providing him with sensational feats such as xenoglossy led to involuntary trances during which she learned Swedish that was then available outside her awareness for use at an appropriate time. Against this hypothesis we have to set the extreme improbability that T.E. could have had such involuntary trances without knowing this fact herself, through awareness of amnesic periods or through noting the effects of some action she could not recall, as actually happened later in 1961 when she could not remember making the notes mentioned earlier. Nor does it seem likely that members of her family would have failed to notice her altered mental state when in such trances or her physical absences if she went off during them for a sufficient length of time to be tutored in Swedish. In cases of multiple personality, it is common to have members of the family (or the patient himself) testify that the patient showed episodes of abnormal behavior which started and stopped abruptly and alternated with normal behavior. T.E.'s family recalled nothing of the kind in her case.

T.E.'s family and she herself might conceivably have failed to notice dissociated states or involuntary trances which she may have undergone prior to 1956. Pickford has reported a case in which he found evidence that a "medium" had acquired some of the contents of his trance messages from reading in public libraries (59). In his trances the subject gave purported communications from great composers. The medium, upon being questioned, said he thought that he had spent some time reading biographies of these men. Pickford infers that the subject was in a dissociated state when he read about the composers, but the evidence for this conjecture derives from the patient's vagueness in recalling what he had read and from a history of his having "wandered about" when he was a soldier during World War I and subsequently.

In any case, Pickworth's subject only communicated information about the great musicians; he did not himself exhibit any musicianship such as skill in playing the piano or composing for it. I shall contend later that the acquisition of a skill requires learning and practice and that a skill and its acquisition require different mental processes from information and its acquisition.

Here we must continue to examine the possibility that T.E. in a dissociated state somehow acquired a knowledge of Swedish and remained unaware in her normal condition that she had learned that language. Then later in another dissociated state (of which we may consider the hypnotized condition to be a type) she might have manifested the earlier acquired skill in speaking Swedish.

Do we have any models encouraging such a hypothesis? Claims have been made that learning can occur during sleep (45). Experiments supporting such claims have often been conducted without adequate control of whether the subjects were in fact asleep or merely drowsy or even more fully awake during the experimental periods. More carefully conducted experiments which included electroencephalographic monitoring of the sleep state have provided no evidence that learning occurs during sleep (31; 79; 80). It remains at least theoretically possible, however, that some learning may take place during sleep and not be accessible to the subject during his later waking periods, but nevertheless become so during another period of altered consciousness.

Some cases of multiple personality perhaps bear on this problem, although I know of none that can settle it. For example, Mary Reynolds in her secondary state forgot what she had learned in her primary state (40, vol. 1, pp. 381–384; 60). Although living in a wooded country, she knew nothing (in her secondary state) of rattlesnakes and their dangers and mistook a bear for a hog, quite in contrast to the understanding of these animals she possessed in her primary state. It is difficult to believe that Mary Reynolds' two personalities remained as impermeable to the contents of each other as described. In other cases of multiple personality, e.g., that of Doris Fischer (65), the secondary personality has had access to the contents of the primary personality's "mind", although the reverse was not the case. Certainly in some cases of multiple personality the secondary personality has had many of the skills of the primary one (14). The skills of the primary personality were, however, learned in the normal state. And our question here is whether a skill learned by a secondary personality (and previously unknown to the primary one) would "leak" to the primary (or a tertiary) personality.

Such evidence as we have does not completely exclude this possibility, but we have none whatever which supports it. And on this hypothesis in the present case we should have to suppose at least three personalities, since no one will imagine that the peasant personality of Jensen could have gone about Philadelphia learning Swedish without attracting attention to T.E.

Paranormal explanations of the case

The decision to favor paranormal explanations in a case of this kind must rest on the probability that the ability to speak a foreign language could not have been normally acquired by the subject to the extent demonstrated. My own opinion is that in this case the capacity to speak Swedish, as this subject did, was not normally acquired by T.E.

I have already listed the various reasons and their supporting data for forming this opinion. But I hasten to add that I do not claim to have proved this. The various possibilities discussed therefore forbid a dogmatic assertion as to paranormality of the acquisition of the knowledge of Swedish. That the subject did converse intelligibly in a Swedish of excellent accent (in some places) and fair vocabulary is incontestable. That she could have learned this much Swedish without herself or someone else knowing this fact seems to me most improbable, but certainly not completely impossible. I have tried to present all of the facts within my knowledge that bear on this question and to offer sufficient detail so that readers may form independent judgments of the case.

The case is not a trivial one. For if my view of it as to authenticity is accepted, then survival of human personality after death is a major hypothesis to be considered in its interpretation. I shall next try to support this statement by considering in detail the main interpretations of the case which (supposing authenticity) require a paranormal explanation for the responsive xenoglossy.

Extrasensory perception from the Swedish-speaking interviewers or other persons

It has sometimes been urged that instances of xenoglossy have less force as evidence of survival if they take place in the presence of someone capable of speaking the foreign language. Theorists who press this point suggest that the communicating personality may acquire its knowledge of the foreign language on the spot from reading the minds of the interviewers through extrasensory perception. This suggestion imposes difficult conditions for the study of cases of responsive xenoglossy.

How can we have a truly responsive xenoglossy unless someone is present who can converse with the ostensible xenoglossist? Are we to ask the xenoglossist to answer questions spoken on a tape recording by the absent questioner? It might be possible to have a person (who knows only English) put questions in English to the subject and record the answers in the foreign language for later translation by someone else. But this would not provide conditions for a natural conversation that would thoroughly test the linguistic agility of the subject. Nevertheless, let us consider further the hypothesis of extrasensory perception from the interviewers.

In the present case this hypothesis has to discard completely the two quite clear phrases in Swedish, "Ja' vill ha" (I want to have) and "Kom med bätarna" (came with the boats), spoken by Jensen in session four when no (other) Swedish-speaking persons were present. If we ignore these phrases, however, the hypothesis becomes stronger since in the three sessions (numbers six, seven, and eight) during which Jensen spoke most Swedish, Swedish-speaking persons were present and talking with him.

Now it is not uncommon—one might almost say it is commonplace—for good mediums to pick up from the subconscious (or conscious) minds of sitters information which they then weave into a coherent personality. This personality is presented as a communicator and frequently seems to "believe in himself" and to be believed in by the control and other communicators of the medium, as in the case of "Bessie Beals", through Mrs. Piper (91), and in a case reported by Heywood (36). If mediums can accomplish this with some kinds of information, what is to prevent their doing it with other kinds, such as the knowledge of a language known by another person present or even absent? I have already cited some evidence of the ability to communicate elements (and even paragraphs) of foreign languages by extrasensory processes (pp. 19–22 above).

I have also mentioned that T.E. developed further as a medium after the Jensen experiments, and although it is not part of the present report to discuss the events of this aspect of her mediumship, there are grounds for believing that it included at least some capacity for extrasensory perception. Hence we need to consider the possibility that T.E. might have acquired her knowledge of Swedish (session four still ignored) from the persons present at later sessions. It is necessary to add that the responses furnished by Jensen to questions asked by the interviewers must, on this hypothesis, have been filched from the subconscious minds of those present rather than their conscious minds only. The person interviewing Jensen was sometimes surprised by answers which certainly had not been present in the conscious mind of the questioner. (See the transcript in the Appendix for examples of such surprise on the part of the interpreters.) In sessions six and seven, the subject might have taken words from the mind of a second Swedish-speaking person present since there were two such persons present at each of these sessions. If the subject obtained the Swedish responses from the conscious mind of the second Swedish-speaking person, the surprise of the interviewer could still have occurred. But in session eight, only one Swedish-speaking person was present, Mr. Sunday, and he also experienced surprise in unexpected answers by Jensen. So in this session at least, the information presumably came, if transferred during it, through extrasensory perception from Mr. Sunday's subconscious mind. But this would still harmonize with what we know of the ways in which mediums rummage in the minds of sitters. In fact, they seem rather more apt to gain knowledge from the subconscious minds than from the conscious minds of their sitters (9, p. 545; 36).

In the current state of knowledge it would be exceedingly difficult either to prove or disprove this hypothesis. It has the merit of not requiring survival of death as a part of it, but the even greater demerit of not really making sense. It is difficult to see what motives could activate the medium's acquisition of Swedish from persons present (or absent) and its expression as emanating from a hitherto unknown and unidentifiable personality. No one present had known or imagined this personality before. He was not a loved deceased person with whom sitters were trying to get in touch through an established medium. In fact, as I have already emphasized, T.E. had, until the manifestation of Jensen, no known capacity for mediumship or extrasensory perception whatever. Incidentally, if T.E. could acquire the ability to speak the Swedish language by extrasensory perception, we would want to ask why she did not also talk Italian when she had Italian-speaking sitters (in early sessions) or Polish when her mother was present. The fact that she did not do so does not, however, exclude the possibility of her having learned Swedish by extrasensory perception since we know subjects show selectivity and fluctuations in their manifestations of paranormal powers.

We must also remember that the personality of Jensen (as opposed to the xenoglossy) emerged fully and spoke in English during two sessions (four and five) when, however, Jensen spoke only two phrases of Swedish. Prior to that in three sessions the personality had partially manifested in the reliving of the closing violent scene of Jensen's life. So we must suppose that the Jensen personality was originally created for some other purpose than that of manifesting an ability to speak Swedish. Furthermore, the Jensen personality, often with strongly expressed emotions, was fully manifested during the sessions when most of the Swedish was spoken. The Swedish spoken was not articulated by a detached tongue and vocal chords, so to speak. It was spoken by Jensen (whoever he was) who expressed strong feelings about his "förste man", war, the Russians, and other subjects, and who smacked his lips loudly when imagining a drink of brandy.

There exist, however, even more severe difficulties for the hypothesis of extrasensory communication from the Swedish-speaking interpreters. As already mentioned, Jensen's language contained a considerable quantity of Norwegian. All the interpreters present and Scandinavian-speaking persons who listened to the tapes commented on this. Dr. Jacobson thought that perhaps Jensen's language was more on the Norwegian than the Swedish side of the linguistic dividing line. And Mr. Sunday actually changed his speech and spoke Norwegian instead of Swedish with Jensen. Yet the interpreters with Jensen were all Swedish-born people who spoke Swedish from preference. Why, we may ask, would Jensen introduce Norwegian words and usages if he was getting the language from the living Swedish interpreters present at the experiments? The Swedish-speaking persons, even though they knew some Norwegian, were certainly not consciously pushing Norwegian on the subject and one cannot reasonably surmise that they were doing so unconsciously either. Nor can we plausibly attribute to the interpreters the grammatical errors and dialect forms found in Jensen's speech. On the other hand, since the interpreters had some knowledge of Norwegian as well as of Swedish dialect forms, Jensen might conceivably have obtained his particular language from them (by extrasensory perception) without their having consciously willed that he speak Swedish with the considerable modifications from standard Swedish which he showed.

At this point I should remind the reader of the Dutch xenoglossy case reported by Suringar (90), in which a living communicator seems to have furnished the medium with the ability to communicate in English, a language ordinarily quite unknown to her (p. 21 above). If the boy in this Dutch case did act as a living communicator, then how do we know that Dr. Sahlin, Mr. Ekman, and Mr. Sunday did not also act as living communicators to provide the Swedish xenoglossy of the present case? The answer is that we do not know positively, but (to sum up the arguments so far developed) this interpretation seems very unlikely for the following reasons: (*a*) Jensen as a personality (and with a little Swedish xenoglossy) manifested *before* these Swedish persons were present; (*b*) the interpreters were not in a trance or sleeping themselves at the time of the sessions at which Jensen manifested and spoke with them; (*c*) it is not easily supposed that at session eight where Mr. Sunday was the only Swedish-speaking person present he acted both as living communicator and interpreter; that is, that Mr. Sunday telepathically pushed Swedish words and phrases into T.E.'s mind which Jensen then spoke and he (Mr. Sunday) then normally answered himself;

instances have occurred in which a sitter at a séance furnished information (telepathically) for the construction of a "communicator" and at the same time responded to the returned information (36); but so far as I know xenoglossy has not entered into any such cases; and (d) it seems unlikely (but not impossible) that the Swedish-speaking persons would (even subconsciously) have communicated the considerable proportion of Norwegian words in the xenoglossy.

The above arguments take account of commonsensical ideas about what is and is not possible in the way of transmission of information by extrasensory perception. I am aware, however, that my arguments include assumptions which may be wrong. For example, some absent person may have been the agent for T.E.'s knowledge of Swedish. After all, the physical distance between a percipient and his source may be of relatively little importance in extrasensory communication (54; 55). On the other hand, personal relationships are of considerable importance and I should think it more likely that the subject learned Swedish from Swedish-speaking persons in her presence, even if she had only met them recently, than from complete strangers at a distance. I also recognize that the agent or agents, whether present or absent, do not have to be consciously (or even unconsciously) desirous of sharing their knowledge with the percipient. He may just reach out and take it from them.

The foregoing arguments have been addressed to what is sometimes called the hypothesis of "super-extrasensory perception". According to this, some humans may be capable of acquiring almost any knowledge with extrasensory perception. And we do have on record some extra-ordinary demonstrations of extrasensory perception with regard both to the "amount" (or sharpness of detail) of the perception (6; 56; 57) and the complexity of the targets designated for detection by the subject (77; 82). At the same time I think there is some danger of erecting the hypothesis of "super-extrasensory perception" into an irrefutable con-jecture that can be used to postpone grappling with fundamental issues. I do not myself believe that we must delay research on the question of survival after death until we learn the limits of extrasensory perception among the living, whatever they may be. There may well be *no* limits to manifestations of extrasensory perception among the living in terms of distance and time. Yet such limits may exist in the ability of living persons to *utilize* information that is otherwise theoretically available by extrasensory perception.

One such limitation may occur in restrictions on the ability of living persons to acquire a skill. The present case provides an example of a skill— the ability to speak a language responsively. The subject integrated the elements of the Swedish language into reasonably correct grammatical forms and, furthermore, understood enough of the language to employ it meaningfully and with good accent in three rather lengthy conversational exchanges with other persons. I emphasize particularly the grammatical integration of the words to form sensible phrases and the accent of the speaker. If it were simply a matter of the subject's acquiring Swedish words by extrasensory perception one could assume these were picked up as readily as any other type of cognitive information obtainable through extrasensory perception. But intelligible sentences and a particular accent constitute skills. Now, a crucial difference exists between information, or "knowledge *that*", and a skill, or "knowledge *how to*". Polanyi has developed and discussed this distinction, which I regard as critical for the evaluation of the present case, in several articles and books (62; 63; 64). He has stated:

There are things that we know but cannot tell. This is strikingly true for our knowledge of skills. I can say that I know how to ride a bicycle or how to swim, but this does not mean that I can tell how I manage to keep my balance on a bicycle or keep afloat when swimming. . . . I know how to carry out these performances as a whole and . . . I also know how to carry out the elementary acts which constitute them, but though I know these acts, I cannot tell what they are (63, p. 601).

Although Polanyi referred to the communication of skills along ordinary sensory routes, his arguments would apply *a fortiori* to communication of skills by extrasensory perception. We need to specify, however, why we cannot communicate skills directly to other people, and what grounds we have for asserting that we must always learn a skill actively and can never acquire one passively as we can acquire information.

A skill does not derive its incommunicability from being largely unconscious, since we know that many unconscious mental contents are communicated through normal sensory channels and also by extrasensory perception; indeed, extrasensory perception seems to occur in two stages of which the first (between agent and percipient) is subconscious. In the second stage the communicated content (or portions of it), more or less distorted, is mediated into consciousness (96).

Neither does the incommunicability of a skill arise from the *complexity* of the motor acts required for its accomplishment, since quite complicated patterns of information seem sometimes to be communicated by extrasensory perception.

We cannot transmit a skill to someone else because it constitutes an organization or pattern of motor acts directed toward a goal and adapted to particular circumstances. These circumstances may be those requiring a tennis ball to be hit with the racket at just the right moment, or a succession of piano keys to be struck in a certain sequence, or an appropriate response made in a conversation. It is this ability to organize and direct adaptively the patterns of our motor acts that we must learn, cannot acquire passively, and cannot communicate to other people. Verbal communications may contribute something to the learning of a skill, as when an instructor tells someone learning a foreign language to pronounce a consonant more or less far back in the throat; but beyond such verbal instructions a skill contains elements which we cannot communicate verbally and which we can only acquire through practice.

It may be objected that we develop skills by imitation of our teachers as when we model ourselves on the instructor in learning to ski or on our parents in learning to speak a language as children. Such modeling accounts, for example, for the fact that persons raised in the southern United States have a different accent in speaking English than do persons raised in other parts of the United States or in other lands where English is spoken. But speaking with a particular accent constitutes a skill in itself and must be learned by practice, as anyone knows who tries to learn a foreign language in adulthood. (Children have to learn to speak with their parents' accent also, but as circumstances favor their doing so almost unconsciously we can easily overlook the process of learning through practice in the acquisition of native languages by children.) In short, mimicry does not imply communication of a skill. It is another case of the communication of information or knowledge *about* what is to be learned, not knowledge of *how* to carry out the act to be learned.*

Another common, but not universal, feature of skills is that they are often almost or completely specific for *particular* persons or minds. Ducasse (25) argued that the occurrence of a particular skill known to have been possessed by one person, which after that person's physical death manifested through the organism of another person who previously had shown no like capacity for that skill, provides evidence of the survival of the original mind that had learned and exhibited it. I agree with Ducasse's position on this question. In the present instance, however, I am not attributing Jensen's skill with language to a particular deceased person, since I have not traced any actual person corresponding to Jensen's statements. Therefore the demonstration by T.E. of a skill she had not normally acquired does not in this case furnish proof that any *identified* person has survived death; but it does, according to the arguments of Polanyi and Ducasse here combined, prove the existence

---

* Recitative xenoglossy may, however, occur without practice. In the case cited by Freeborn (34), the woman in question sang a song in Hindi which as a child she had heard her nurse sing, but which almost certainly she herself would not have sung as a child. Likewise, the girl in Coleridge's case (13) almost certainly never *spoke* the material she heard her foster father reciting until her delirium years later. According to the definitions I have used, recitative xenoglossy does not constitute a skill, but simply the revival of cognitive memories.

of *some* deceased personality, assuming T.E. did not learn Swedish normally.

If we believe the subject and all around her who testify on this point, T.E. did not learn to speak Swedish by normal means prior to the sessions of 1955–56. Yet she then exhibited the definite skill of speaking responsively in Swedish. And if we agree with Polanyi that we can communicate *about* a skill, but cannot communicate the *skill itself*, and if we acknowledge that we can acquire no skill without practice in the associated motor acts, then we can reject extrasensory perception from the interpreters (or anyone else) as an explanation of the responsive xenoglossy.*

It remains true, nevertheless, that Jensen spoke more and better Swedish in the presence of Swedish-speaking people and extremely little in their absence. We could explain this on the basis of either (*a*) a fuller manifestation of the Jensen personality during the later sessions; or (*b*) the activation of some of Jensen's memories for the language by practice in speaking it; or (*c*) the belief which he might reasonably entertain that it is worth speaking a particular language if you are in the presence of people who will speak it with you and not of much value if no such persons are available. Perhaps a combination of these factors accounts for Jensen's greater fluency in Swedish in sessions seven and eight than in the preceding ones.†

My extensive review of the literature has failed to bring to attention any case of responsive xenoglossy in which the hypothesis of extrasensory

---

* I am aware (and have been made more so by two colleagues who read earlier versions of this monograph) that Polanyi's definition of a skill as a type of incommunicable knowledge is a stated general principle or perhaps simply an assumption. Polanyi derived the principle of tacit knowing by inference from many different types of observation which he cited in expounding his concept. Many observations and some results of experiments are harmonious with the concept of tacit knowing, but it cannot be said as yet to rest on any critical experiment or experiments designed exclusively to test it, if testable it be, which I think Polanyi inclined to doubt. It is also by no means accepted by all philosophers who have considered the question of the incommunicability of skills (111).

I have made a considerable search for reports of experiments in which the acquisition of skills through imitation or instruction without practice has been studied. Three psychologists, experts in the area of the learning of skills, have been unable to direct me to reports of relevant experiments and it seems unlikely that any have been conducted. And indeed it may be difficult to devise one that would test the point at issue here. I am certainly *not* asserting that instruction in acquiring a skill cannot help in its acquisition. All our experience with the value of instructors in learning languages, dancing, swimming, skiing, etc., is not declared worthless by what I am here contending. This is simply that, however much one may be assisted by the advice of other more experienced persons, one cannot actually acquire any skill, including that of speaking a foreign language, without having practiced it.

† This analysis fails perhaps to give adequate credit to the interpreters for the personal relationship they established with Jensen. From the recording of session seven, one learns easily that Mr. Ekman particularly achieved a friendly contact with Jensen. He addressed him with the familiar "Du" and obviously felt a warmth toward Jensen to which the latter seems to have responded. Some of the interpreters' friendliness is apparent even in the verbal transcript given in the Appendix.

perception seems adequately to explain the phenomena. The present case
may provide the first example, but in the meantime it seems worth while
to consider other explanations such as those which suppose that a deceased
person called Jensen had in fact returned in one way or another to communicate in Swedish.

Reincarnation or discarnate influence on the subject

If we set aside each of the previously considered hypotheses, e.g.,
fraud, cryptomnesia, and extrasensory perception, we find ourselves
incapable of understanding the responsive xenoglossy without supposing
some form of survival of physical death by a personality who learned
Swedish before 1956 and communicated at the experimental sessions.
This personality could be a discarnate entity temporarily speaking as
a communicator through the entranced T.E. Or "he" could be an aspect
of T.E.'s own personality residual from a previous life; in short, a manifestation of reincarnation. I find it convenient, and I hope it will be
helpful, to discuss these two hypotheses together.

Between these two hypotheses I have no firm opinion and I do not
believe the available data will permit an incontestable decision. In
weighing the two possibilities, the following facts need to be taken into
consideration.

In the first place, Jensen gave very little account of himself as an independent personality. Unfortunately, he was not questioned specifically
on this point. However, most mediumistic communicators (whatever
they may ultimately prove to be) seem to conceive of themselves as
existing after death and having a life in between their communications
even though their accounts of that life often leave much to be desired
in the way of clarity and consistency. On the other hand, a small number
of mediumistic communicators, popularly called "earthbound", do not
so conceive themselves. They act, in fact, as if they were still living and
seem not to know they have died. Jensen could be an entity of this type;
the apparently violent end to his life is a feature often found in the
accounts of the so-called "earthbound" spirits.

Secondly, Jensen's knowledge of English seems more in keeping with
a regression to the personality of a previous incarnation than with a
possessing spirit. Supposing Jensen were indeed a discarnate entity, one
would not be surprised that he could continue to speak his native language
after several hundred years. But one *is* surprised that he can speak some
English and that he can respond to English questions, instructions, and
suggestions.* Such responses, however, would be entirely harmonious

* This difficulty is taken care of on the hypothesis mentioned earlier that Jensen lived in
the seventeenth century, was born in Sweden, and emigrated from there to New Sweden
where he learned English.

with a regression to a previous life. The subject could then manifest, say, nine-tenths of a previous male, Swedish-speaking personality and still retain one-tenth of her present female English-speaking personality. We know that something of this kind can occur in hypnotically induced regressions to the early years of the present life. A subject, for example, may lose his knowledge of a vocabulary he has acquired after the age to which he is regressed, but he may at the same time preserve the capacity to respond to instructions spoken to him in the richer vocabulary acquired later. Clearly such a subject is not totally regressed. If he were, the words he only learned later would be unintelligible to him just as would words of a foreign language to someone who has never learned that language. A partial regression of this kind may have also occurred in the case of "Bridey Murphy" (5). The personality of "Bridey Murphy" generally exhibited an Irish vocabulary and accent. This personality also showed a knowledge of certain obscure places and names in Ireland which knowledge it seems unlikely the subject could have acquired through normal means (24). At the same time, "Bridey Murphy" occasionally used words and phrases which were characteristically American and quite inappropriate to the vocabulary of a nineteenth-century Irish woman.

Along these lines it is possible to conceive also that a word or phrase heard in English by the present subject may have evoked images which, in the particular condition of the hypnotized subject, "aroused" or "resonated with" words in Swedish representing the same images. Thus if I get into a French mood, I can look at objects around the room I am in and easily think of all the words for these objects in French, although ordinarily I attach English words to them.

A blending of two personalities, an earlier one manifested fully in a previous incarnation and the present one, could perhaps then account for the ability of the Jensen personality to speak some English. Although I have expressed my conviction that the Swedish spoken during the sessions came from a discarnate Jensen personality (whoever he was), I believe the English understood and spoken by the Jensen personality derived from the knowledge of that language possessed by the subject, T.E. (There is also the possibility that Jensen himself had learned some English in New Sweden, if he lived there.)

This kind of blending of the manner and abilities of one personality with those of another can occur in the mediumistic phenomena of "direct control". Under these conditions a communicator may achieve representation in the communications of voice and manner strong enough to make these features clearly distinguishable by the sitters from the comparable expressions of the medium, her control, or other communicators. Sitters may easily be deceived when this seems to happen. Their

expectations may lead them to believe they have recognized characteristic, or even specific, traits of a particular person when more critical
observers could not do so.

The phenomenon of blending of modes of expression of two personalities, however, has been observed in cases in which from other
evidence, e.g., in the communication of material unknown to the sitters,
one could believe that the communications were derived from the
deceased personality of whom the communicator claimed to be a con-
tinuation. When losing control, one such communicator (through
Mrs. Osborne Leonard) complained that her accent was taking on the
quality of the medium's accent and thus ceasing to represent her (the
communicator) as she wished. The communicator said, at one point:
"Oh! now the power is going, can't you hear my voice getting Mrs.
Leonardy again?" The sitters thought this in fact was happening (67,
p. 480).

The case of approximately simultaneous similar communications in
French and English mentioned earlier (pp. 21–22) seems relevant here.
Whether on the hypothesis of a discarnate communicator or that of a
living communicator (Mme Bricout herself) the English medium seems
to have had impressed on her what we may call "supralingual thoughts"
which she then translated into English script. This raises the possibility
then that a discarnate Jensen might first have communicated his thoughts
to the medium who translated these into English. Later the Jensen personality assumed "personal control" of the subject (T.E.) and spoke
Swedish directly. In principle, the process would be no different than
that described for communications by discarnate communicators through
Mrs. Leonard's control, Feda. The communicators seemed usually to
communicate to Feda in words or other symbols and Feda then translated
what she perceived into her own words, which were uttered through
Mrs. Leonard's vocal apparatus. But sometimes the communicators themselves seem to have assumed direct control of Mrs. Leonard and displaced
Feda (67; 92; 93; 94). It then seemed that they controlled Mrs. Leonard's
brain and vocal apparatus.

Thirdly, Jensen was evoked by and only by suggestions of regression
and "going away back". As previously mentioned, T.E. subsequently
developed a more conventional mediumship through which a number
of communicators have expressed themselves. Jensen never turned
up as one of these, although the way would presumably have been open
for him to do so according to the method of conducting the mediumistic
experiments.

Fourthly, the occurrence of the case in Philadelphia has no weight with
regard to choosing between reincarnation and possession by a discarnate
personality. On the reincarnation hypothesis we have no difficulty in

accounting for what Jensen was doing in Philadelphia, for "he" would then simply be a previous personality of which T.E. is the present personality. But on the possession hypothesis we have to ask why a Swedish peasant would communicate in Philadelphia. If, however, Jensen was a Swedish settler in New Sweden and was killed there in a skirmish of some kind, he might have become an "earthbound" spirit and simply hung around the area of his violent death until a suitable occasion for his mediumistic appearance occurred. If we reject the conjecture that Jensen lived some part of his life in New Sweden, then the possession hypothesis cannot very easily account for how a peasant of (old) Sweden appeared at a mediumistic séance in Philadelphia. He certainly had no obvious connection whatever with any of the persons present. Communicators unknown to medium and sitters ("drop-in" communicators) do, however, sometimes communicate in foreign countries. Bozzano published one case of this type in which an Italian "drop-in" communicator manifested in Paris (8).

Fifthly, T.E. made some comments in transitional stages as the manifestations of Jensen began that suggest awareness on her part of at least partial identity with the Jensen personality. Thus as the Jensen personality came on in session four, the subject when asked her name said, "Jensen myself, but I am here", and a moment later, "I am here and I know it, but I can't see myself". Then followed the fuller development of the Jensen personality. A little later the personality speaking said, "I am a man" and when asked his name said "Jensen".

In session five with the coming of the Jensen personality, the following exchange took place:

K.E.:	What's your name?
Subject:	Jacoby.
K.E.:	Jacoby what?
Subject:	Jensen Jacoby.
K.E.:	Is that your full name?
Subject:	Ja.
K.E.:	Now when you say you were not Jensen, who were you?
Subject:	I was me.
K.E.:	Me who?
Subject:	I was talking about him, I was me.
K.E.:	Who is me?
Subject:	Me.

This passage suggests that the subject was perplexed and assailed by doubts about his (her) identity. Possibly the questioning about identity further disturbed the balance toward the reemergence of the T.E. personality. At any rate, K.E. sensed that when the subject said, "I was talking about him, I was me", T.E. and not Jensen was talking. He thereupon brought her fully back to the present and again induced the Jensen personality by suggestions of regression. This time as Jensen began to manifest, the subject said, "I see myself as a . . . as a man". In session eight, Jensen was asked: "Is this your own body?" and he replied (after some hesitation): "Very strange". Unfortunately, remarks of this type were extremely rare in the sessions with this subject. In any case, such statements probably do not entitle us to say much about the status of a manifesting personality with regard to the differentiation between a discarnate entity and the expression of an aspect of the personality residual from a previous incarnation. The communicators already mentioned who seem to take over the "personal control" of the medium sometimes comment on the strangeness of the medium's body through which they manifest. For example, when a communicator, who was accepted by C. D. Thomas as his father, controlled Mrs. Leonard, he (the communicator) remarked on the absence of his beard in Mrs. Leonard (94, p. 35).*

Possibly we can and should separate the evidence for the xenoglossy and that for a real, fully formed surviving personality. The xenoglossy, if we accept the testimony of informants that T.E. did not learn Swedish by normal means, strongly indicates, in my opinion, survival of *some part* of human personality. The personality exhibiting this xenoglossy, however, manifested incompletely. This is not to say that Jensen exhibited no emotions. On the contrary he expressed intense ones in his antagonism towards war and in his vigorous approval of "förste man Hansen" or "Johansen". But his characterization was limited, since he showed a comparatively narrow range of personal attributes. This aspect of the case might arise from several possibilities: (a) the real Jensen, if he existed, was a peasant of extremely constricted interests and "personality", and his manifestations several centuries later would reflect this impoverishment; (b) the conditions of the experiments failed to provide adequate opportunities for the complete expression of a much richer Jensen personality which survived but could not present itself fully; or (c) the manifested Jensen personality had no existential status, but was a dream personality constructed by T.E. subconsciously and therein perhaps resembled the controls and communicators of Mrs. Piper, whose ontological status Mrs. Sidgwick effectively criticized (78).

An obstacle for this explanation, however, occurs in the difficulty of tying in the personality of Jensen and the xenoglossy, both of which seem obviously to be part of the same process, whatever that may be.

---

* Child subjects of reincarnation cases not infrequently allude to their awareness of being in a physical body of a shape and other appearance different from the one they remember being in during the previous life recalled.

Perhaps Jensen exists only as a partial personality or what in German we might call "ein Persönlichkeitchen". But this personality has at least enough of its former organization to handle speech intelligently and to show strong emotions at times.*

Jensen's tendency to sluggish responses and to perseveration suggestive of an organic brain syndrome does not seem to me to help in discriminating between reincarnation and possession. Some of the child subjects of reincarnation cases show a similar tendency to dwell on one topic and to relive, almost like a delirious person, the events they seem to be remembering of previous lives. And some mediumistic communicators also have complained that, when they are actually controlling a medium (as they believe), their memories are impaired and their responses more limited than is the case when they are in their "free state" away from the medium (92; 93). We should remember also that deeply hypnotized persons, whether "regressed" or not, usually exhibit sluggish responses and answer questions slowly and with apparent effort. They do not, however, ordinarily show the perseveration which Jensen often manifested.

As I stated at the beginning of this section, I do not believe I can myself decide between the hypothesis of possession and that of reincarnation in this case, although I do favor either of these over all other hypotheses as being (one or other) the most probably correct interpretations of the case. When I first studied the case I inclined to think reincarnation the more likely explanation, but in recent years as I have continued to think about it I find I have changed my opinion so that I now think possession slightly more suitable as the correct interpretation. I am not sure that I can say what has brought about this shift. No doubt it is partly due to my having (since I first took up this case) greatly expanded (and I hope deepened) my studies of cases of the reincarnation type. I know that some critics think most or all of them are best explained as instances of possession and I have given elsewhere my reasons for not thinking so (86). The apparent long interval or "intermission" between death and presumed rebirth, if the Jensen case is one of reincarnation, does not argue

---

* A colleague who read an earlier version of this monograph pointed out that postulating survival of a human personality after death in this case (or any other similar one) does not *explain* the xenoglossy. It does not explain how the hypothetical surviving personality accomplishes the motor acts involved in making the subject's vocal organs express sounds that communicate the xenoglossic language to other persons. I agree, but then, linguists and neurologists have no adequate explanation anyway of how living persons convert a thought into a spoken word intelligible to another person. Explanations of this order must await further appropriate research and I do not claim that an authentic case of responsive xenoglossy, such as I believe the case of T.E. to be, contributes to them. Survival of human personality after death does not explain responsive xenoglossy, but responsive xenoglossy may nevertheless require us to postulate that survival. If this proves correct, it would not be the first time a new fact is forced into acceptance before associated processes are understood.

for me against reincarnation. For although it is true that in most of the authentic reincarnation type cases of which I have published reports (84; 85; 86; 88; 89) the "intermissions" are very much shorter than the several centuries (minimally) which the Jensen case calls for, I have studied (and plan to publish) some cases with much longer "intermissions" than those reported for my already published cases. In such instances, however, it is difficult if not impossible to exclude the occurrence of one or more intermediate lives between that of the subject and the one apparently remembered.

In reincarnation type cases with longer "intermissions" one often finds, however, a kind of correspondence between the previous personality and the subject either in character or in circumstances or in both. But in the Jensen case such connections are missing or very obscure if present. The life and personality of Jensen simply do not seem to fit anywhere in the life and personality of T.E. It is, I think, this irrationality, so to speak, of Jensen's life in relation to that of T.E. which makes me slightly favor the possession hypothesis over the reincarnation one at present.

The potential contribution of cases of responsive xenoglossy to the evidence for survival after death

In the early days of scientific psychical research, reincarnation was considered favorably as a possible mode of survival after death, but as F. W. H. Myers correctly pointed out, there was not then any published evidence to support it (52, vol. 2, pp. 134–135).* The situation has altered somewhat, and since the turn of the century a considerable number of cases have occurred (and been reported) in which reincarnation seems at least a plausible hypothesis, among others, for explaining them. In recent years I have devoted a major portion of my energies to the investigation, analysis, and reporting of cases of the reincarnation type from many parts of the world (84–89). I believe that reincarnation seems the best explanation for some of these cases, although by no means for all.

The data available on many cases suggestive of memories of previous incarnations do not permit an absolute rejection of the possibility that the information allegedly remembered was acquired through normal means in this life. Often the memories have to do with items of personal information about a deceased person, such as his name, address,

---

* This is not strictly true, for even before Myers' death in 1901 a very few cases of the reincarnation type had been published, but in somewhat out-of-the-way places. And although these cases can now be seen to correspond in many respects to cases studied more recently, it remains correct that in Myers' day there was almost no published evidence that could be said to support the reincarnation hypothesis.

occupation, and family. One can only rarely feel absolutely positive that the subject could not have learned about such matters through normal means. Brief contacts with visitors from the town of the "remembered" deceased person might suffice to implant some of such "memories". Many cases suggestive of reincarnation cannot, I believe, be dismissed by such a simple explanation; nevertheless, this possibility, extremely difficult to exclude absolutely, seriously weakens some cases of the type. When, however, a subject recalls not merely a few items of information, but a complex skill such as an alien language, explanations along normal lines become much more difficult and the case accordingly becomes more important as evidence of the survival of human personality after physical death. I regard the present case as contributing substantially along this line. I do not think normal explanations suffice to account for the case and therefore regard it as strengthening the evidence for survival. A single case of this kind can carry us only a little farther. Yet I think this case does take us a small step. Although many instances of xenoglossy have been published in the various reports mentioned in my review of the subject (Chapter I), so far as I know, only three cases of xenoglossy have received anything approaching thorough contemporary recording and investigation. These are Richet's case (69), the Egyptian xenoglossy of "Rosemary" (38; 108; 109), and the present case. Richet's case exhibited (with a few doubtful exceptions) a recitative rather than a responsive xenoglossy and paranormal explanations, unless we include cryptomnesia here, hardly entered into the discussion of the possibilities. The "Rosemary" case of apparent Egyptian xenoglossy has suffered from the disadvantage (as well as the advantage) of providing the communication of a dead language for investigation. And the occurrence of an Egyptian xenoglossy in the case has not yet been accepted by students of Egyptian other than Hulme and Wood. In the present case, the subject communicated in a modern (or largely modern) language; tape recordings or notes were made of nearly all the Swedish xenoglossy; and three interpreters and five other scholars (not including myself) devoted their talents to the investigation of the case. It is presented, therefore, as a type of case belonging to a group with few other examples, but with a great deal of potential importance.*

If any reader, having come this far, has rejected the idea that the case involves a clever fraud whose subtle ingenuity somehow eluded my

---

* As I was preparing this book for the press I began investigation of another case of responsive xenoglossy. I have myself spoken German with the trance personality of the subject, an American woman who claims never to have studied or otherwise learned German. I received sensible replies in German to my questions spoken in German. I hope to publish a full report of this case at a later time. At present it would be premature to make any further comment beyond stating that I believe this case of German xenoglossy deserves a thorough investigation comparable or superior to that given the principal case presented in this book.

efforts to detect it, but nevertheless balks at accepting the interpretation of the case as evidence of the survival of human personality after physical death, he will then find himself (almost certainly) believing that somehow T.E. learned Swedish, more or less *ad hoc*, by extrasensory processes from living persons who could speak Swedish. In espousing this theory he is, however, acknowledging the existence of a far greater "amount" of extrasensory perception than he is probably accustomed to finding in the usual reports of parapsychological experiments either with unselected subjects or with specially gifted sensitives and mediums.

He will be forced to choose then between an interpretation involving the survival of human personality after physical death and one involving "super-extrasensory perception". I have earlier referred to the hypothesis of "super-extrasensory perception" as being itself a conjecture rather than a fact that all can acknowledge. This idea of "super-extrasensory perception" is often mooted by parapsychologists as a potential capacity of all human beings and an actual capacity of some. The existence of this ability, assumed by its advocates, would adequately account for all cases suggestive of survival after death, because its possessor becomes credited with an omnipotent endowment for paranormal cognition. The promoters of the hypothesis of "super-extrasensory perception" rarely mention it, however, except in cases where survival after death is at issue. The hypothesis sometimes seems to provide for them an escape from contemplating the possibility that survival after death is also a meritorious interpretation of many cases. If the advocates of "super-extrasensory perception" would bring forward a case in which it would seem to apply, although the case had no suggestion of survival in it, they would strengthen their argument. In the meantime, however, it seems to me that survival of human personality after death is not a more extravagant conjecture than "super-extrasensory perception". Belief, as Richet pointed out many years ago (70), is largely a matter of habit.* Our generation has become (or is becoming) habituated to the idea of extrasensory perception, but not yet to that of survival after physical death. And if two hypotheses seem otherwise equally valid most persons will choose the one that is least mind-stretching.

I shall myself be content if the present case serves to force review and discussion of these issues without claiming that it should settle them. But if any reader, accepting that the case calls for *some* paranormal interpretation, rejects one including survival and favours that of "super-extrasensory perception", he will surely acknowledge that the subject of the present case is a most remarkable demonstrator of it.

---

* "Pour croire complètement à un phénomène, il faut y être habitué" (70, p. 441).

Summary of the case and conclusions

In conclusion, I shall briefly summarize the principal features of the case and the main arguments which lead me to believe it provides important evidence of the survival of human personality after death.

Three native-born Swedish-speaking persons conversed with the subject in Swedish and testified to the occurrence of a responsive Swedish xenoglossy. Three additional Swedish-speaking persons who studied copies of the original tapes have also agreed that these tapes demonstrate a responsive xenoglossy. A seventh person, an American who understands Scandinavian languages, has also concurred in this opinion, based on his examination of the tape recording of one session.

Fraud seems most improbable from a careful examination of the character of the subject, and of the motives and opportunities available to her for the covert learning of Swedish and its later exhibition. Extensive interviews with the subject and members of her family as well as psychological tests and a polygraph test for lie detection did not elicit any indications of fraud.

Cryptomnesia seems extremely improbable from the testimony of the subject's mother, older sister, and older brother with regard to the close observation of the subject as a child, as well as from the subject's low aptitude for foreign languages.

Extrasensory perception from Swedish-speaking persons seems unlikely in the first instance because it would suppose a degree of amount and accuracy of extrasensory perception far beyond anything so far reported. And in the second instance, if a skill cannot be communicated even normally, but can only be acquired through practice, then a communication by extrasensory perception of the skill of speaking a language is impossible.

I conclude, therefore, that the case offers strong evidence of the survival of physical death by some aspect of human personality. As to how strong the evidence is, I would say that it definitely falls short of proof because of the impossibility of reaching absolute certainty in human testimony based on memories of past events. At the same time, I think it approaches proof according to the confidence given to the testimony in the case. This approach includes four stages. Of these, one is a question of fact established beyond dispute; one is an assumption or stated principle about the nature of skills; one is an assumption about the limits of telepathy between living persons; and one requires judgment about the reliability of human testimony in the case. The stages are as follows:

1. The subject exhibited a responsive xenoglossy. I regard this as a fact established beyond dispute by the concordant testimony of the seven

Swedish-speaking linguists, three of them actual interpreters at sessions with the subject.

2. The ability to speak any language in a sensible conversation is a skill and a skill as defined by Polanyi and described in this report is incommunicable and can only be acquired through practice. This is a definition or, if you prefer, an assumption of a general principle true of all skills.

3. A skill as defined in (2) above cannot be transmitted telepathically from one living person to another. This is another assumption based on (*a*) the essential incommunicability of all skills and (*b*) the absence of any authentic cases in which skills seem to have been paranormally communicated from living persons to a subject.

4. The medium of the present case had not herself learned Swedish normally prior to the hypnotic sessions of 1955–56. If the above stages of the argument are passed, and if the testimony presented is accepted as establishing that the subject did not learn Swedish normally, then there seems no escape from considering the case as best explained by the actual survival after death of the Jensen personality with its later manifestation in the sessions described.

References

1. ABERCROMBIE, J. (1831), *Inquiries Concerning the Intellectual Powers and the Investigation of Truth*. 2nd ed. Edinburgh: Waugh & Innis.

2. AKSAKOV, A. N. (1890), *Animismus und Spiritismus*. 2 vols. Leipzig: Druck und Verlag Oswald Mutze (1919).

3. ANDERSSON, I. (1956), *A History of Sweden*. Trans. C. Hannay. New York: Praeger.

4. ÅS, A. (1962), The recovery of forgotten language knowledge through hypnotic age regression: A case report, *American Journal of Clinical Hypnosis*, **5**, 24–29.

5. BERNSTEIN, M. (1956), *The Search for Bridey Murphy*. New York: Doubleday. (Rev. ed., 1965.)

6. BESTERMAN, T. (1932) An experiment in "clairvoyance" with M. Stefan Ossowiecki, *Proceedings S.P.R.*, **41**, 345–351.

7. BOZZANO, E. (1932), *Polyglot Mediumship (Xenoglossy)*. Trans. I. Emerson. London: Rider.

8. —— (1940), Di un caso importante d'identificazione spiritica. Chapter in *Indagini sulle Manifestazioni Supernormale*. Pieve: Dante. (This case was also published in E. Bozzano, *Casos de Identificación Espirita*. Trans. C. Postiglioni. Buenos Aires: Editorial Constancia, 1959.)

9. BROAD, C. D. (1925), *The Mind and its Place in Nature*. London: Kegan Paul, Trench & Trubner.

10. CARROLL, J. B., AND SAPON, S. M. (1955), *Modern Language Aptitude Test Manual*. New York: The Psychological Corporation.

11. CHARLTON, M. H. (1964), Aphasia in bilingual and polyglot patients—A neurological and psychological study, *Journal of Speech and Hearing Defects*, **29**, 307–311.

12. CLAY, J. C. (1938), *Annals of the Swedes on the Delaware*. Chicago: John Ericsson Memorial Committee.

13. COLERIDGE, S. T. (1817), *Biographia Literaria*. New York: Macmillan (1926).

14. CONGDON, M. H., HAIN, J. D., AND STEVENSON, I. (1961), A case of multiple personality illustrating the transition from role playing, *Journal of Nervous and Mental Disease*, **132**, 497–504.

15. CORY, C. E. (1919), A divided self, *Journal of Abnormal Psychology*, **14**, 281–291.

16. CRANE, H. W. (1915), A study in association reaction and reaction time. With an attempted application of results in determining the presence of guilty knowledge, *Psychological Monographs*, **18**, 1–75.

17. CROSLAND, H. R. (1929), The psychological methods of word association and reaction time as tests of deception, *Psychology Series*, University of Oregon Publications, **1**, 1–104.

18. CUTTEN, G. B. (1927), *Speaking with Tongues*. New Haven: Yale University Press.

19. DAHLSTROM, W. G., WELSH, G. S., AND DAHLSTROM, L. E. (1972), *A Minnesota Multiphasic Personality Inventory Handbook*. Rev. ed. Minneapolis: University of Minnesota.

20. DEARMAN, H. B., AND SMITH, B. M. (1963), Unconscious motivation and the polygraph test, *American Journal of Psychiatry*, **119**, 1017–1020.

21. DELANNE, G. (1924), *Documents pour servir à l'étude de la réincarnation*. Paris: Editions de la B.P.S.

22. DENIS, L. (1924), Cited in G. Delanne, *Documents pour servir à l'étude de la réincarnation*. Paris: Editions de la B.P.S.

23. DREIFUSS, F. E. (1961), Observations on aphasia in a polyglot poet, *Acta Psychiatrica et Neurologica Scandinavica*, **36**, 91–97.

24. DUCASSE, C. J. (1960), How the case of "The Search for Bridey Murphy" stands today, *Journal A.S.P.R.*, **54**, 3–22.

25. —— (1962), What would constitute conclusive evidence of survival after death? *Journal S.P.R.*, **41**, 401–406.

26. DUMAS, A. (1950), Quelques cas de phénomènes spirites, *Revue Métapsychique*, Nouvelle série, **12**, 205–222.

27. ECKERMANN, J. H. (1848), *Gespräche mit Goethe in den letzten Jahren seines Lebens*. 3 vols. Leipzig: Theodor Huth.

28. ECKMAN, J. (1958) *Crane Hook on the Delaware*. Newark, Delaware: Institute of Delaware History and Culture.

29. —— (1968), Personal communication, October, 1968.

30. EDWARDS, A. L. (1958), *Statistical Analysis*. Rev. ed. New York: Rinehart.

31. EMMONS, W. H., AND SIMON, C. W. (1956), The non-recall of material presented during sleep, *American Journal of Psychology*, **69**, 76–81.

32. FLOURNOY, T. (1900), *Des Indes à la planète Mars. Etude sur un cas de somnambulisme avec glossolalie*. Paris: Librairie Fischbacker, 1900. English ed., trans. D. B. Vermilye: New York: Harper's (1900). Reprinted with an introduction by C. T. K. Chari: New Hyde Park, New York: University Books (1963).

33. —— (1901), Nouvelles observations sur un cas de somnambulisme avec glossolalie, *Archives de Psychologie*, **1**, 102–255.

34. FREEBORN, H. (1902), Temporary reminiscence of a long-forgotten language during delirium, *Journal S.P.R.*, **10**, 279–283. (Originally published in *The Lancet*, June 14, 1902, 1685–1686.)

35. GUIRDHAM, A. (1970), *The Cathars and Reincarnation*. London: Neville Spearman.

36. HEYWOOD, R. (1948), Emergence of an apparent pseudo-communicator, *Journal S.P.R.*, **34**, 175–177.

37. HOPE, O. (1941), Case: Greek script by a child of four, *Journal S.P.R.*, **32**, 116–119.

38. HULME, A. J. H., AND WOOD, F. H. (1937), *Ancient Egypt Speaks*. London: Psychic Book Club.

39. INBAU, F. E., AND REID, J. E. (1953), *Lie Detection and Criminal Interrogation*. 3rd ed. Baltimore: Williams & Wilkins.

40. JAMES, W. (1890), *Principles of Psychology*. 2 vols. New York: Henry Holt.

41. JOHNSON, A. (1911), *The Swedish Settlements on the Delaware. Their History and Relation to the Indians, Dutch, and English, 1638–1664*. 2 vols. New York: Appleton.

42. — — (1927), *The Swedes on the Delaware, 1638–1664*. Philadelphia: International Printing Co.

43. JUNG, C. G., AND RIKLIN, F. (1904), Diagnostische Assoziationstudien. I. Beitrag. Experimentelle Untersuchungen über Assoziationen Gesunder, *Journal für Psychologie und Neurologie*, **3**, 193–215.

44. KELSEY, M. T. (1964), *Tongue Speaking: An Experiment in Spiritual Experience*. Garden City, New York: Doubleday.

45. KULIKOV, V. N. (1964), Psychology of sleep, *Soviet Psychology and Psychiatry*, **3**, 13–22. (Originally published in *Voprosy psikhologii*, **2**, 1964.)

46. LÁRUSDÓTTIR, E. (1970), *Hvert Liggur Leidin?* Reykjavik: Skuggsjá. (Relevant passages translated by Erlendur Haraldsson.)

47. LAURING, P. (1960), *A History of the Kingdom of Denmark*. Trans. D. Hohnen. Copenhagen: Høst & Son.

48. LEBARON, A. (pseud.) (1897), A case of psychic automatism, including "speaking with tongues", *Proceedings S.P.R.*, **12**, 277–297.

49. LODGE, O., AND OTHERS (1905–07), Discussion of Professor Richet's case of xenoglossy, *Proceedings S.P.R.*, **19**, 195–266.

50. MELVILLE, H. (1851), *Moby Dick*. New York: Random House (1926).

51. MONBODDO, LORD (1782), *Ancient Metaphysics, or the Science of Universals*. 2 vols. London: T. Cadell.

52. MYERS, F. W. H. (1903), *Human Personality and its Survival of Bodily Death*. 2 vols. New York: Longmans, Green.

53. ORNE, M. T. (1959), The nature of hypnosis: Artifact and essence, *Journal of Abnormal and Social Psychology*, **58**, 277–299.

54. OSIS, K. (1965), ESP over distance: A survey of experiments published in English, *Journal A.S.P.R.*, **54**, 22–42.

55. — — AND TURNER, M. E., Jr. (1968), Distance and ESP: A transcontinental experiment, *Proceedings A.S.P.R.*, **27**, 1–48.

56. OSTY, E. (1923), *La connaissance supra-normale*. Paris: Librairie Alcan. English ed., trans. S. de Brath: *Supernormal Faculties in Man*. London: Methuen (1923).

57. PAGENSTECHER, G. (1922), Past events seership: A study in psychometry, *Proceedings A.S.P.R.*, **16**, 1–136.

58. PAL, P. (1968), Personal communication, August, 1968.

59. PICKFORD, R. W. (1943), An "hysterical" medium, *British Journal of Medical Psychology*, **19**, 363–366.

60. PLUMMER, W. S. (1887), *Mary Reynolds: A Case of Double Consciousness*. Chicago: Religio-Philosophical Publishing House.

61. PODMORE, F. (1902), *Modern Spiritualism*. 2 vols. London: Methuen.

62. POLANYI, M. (1958), *Personal Knowledge*. London: Routledge & Kegan Paul.

63. — — (1962), Tacit knowing: Its bearing on some problems of philosophy, *Reviews of Modern Physics*, **34**, 601–616.

64. — — (1966) *The Tacit Dimension*. Garden City, New York: Doubleday.

65. PRINCE, W. F. (1915–16), The Doris case of multiple personality, *Proceedings A.S.P.R.*, **9–10**, 9–1419.

66. — — (1929), *The Case of Patience Worth*. Boston: Boston Society for Psychic Research.

67. RADCLYFFE-HALL, M., AND TROUBRIDGE, U. (1919), On a series of sittings with Mrs. Osborne Leonard, *Proceedings S.P.R.*, **30**, 339–554.

68. RAO, K. R. (1963), Studies in the preferential effect. II. A language ESP test involving precognition and "intervention", *Journal of Parapsychology*, **27**, 147–160.

69. RICHET, C. (1905–07), Xénoglossie: L'écriture automatique en langues étrangères, *Proceedings S.P.R.*, **19**, 162–194.

70. — — (1926), Des conditions de la certitude, *Proceedings S.P.R.*, **35**, 422–444.

71. RISING, J., *Een beskrefningh om Nova Svecia*, etc. Manuscript copy. Cited by A. Johnson, *op. cit.*, ref. 41, vol. 1, p. 353.

72. RODNEY, J. (1959), *Explorations of a Hypnotist*. London: Elek Books.

73. ROLL, W. G. (1969), The Newark disturbances, *Journal A.S.P.R.*, **63**, 123–174.

74. ROSEN, H. (1956), Introduction. In *A Scientific Report on "The Search for Bridey Murphy"*, ed. M. V. Kline. New York: Julian Press.

75. SALTER, H. W. (1932), The history of George Valiantine, *Proceedings S.P.R.*, **40**, 389–410.

76. SAMARIN, W. J. (1969), Forms and functions of nonsense language, *Linguistics*, **50**, 70–74.

77. SCHMEIDLER, G. R. (1964), An experiment on precognitive clairvoyance. Part I. The main results, *Journal of Parapsychology*, **28**, 1–14.

78. SIDGWICK, E. M. (1915), A contribution to the study of the psychology of Mrs. Piper's trance phenomena, *Proceedings S.P.R.*, **28**, 1–652.

79. SIMON, C. W., AND EMMONS, W. H. (1955), Learning during sleep? *Psychological Bulletin*, **52**, 328–342.

80. SIMON, C. W., AND EMMONS, W. H. (1956), Responses to material presented during various levels of sleep, *Journal of Experimental Psychology*, **51**, 89–97.

81. SINCLAIR, U. (1930), *Mental Radio*. Springfield, Illinois: Thomas (1962).

82. SOAL, S. G., AND BATEMAN, F. (1954), *Modern Experiments in Telepathy*. London: Faber.

83. STEVENS, W. O. (1945), *Beyond the Sunset*. New York: Dodd, Mead.

84. STEVENSON, I. (1960a), The evidence for survival from claimed memories of former incarnations, Part I, *Journal A.S.P.R.*, **54**, 51–71.

85. — — (1960b), The evidence for survival from claimed memories of former incarnations, Part II, *Ibid.*, **54**, 95–117.

86. — — (1966) Twenty cases suggestive of reincarnation, *Proceedings A.S.P.R.*, **26**, 1–362.

87. — — *Cases of the Reincarnation Type*. (In preparation.)

88. — — AND STORY, F. (1970), A case of the reincarnation type in Ceylon: The case of Disna Samarasinghe, *Journal of Asian and African Studies*, **5**, 241–255.

89. STORY, F., AND STEVENSON, I. (1967), A case of the reincarnation type in Ceylon: The case of Warnasiri Adikari, *Journal A.S.P.R.*, **61**, 130–145.

90. SURINGAR, J. V. (1923), A case of thought-transference, *Journal S.P.R.*, **21**, 170–175.

91. TANNER, A. (1910), *Studies in Spiritism*. New York: Appleton.

92. THOMAS, C. D. (1928), *Life Beyond Death with Evidence*. London: Collins.

93. — — (1928–9), The "modus operandi" of trance communication according to descriptions received through Mrs. Osborne Leonard, *Proceedings S.P.R.*, **38**, 49–100.

94. — — (1950), Personal control in trance sittings. In W. H. Salter, *Trance Mediumship*. London: Society for Psychical Research.

95. THURMOND, C. T. (1943), Last thoughts before drowning, *Journal of Abnormal and Social Psychology*, **38**, 165–184.

96. TYRRELL, G. N. M. (1946), The "modus operandi" of paranormal cognition, *Proceedings S.P.R.*, **48**, 65–120.

97. UNDERHILL, A. L. (1885), *The Missing Link in Modern Spiritualism*. New York: Thomas R. Knox.

98. VAN EEDEN, F. (1901–3), Account of sittings with Mrs. Thompson, *Proceedings S.P.R.*, **17**, 75–115.

99. VON REUTER, F. (1928), *Psychical Experiences of a Musician*. London: Simpkin Marshall.

100. WARD, C. (1930), *The Dutch and Swedes on the Delaware, 1609–1664*. Philadelphia: University of Pennsylvania Press.

101. WEINSTEIN, E., ABRAMS, S., AND GIBBONS, D. (1970), The validity of the polygraph with hypnotically induced repression and guilt, *American Journal of Psychiatry*, **126**, 143–146.

102. WELSH, G. S., AND DAHLSTROM, W. G. (1956), *Basic Readings on the Minnesota Multiphasic Personality Inventory in Psychology and Medicine*. Minneapolis: University of Minnesota Press.

103. WEST, D. J. (1948), Investigation of a case of xenoglossy, *Journal S.P.R.*, **34**, 267–269.

104. WHITAKER, T. (1900), Automatic phenomena in a case of hysteria, *Journal S.P.R.*, **9**, 333–339.

105. WHYMANT, N. (1928), Some Valiantine sittings and oriental voices, *Journal A.S.P.R.*, **22**, 225–229.

106. — — (1931), *Psychic Adventures in New York*. London: Morley & Mitchell Kennerley.

107. WOLFF, H. G., AND CURRAN, D. (1935), Nature of delirium and allied states, *Archives of Neurology and Psychiatry*, **33**, 1175–1215.

108. WOOD, F. H. (1935), *After Thirty Centuries*. London: Rider.

109. — — (1955), *This Egyptian Miracle*. 2nd ed. London: Watkins.

110. YOST, C. S. (1929), The evidence in *Telka*. In W. F. Prince, *The Case of Patience Worth*. Boston: Boston Society for Psychic Research.

111. ZAFFRON, R. (1970), Review of *Knowing and Being: Essays by Michael Polanyi*. (ed. M. Grene. Chicago: University of Chicago Press, 1969). *Science*, **168**, June 19, 1970, 1440–1442.

112. ZIRKLE, C. (1954), Citation of fraudulent data, *Science*, **120**, July 30, 1954, 189–190.

Appendix

Introduction

The transcript of session number seven here provided has been carefully developed from the original transcript made from the tape recordings by Mrs. Britta Warbert and Mrs. Eva Hellström in Stockholm. However, a number of words and phrases not included in that transcript have been distinctly heard by myself or others on the tapes and these words and phrases have been included. Mrs. Birgit Stanford, a native of Sweden, and I have listened to the tapes separately and together many times. We listened to doubtful portions until we could (except in a very few instances) agree on what we had heard and its meaning. We have also gone over the present transcript carefully and repeatedly.

In the transcript of the Swedish (left-hand column) all phrases, words, and parts of words that cannot be distinctly heard are placed in brackets. Many of these words in brackets can, however, be heard at least partially. In a few places I have added in brackets words, e.g., pronouns, that are not heard at all, but which may be safely conjectured. Indications of emotions and other "stage directions" are placed in parentheses. No word has been omitted from the transcript if it could be identified, except for irrelevant material at the beginning and end of the session in which the hypnotist is giving suggestions to the subject and some of the background comments in English. Occasionally the interpreter or the hypnotist and the subject spoke at the same time. In these few instances, an arbitrary order of the remarks has been assigned in the transcript to remarks that were made simultaneously or almost so.

Identified words of both the subject and interpreters have usually been transcribed with correct Swedish spelling. This does not do justice to the peculiarities of Jensen's pronunciation, especially his habit of adding a vowel at the end of words ending in a consonant, e.g., saying "Brännvine" instead of "Brännvin".*
Also in many places one cannot be certain whether Jensen is giving a Swedish or a Norwegian pronunciation to a word that (with small variations) belongs to both languages. In most cases I have given the Swedish spelling. In a number of other instances, e.g., "plass", "klærne", and "fjær", Jensen's pronunciation is so clearly on the Norwegian side that I have given the Norwegian spelling. And in some other places I have given words that are clearly dialect forms or words that cannot be definitely identified with as approximate a spelling as possible to

---

* This example illustrates a common difficulty in understanding precisely what Jensen says. The vowel added at the end of his word could be a superfluous vowel sound often heard in dialects. But it could also be the final vowel of "brännvinet" with the suffixed definite article and the final consonant not pronounced or at least not heard.

represent the sounds heard. Only a complete phonetic transcription could adequately convey Jensen's peculiarities of pronunciation and rather than attempt this partially, I decided instead to draw attention to the main oddities of his pronunciation in the Comments.

In a small number of places Jensen's words have not been identified at all. In these instances also I have tried to represent Jensen's sounds with approximately corresponding spelling using the English alphabet.

Careful readers who compare the text of this transcript with some of the citations given earlier, in the summary account of Jensen's language, may notice some discrepancies. These are due to my reluctance to change the spelling given by some commentators, e.g., Dr. N. G. Sahlin and Mr. W. G. Roll, and also to the fact that different listeners have heard some of the words differently.

The English translation of the transcript was made in the first place by myself and then revised by Mrs. Stanford and Dr. Sahlin. In a number of places the translation is loose and vague because Jensen sometimes pronounced only the stumps of sentences or words, so to speak, and it was difficult to know what he was actually trying to say. In many places we have given an idiomatic English rendition instead of a more literal, but stiffer translation.

Occasionally I have added to the translation a word in brackets, usually an article or a pronoun, that does not have a corresponding word in the Swedish. Such additions are to improve the meaning of the translation for the reader. The word (untranslatable) or the indication (?) appears in the translation (middle) column on the same line as untranslatable utterances in the transcript. I have also used the symbol (?) adjoining translations that seem doubtful. Other places of difficulty in the translation are indicated in the column (right-hand) of Comments.

English words spoken in the interview and included in the transcript are not reproduced in the translation column. Nor are most proper names unless they occur in a sentence.

In addition to my own observations, the Comments include many contributions by Dr. Sahlin, Mrs. Hellström, Mr. Ejvegård, Mr. Roll, Dr. Jacobson, Dr. Coates, and others.

Both Dr. Sahlin and Mr. Ejvegård reviewed the entire transcription, translation, and comments and made many further suggestions for improvements.

The following abbreviations have been used in the Transcript and in the Comments:

S: the Subject, T.E., or the Jensen personality.

H: the Hypnotist, K.E.

I: the Interpreters, Dr. Sahlin and Mr. L. Ekman. I have not indicated (except occasionally) which interpreter was speaking as to do so seemed unnecessary and possibly confusing to the reader.

V: Unidentified voices, usually in the background, and most often the interpreters translating *sotto voce* for the hypnotist, or the participants discussing further tactics for the interview.

At one point for an interval of undetermined length, the tape recorder was turned off or not functioning, probably because the tape had come to an end without this being noticed by the participants. It seems that during this unrecorded period the conversation went on and some other objects were shown to Jensen.

This accounts for the fact that Dr. Sahlin mentioned in his notes and conversations with me some few objects that were shown to the subject but which cannot be identified or otherwise inferred from the remarks recorded on the tape.

Unfortunately, the interviewers kept no list of the objects and pictures shown Jensen. In most instances I have been able to indicate these correctly either from notes of my interviews with K.E. and Dr. Sahlin or from notes furnished by Dr. Sahlin. In a few instances it has been impossible to say exactly what object was shown to Jensen at a particular time. Some of the most interesting and important details of the session occurred when Jensen responded to an object or picture shown him either with the correct name or some other appropriate response in Swedish.

In a few instances I have included in the Comments some additional information about Jensen's reactions, for example, to the objects shown. This part of the Comments derives from interviews with K.E., the hypnotist, and Dr. Sahlin, or from notes by Dr. Sahlin.

The transcript of session number seven follows.

Transcript

H: You feel as if you have lived again in the past. You feel as if you are living that life that you have lived a long time ago again. You are right there. You are getting closer to the time that you have lived in the past.

Three! You are in the past. You are now living. You are living a life. When I snap my fingers you will know who you are. You are living a life. (snap) Who are you? Who are you?

S: (whispering) A man.

H: What?

S: A man.

H: All right, you are feeling very relaxed as that man. You feel very good. You are going back further a little bit. He is a young man.

He is a young man, he is a young man. He is a young man and you are feeling good. You feel very good, you feel happy. You don't know why, but you are feeling happy. What's your name?

Translation

Comments

Considerable preliminary material consisting of suggestions to the subject to relax and get ready to return to another point in time has been omitted. The transcript has been given from near the point where the Jensen personality first emerges in the session.

H. has previously told S. he will count up to three as S. goes back to the previous life.

At this point the subject responds in English.

Here the hypnotist is trying to regress the subject in the Jensen personality to avoid the closing scene of Jensen's life in which he seems to be killed by a blow on the head. This scene had caused the subject much distress on other occasions.

Transcript	*Translation*	*Comments*
S: Jensen.		
H: Now Jensen, what is your second name? You have another name?		
S: Ja.	Yes.	
H: What is it? Talk louder, Jensen, I can't hear.		
S: Jacoby.		Jensen pronounces this name: Yah'-ko-bee.
H: And what is your father's name?		
S: Jacoby.		
H: Does he have another name?		
S: [Inaudible few words]		
H: All right, Jensen. You feel very good. You are relaxed. I am going to ask you a lot of questions about your life. You are right there. You are living, Jensen. You are enjoying life. You are forty years old, forty years old. You feel forty years old. You feel forty years old. You feel forty years old, Jensen. You feel		

very good. Just relax, Jensen. You feel very good. Now Jensen, I am going to ask you questions, and you are going to find that you want to talk to me, because you feel as if I am your friend. You want to talk to me. What do you do for a living, Jensen? What do you do for a living?

S: En bonde.

"En bonde" may perhaps be better translated by the word "peasant". This is the first of many instances in which Jensen responds in Swedish to a question asked in English.

A farmer.

H: What?

S: En bonde.

A farmer.

H: What?

The hypnotist repeats "What?" because he knows no Swedish and does not understand what Jensen has said.

S: En bonde.

A farmer.

I: En bonde.

A farmer.

The interpreter here repeats what Jensen has said more for the benefit of the hypnotist than otherwise since Jensen's utterance of "en bonde" seems distinct enough.

Transcript	*Translation*	*Comments*
H: All right, now my voice is going to change to other types of voices, and you are going to talk because you like my voice, don't you? I am your friend, Jensen. I am your friend. I like you very much. We are friends. What's your best friend's name, Jensen? What's your best friend's name? Do you have a friend? What's his name?		
S: Ja då, ja, ja.	Oh yes, yes, yes.	"Ja då" is roughly equivalent to "Oh yes", or "Well, yes".
H: What's his name?		
S: Jensen.		
H: That's your name, isn't it? What's *his* name?		
S: Jensen.		
H: Is your friend's name Jensen? What's his second name?		Here occurs the first of a number of instances of perseveration on the part of Jensen. Asked for his friend's name he goes on repeating or giving his own name as if he cannot get off that topic.
S: Jensen Jacoby.		The hypnotist is puzzled.
H: That's *you*!		

S: Ja.

Yes.

H: But, what's your friend's name?

S: Jensen är vän.

Jensen is [a] friend.

H: Jensen who?

S: Jensen min vän.

Jensen [is] my friend.

The verb cannot be heard.

H: Say that name again.

S: Jensen är min vän.

Jensen is my friend.

V: (repeating) Är min vän.

Is my friend.

Here the verb is distinctly put in.

H: All right now, I am going to feel . . . You are going to feel as if I am that friend. I am your best friend. I sound just like him.

S: Jensen.

H: His name is Jensen, too? All right.

S: Magda. Magda. Magda.

"Magda" is a woman's name in Swedish, but not heard much in modern Sweden. It is short for "Magdalena".

H: All right, all right. Now here are some friends of mine, and they are going to talk to you.

I: Du säger att du är en bonde, Jens?

You say you are a farmer, Jens?

S: Ja.

Yes.

Transcript	Translation	Comments
I: Var bor du?	Where do you live?	
S: I huset.	In the house.	The article is correctly placed at the end of the noun.
I: Du bor i huset?	You live in the house?	
S: Ja.	Yes.	
I: Var ligger huset?	Where is the house located?	
S: I Hansen.	In Hansen.	
I: Var ligger huset? Vad heter platsen?	Where is the house located? What is the place called?	
S: Hansen.	Hansen.	
I: Huset ligger i Hansen?	The house is located at Hansen?	
S: Ja då.	Oh yes.	
I: Bor det många människor där? Bor det mycket folk där? I Hansen?	Do many persons live there? Are there a lot of people there? In Hansen?	
S: [Hansen.] Ja, Hansen.	Hansen. Yes, Hansen.	
I: Har du mycket land?	Do you have a lot of land?	
S: Har..s..landet.	Have the land.	The "s" heard between "har" and "landet" seems extraneous and its use is not understood.

I: Har du mycket skog, Jens? På din gård? ....

S: Har jugo skog.

Do you have a lot of woods, Jens? On your farm? ....

Have (? twenty) woods.

The meaning of "jugo" is unclear. Jensen's final vowel sounds like "a", as if he pronounces "juga". Although no "t" sound is heard, he may be trying to say "tjugo", the Swedish word for "twenty". Here as often elsewhere, Jensen adds a vowel after the final consonant of "skog", making the word sound like "skoga". But he might have been trying to say (correctly) the plural "skogar".

I: Du har mycket skog?

S: [T] jugo.

Do you have a lot of woods?

Twenty.

In Jensen's word here the "t" sound is faintly heard, and he is almost certainly trying to say the Swedish word for "twenty". The final vowel still sounds like an "a".

I: Vart går du någonstans, Jensen, när du går till byn? Vad heter byn?

S: Mörby Hagar.

Whereabouts do you go, Jensen, when you go to the village? What is the village called?

Mörby Meadows.

The translation is somewhat conjectural since Jensen makes the second word sound like "hargar". But I have supposed that the place where he lived might have been called "Mörby Meadows". "Hage" in Swedish (and also Norwegian) refers to an enclosed pasture, a grove, orchard, or paddock. I have chosen the word "meadows", as perhaps the most suitable translation.

Transcript	Translation	Comments
I: Säg det igen?	Say that again.	
S: Mörby Hagar.	Mörby Meadows.	See text (p. 29) for another possible identification of the name of Jensen's village.
I: Jag förstår dig inte . . . Vad heter byn? Du bor i Hansen.	I don't understand you. What is the name of the village? You live in Hansen.	
S: Hansen.	Hansen.	
I: Du bor i Hansen? Ja.	You live in Hansen? Yes.	
S: Ja. [Indistinct murmuring]	Yes.	
I: Kan du tala litet högre? Jens?	Can you speak a little louder? Jens?	
S: [Jag] är trött, [jag] är trött, [jag] är trött.	I am tired. I am tired. I am tired.	
I: Är du trött, ja?	You're tired, are you?	This is the first of several occasions when Jensen complains of being tired. His sighs seem to confirm his statement.
S: Ja. (sighs)	Yes.	
I: Du är inte trött, nu inte. Ja. Du känner dig bättre nu, gör du inte? Eller hur? Ja, mycket bättre. Så. Tala om för mig nu, Hansen! Vart går du när du vill ha . . . köpa salt?	You're not tired now; not at all. Yes. You feel better now, don't you? Don't you? Yes, a lot better. So. Tell me now, Hansen. Where do you go when you want to have . . . to buy salt?	The interpreter makes a slip here in addressing Jensen as "Hansen".
S: Haverö.	Haverö.	Here Jensen introduces the name of the nearby town where he goes to market.

I: Till Haverö?	To Haverö?	
S: Ja.	Yes.	
I: Är Haverö en stor plats?	Is Haverö a big place?	
S: En stort? Nej.	A big [place]? No.	Since "plats" is of common or non-neuter gender, Jensen's addition of "t" at the end of "stor" is ungrammatical.
I: Är det långt till Haverö? Hur går du dit? Tala om för mig vägen. Jag vill gå till Haverö. Säg mig! Hur kan jag gå dit? Är det långt från här?	Is it far to Haverö? How do you go there? Show me the way. I want to go to Haverö. Tell me. How can I get there? Is it a long way from here?	
S: Nej, nej ... morgon.	No, no ... morning.	Jensen may mean to say you can reach Haverö in half a day. He may also mean to say: "I will show you tomorrow".
I: Hur många gånger går du till Haverö? Går du dit ofta?	How often do you go to Haverö? Do you go there often?	
S: Ja, ja. Här torv.	Yes. Yes. Here [is a] market.	Jensen seems to omit the verb in the sentence. He also adds a vowel at the end of "torv", saying "torve". "Torv", is Norwegian for market. The Swedish equivalent is "torg".
I: Tala högre!	Speak up!	
S: Här till torv.	Here to market.	Again Jensen apparently omits the verb of the sentence.

Transcript	Translation	Comments
I: Jag förstår dig inte. Säg mig igen! Säg mig, Jens! Vad gör du i Haverö? Vad gör du i Haverö?	I don't understand you. Tell me again. Tell me, Jens. What do you do in Haverö? What do you do in Haverö?	
S: Här torv.	Here [is a] market.	No verb can be heard.
I: Högre! Säg det igen! Vad gör du i Haverö?	Louder! Say that again. What do you do in Haverö?	
S: Här torv.	Here [is a] market.	No verb can be heard.
I: En gång till... Har du hört... Har du hört talas om Uppsala?	Once more... Have you heard of... Have you ever heard Uppsala mentioned?	Here the interpreter changes the topic and asks another question.
S: Nej.	No.	
I: Ligger Haverö vid havet?	Is Haverö on the coast?	Here the interpreter returns to press for more information about Haverö, but the hypnotist comes in with further suggestions in English.
V: [Indistinct in background]		
H: Now you will find, Jensen, that when I touch your head you are going to feel relaxed. You won't even have to try to remember. It's all going to come back to you. Everything that you did is coming back to you. You remember very well. Oh, your mind is very good, Jensen, you are a smart man! Everything you		

want you can remember. You are feeling better now, aren't you? You are feeling much better. Very good. You don't even have to think. It's right there. When I snap my finger, you will be able to answer our friend ... all his questions without even having to think. It's right there in your mind. Watch that happen. (snap) Ah! Now you can answer. You can answer them very easily and you feel relaxed. And you can talk loud just like Jensen talks, Jensen is a strong man.

I: Jensen, kan du höra mig? Hör du mig?

Jensen, can you hear me? Do you hear me?

S: Ja.

Yes.

I: Hur gammal är du?

How old are you?

S: [Unclear muttering]

Although the interpreter repeats the number he thinks Jensen spoke, it cannot be heard distinctly on the recording.

I: Trettio? Säg det igen! Hur gammal är du?

Thirty? Say that again! How old are you?

S: Långsam. Nej.

Slow. No.

Jensen may here be trying to get the interpreter to speak more slowly.

I: Jag förstod inte. Säg det igen! Hur gammal är du? Tio? Tjugo? Trettio? Fyrtio? Är du fyrtio? Är du fyrtio år gammal? Förstår du [mig]?

I did not understand. Say that again. How old are you? Ten? Twenty? Thirty? Forty? Are you forty? Are you forty years old? Do you understand me?

5

Transcript	Translation	Comments
S: Trettio.	Thirty.	
H: Now you feel very good, Jensen. Now I am going to show you how you are going to feel good. Jensen, you have a lot of "potty seed" and you are taking it to Haverö and you feel very good. How are you taking it to Haverö? How are you going to Haverö?		The hypnotist is here trying to draw Jensen out in connection with the "potty seed" or "batty seed" which he described as a source of an intoxicating beverage and seeds made into cakes. This may in fact have been "poppy seed" (see text).
S: Hästkrafter.	Horsepowers.	Presumably Jensen means on horseback. See text (p. 31) for discussion of the possible anachronism in the use of the word "hästkrafter".
H: Go ahead, tell me, how are you going into Haverö? Huh?		
I: (repeating S's word) Hästkrafter.	Horsepowers.	
H: Go ahead, now you are going to Haverö? Huh? Tell me, what's on your mind, Jensen? You are feeling good. You are going to Haverö. You are going to have a good time. Now you are in Haverö. You are right in Haverö. You just got there and you want to trade. You understand me, don't you,		

Jensen: You want to trade ... you ... you ... you want to sell your "potty seed", and you want to get something else, don't you? Do you? Uh? Go ahead, you can talk loud. Now you are in Haverö. There is somebody coming up to you. He wants to trade with you. He wants to ask you what you have.

I: Vad har du att ge mig? Säg mig, Jens! Vad har du att ge mig?

What do you have to give me? Tell me, Jens. What do you have to give me?

S: Kornet.

The grain.

A very clear example of a response with a word not in any way offered by the interpreter. The definite article is correctly suffixed.

I: Säg det igen! Jag förstår dig inte.

Say that again! I don't understand you.

S: Kornet.

The grain.

I: Kornet? O! Vad vill du ha av mig?

The grain? Oh! What do you want from me?

S: En tupp.

A rooster.

Jensen adds a vowel at the end of the word and pronounces "tuppe".

I: (repeating *sotto voce* in background) En tupp.
(out loud) Ja, vill du ha salt? Behöver du någon salt? Vill du ha tyg? Vill du ha något att dricka, Jens? Har du några pengar?

A rooster. Yes. Do you want some salt? Do you need any salt? Do you want some cloth? Would you like something to drink, Jens? Have you any money?

The interpreter makes a grammatical slip here when he says "någon salt" instead of "något salt".

Transcript	Translation	Comments
S: Nej pengar.	No money.	Jensen's reply here is ungrammatical and corrected by the interpreter in his response.
I: Inga pengar?	No money?	
S: Nej.	No.	
I: Varför har du inte pengar?	How is it you don't have any money?	
S: Fattig. [Kornet.]	Poor. The grain.	Another appropriate response. The addition of "kornet" provides an example of which there will be many more of Jensen's tendency to perseveration, the repeating of a word or phrase in a more or less automatic way.
I: Kornet, bara kornet, inget annat. Har du några djur på din gård? Säg mig, Jens, har du många getter? Har du häst?	Grain, only grain and nothing else. Have you any animals on your land? Tell me, Jens, have you many goats? Do you have [a] horse?	
S: Ja.	Yes.	
I: Har du en häst?	You have a horse?	The indefinite article "en" is not required before "häst" in the Swedish.
S: Ja.	Yes.	
I: Har du hästen här i Haverö?	Do you have the horse here in Haverö?	
S: Ja.	Yes.	

I: Vill du sälja den hästen? Nej? Du vill inte sälja din häst.	Would you like to sell that horse? No? You don't want to sell your horse.	N. Sahlin remembered that Jensen shook his head emphatically when asked if he wanted to sell his horse.
S. (emphatically) Nej!	No!	
I: Varför inte? Säg mig varför! Är det en bra häst?	Why not? Tell me why not. Is it a fine horse?	
S. God.	Excellent.	Jensen does not copy the interpreter's word "bra", but replies with a near synonym "god", which he pronounces close to "gote".
I: Den är god?	So it is excellent?	
S: God.	Excellent.	
I: När skall du åka hem igen? Säg, har du en flicka här i Haverö? Säg mig, Jens, vad heter hon? Tala högre! Jag hör dig inte. Säg mig, vad heter flickan? Du förstår mig, gör du inte?	When will you drive back home again? Say, do you have a girl friend here in Haverö? Tell me, Jens, what's her name? Speak up! I can't hear you. Tell me, what's the name of the girl? You understand me, don't you?	
S: Nej, trött.	No, tired.	Jensen puts a vowel at the end of the word, making "trötte".
I: Nej, du är inte trött. Du är inte trött alls, Jens. Du mår bra. Ja, du känner dig fin. Ja. Du tycker det är roligt här. Tycker du inte om Haverö?	No, you are not tired. You are not one bit tired, Jens. You feel great. Yes, you feel fine. Yes. You think it is fun to be here. Don't you like Haverö?	The general policy of the interviewers is to ignore, or deny, Jensen's repeated complaints of being tired.
S: [Indistinct murmuring] [Jag sover.]	I am sleeping.	

Transcript	Translation	Comments
I: Vad säger du?	What are you saying?	
S: (indistinctly) Jag sover.	I am sleeping.	
I: Jaså du...? Vad? Du sover? Nej. Du sover inte. Du är i Haverö nu. Du har ditt korn. Du har kornet här. Vad vill du ha av mig nu? Säg mig! Säg mig, Jens! Vad vill du ha för ditt korn?	So you...? What? You are sleeping? No. You're not asleep. You are in Haverö now. You have your grain. You have [your] grain here. What would you like from me now? Tell me! Tell me, Jens! What do you want for your grain?	
S: Tepper.	Covers.	"Tepper" in Norwegian refers to rugs and also to bedcovers. It is unlikely Jensen bought rugs, but he might have wanted bedcovers. It is also possible that Jensen might have been trying to say "Tupper" (English: "roosters"). "Tupp" (rooster) had been his response earlier to a similar question.
I: Jensen, hör på mig! Hör på mig! Vet du om Stockholm? Vet du om Stockholm? Har du hört ordet Stockholm?	Jensen, listen to me. Listen to me. Do you know about Stockholm? Do you know about Stockholm? Have you heard the word "Stockholm"?	
Inte det. Har du hört Sigtuna? Har du hört namnet Sigtuna? Tala litet högre! Hör på mig nu! Tala högre! Så där ja! Smile a little. You are very relaxed. Smile a little.	No. Have you heard of Sigtuna? Have you heard of the name Sigtuna? Speak up a little! Listen to me now! Speak up! There now!	The interpreter here speaks a little English to Jensen as he occasionally does elsewhere.

Förstår du Björkö? Nej. Förstår du Haverö? Vad heter din flicka i Haverö?

Are you familiar with Björkö? No. Are you familiar with Haverö? What's the name of your girl in Haverö?

Here the interpreter, in an attempt to date Jensen's lifetime, asks him about Björkö, a town or trading post antedating Stockholm, but also on Lake Mälar. Björkö was the chief town of the Svear or central Swedes.

S: Jag heter Hansen.

My name is Hansen.

I: Ja, du heter Hansen? Du heter Jens Jacoby.

Yes, you're called Hansen? Your name is Jens Jacoby.

S: Ja.

Yes.

I: Vad heter din flicka?

What is your girl called?

S: Hansen [själv].

Hansen himself. (?)

Jensen has possibly not understood the question, or may be trying to emphasize that the girl's name really is Hansen also.

H: All right, Jensen, now you recognize my voice, don't you? I am another friend of yours. I am your good friend, Jensen, I am your friend and you feel very good. Ha, let's have a good time, Jensen. What are you laughing about? You feel happy. You feel good.

During this section chuckles may be heard in the background. Some of these seem to have been expressed by Jensen and the others present laugh lightly with him.

V: (in background) He is thinking about that girl.

Transcript	Translation	Comments
H: Jensen, let us go out and have a good time with the girls, huh? Do you want to go and get drunk? What would you like to drink? We are in Haverö.		
S: Brännvin.	Brandy.	Again Jensen adds a vowel to the end of the word, pronouncing "Brännvine". This word is an excellent example of an appropriate response in Swedish to a question posed in English.
H: What?		
S: Brännvin.	Brandy.	
I: (repeating) Brännvin?	Brandy?	The interpreter pronounces the word as does Jensen. One interpreter can be heard saying in background in English: "Shame on you, Jensen!"
H: What kind of liquor do you like, Jensen? What kind of "vina" do you like?		In saying "vina", the hypnotist partly mimics Jensen's pronunciation of "Brännvin" with a vowel at the end of the word.
I: (*sotto voce* to H.) Brännvin. Brännvin.	Brandy. Brandy.	
H: Brännvin? What kind do you like? Huh? Come, let's go into the inn and we'll have some. Huh? Come on.		
S: [Inga] pengar.	No money.	Jensen's word "inga" cannot be heard distinctly on the tape, but evidently was

I: (repeating) Inga pengar. Inga pengar.	No money. No money.	heard by the interpreter who repeats it. Jensen's phrase is now grammatical, but he has already heard it once before spoken by the interpreter. Note that Jensen makes an appropriate response in Swedish to the hypnotist's question spoken in English.
H: Well, I have money. You don't have to worry. I have got plenty of money. Yea, yea, I have got money. Come, I will show you. Do you want to see the money? You believe me, don't you? (S. sighs) Let's go into the inn. Now we are going in the inn. Go ahead, Jensen. You ask for the drink. Go ahead. We are up to the bar. We are up to the place where they give the drink. Somebody is asking you what kind of drink you want.		
I: Vad vill du ha, Jens? Vad vill du ha att dricka?	What would you like, Jens? What would you like to drink?	
S: Brännvin.	Brandy.	
I: Brännvin? Hur mycket vill du ha? Stort glas?	Brandy? How much would you like? A large glass?	Jensen again adds a vowel at the end of the word saying "Brännvine". But perhaps he is saying "Brännvinet" with the definite article suffixed and its final "t" unheard.

Transcript	Translation	Comments
S: Stört.	Large.	
I: Stort glas? Ja, du skall få det, Jens.	[A] large glass? All right, that is what you will have, Jens.	
S: Stört.	Large.	Another example of perseveration. Jensen keeps repeating the word "stört" almost as if to himself. The umlaut-slurred "o" in "stört" appears to be Jensen's own word. He does *not* use I's pronunciation even in the repetition.
I: Tala om för mig, Jens! Vad skall du göra i kväll? Vad skall du göra i kväll? Skall du gå ut och träffa din flicka?	Now tell me, Jens. What are you going to do tonight? What are you going to do tonight? Are you going out and meet your girl?	
S: Ut är hon.	She is out.	Jensen reverses the correct word order which should be "Hon är ute".
I: Drick! Drick ditt brännvin!	Drink! Drink your brandy!	
S: Drick det?	Drink that?	
I: Ja, tycker du om brännvinet? Det är gott.	Yes, do you like the brandy? It's good.	Here as sometimes elsewhere the interpreter adopts Jensen's pronunciation and says "brännvine". He does this apparently to facilitate communication with Jensen.
S: Ja.	Yes.	

Swedish	English	Notes
I: Är det inte? Smakar det inte gott, brännvinet? Drick det nu! Ja, drick ditt brännvin nu!	Isn't it? Doesn't it taste good, the brandy Drink it up! Yes, drink your brandy now	
S: (Sound of S. smacking lips.)		They go through the motions of drinking, but without glasses.
I: Ja, det var starkt, var det inte?	Yes, that was strong, wasn't it?	
S. Bra! Bra! Bra! (Sounds of S. smacking lips.) Ah. Ah.	Fine! Fine! Fine!	
I: Vill du ha mera?	Would you like some more?	
S: (emphatically) Nej!	No.	
I: Var det starkt nog?	Was it strong enough?	
S: (Sounds of S. still smacking lips.) Ja.	Yes.	
I: Vill du sjunga en stump nu? Sjung en visa nu, Jens! Får vi höra något nu?	Do you want to sing a bit now? Sing a song now, Jens. May we hear something now?	"Stump" is here used colloquially to mean "a bit" or "a little".
S: Nej.	No.	
I: Vill inte Jens sjunga? Ja, du tycker om att sjunga. Du vill sjunga nu.	Doesn't Jens want to sing? Yes, you like to sing. You want to sing now.	The written transcript here conveys little of of the drama heard on the tape as the seemingly drunken Jensen laughs uproariously and refuses (at first) to be talked into singing.
S: Hm.	Hm.	
I: Ja, du vill sjunga, Jens.	Yes, you want to sing, Jens.	
S: Nej.	No.	

Transcript	Translation	Comments
I: Sjung nu!	Sing now!	
S: Nej.	No.	
I: Jo, Jens!	Yes, Jens!	
S: Nej.	No.	
I: Får vi höra det?	May we hear it?	
S: (laughs loudly) Nej! Nej! Nej! Nej!	No! No! No! No!	Jensen's laughter can be heard in the background through this section. He slurs his words and provides a marvelous simulation of someone who is drunk. His "Nej" is drawn out for emphasis, and sounds like "Neeej". N. Sahlin commented that this drawn-out and emphatic "Neeej" is normal Swedish, but not a style Jensen could have picked up from the interpreters.
I: Ja, du skall sjunga nu!	Yes, you are going to sing now.	
S: Nej . . . inte.	No . . . not.	
I: Jo, jag vet att du kan det. Du kan det så bra.	Yes, I know you can do it. You can do it very well.	
S: (laughter) Nej.	No.	
I: Nu, nu. Ja. När vi knäpper med fingrarna, så skall du sjunga nu. (snap)	Now, now. Yes. When we snap our fingers, you will begin singing.	
S: (loud laughter) Nej.	No.	
I: Får vi höra nu?	May we hear you now?	

S: (loud laughter) Nej. Nej. Nej.

No. No. No.

Some other remarks of the interpreter here are inaudible because of Jensen's loud laughter which continues throughout. Jensen sometimes spreads his negative into "Neeej".

I: Du kan sjunga.

You can sing.

S: Nej. Nej ... nu sjungit.

No. No ... now [have] sung. (?)

Jensen's expression is ungrammatical. "Sjungit", is the supine form of "sjunga" (English: "to sing"). Jensen may be trying to say something like: "I have sung". If so, he omits the auxiliary verb, which should not be done in a main clause.

I: Vad?

What?

S: (loud laughter) Nej.

No.

I: Gör det! Du skall sjunga nu.

Go to it. Now you're going to sing.

S: (laughter) Nej! Nej!

No! No!

H: When I snap my fingers, Jensen.

S: Morsom.

Funny.

An entirely spontaneous, appropriate response. "Morsom" is Norwegian meaning "funny", "amusing", or "droll". It is not Swedish and has no Swedish cognate. Jensen's seemingly uncontrolled and drunken laughter can be heard throughout this section as the hypnotist and interpreter try to give him further directions which he largely ignores or rejects.

Transcript	Translation	Comments
I: Du . . . morsom	You . . . funny. . . .	
H: All right, Jensen. When I snap my fingers, you are going to sing, you will sing. Everybody wants you to sing. Here you go, you must sing. There you are, now you are singing. All right, now you can stop laughing. All right, now you can stop laughing. You are just feeling good. All right, now just sign. You want to sing, You are feeling good. Go ahead.		
S: Nej.	No.	
H: Everybody is looking at you. They all want you to sing.		
S: Nej, sjungit. Nej, sjungit. Nej.	No, [have] sung. No, [have] sung. (?) No.	The translation is quite conjectural. See previous note on "sjungit", on p. 121.
H: Everybody likes you. Everybody likes Jensen. They all want him to sing. Go ahead. Go ahead, you want to sing. You will find that when I touch your head you can't stop. You have got to sing, You are going to sing. Go ahead, sing, sing, sing.		
S: (loudly) Nej! Nej! Nej!	No. No. No.	

V: [Indistinct in background]

H: All right, now you are going to remember a song that your mama taught you. You are going to want to sing it. Go ahead. Now that song is coming back. It's right in your mind. You want to sing it. It is a song that you learned when you were a little child and now you want to sing it. You don't know why, but you want to sing it. You want to sing it loud. You are having a good time. Your friend is with you. You are feeling good. And now when you feel my finger touch your head, you are just going to start singing. You can't stop. Now! Go ahead.

S: Jeg bodde . . .

I lived . . .

Jensen begins to sing here but stops almost immediately. "Jeg" is Norwegian.

H: Now Jensen, all the words are coming back to you.

I: Det är fint, Jensen! Du kan sjunga!

That's great, Jensen. You can sing!

S: Nej . . . (laughter) [Inaudible words] vinet.

No . . . the wine.

H: Let's get out of the inn. Come on, let's go home. Now you are going home with me. We are going home. Tell me, are you going to walk home or did you bring an animal?

Transcript	Translation	Comments
S: [Min] häst, [min] häst.	My horse, my horse.	Another example of Jensen's preference for answering in Swedish even when questioned in English. The response is quite appropriate to the question.
I: Skall du åka hem med din häst?	Are you going to drive home with your horse?	
S: Ja.	Yes.	
I: Hur lång tid tar det? När kommer du att vara hemma? I morgon? Är du hemma i morgon? Springer din häst fort?	How long is that going to take? When will you be at your house? By tomorrow? Will you reach home tomorrow? Does your horse go fast?	
S: Ja.	Yes.	
I: Det gör han? Så du skall vara hemma i morgon? Du vet inte hur lång tid det tar? Säg mig, Jens, vad skall du göra när du kommer hem?	Does he really? So you will be home tomorrow? Don't you know how long it will take? Tell me, Jens, what are you going to do when you reach home?	
S: [Indistinct murmuring] Nej.	No.	
I: Jag hör dig inte. Tala högt! Tala högt, Jens!	I can't hear you. Speak up! Speak up, Jens!	
H: Now you want to talk. You want to talk, Jensen. Go ahead, talk to him. He is your friend.		
S: Hansen. (sighs)		
H: Tell me, did you ever hear of a church?		

S: En körk.

A church.

The first "k" is distinctly hard. Jensen has evidently understood the question but repeats the word in his language without otherwise answering. He pronounces the word close to "körk" and away from both "kyrka" (Swedish) and "kirke" (Norwegian). His pronunciation is close to "kirk" (Scottish) with both "k's" hard. Correct Swedish pronunciation may be represented for speakers of English by "shur'ka" with the first "k" soft, the second one hard and some accent on both syllables. R. Ejvegård states that "körka" is a form of the word found in northern Sweden, but there, too, the first "k" is soft. Jensen's pronunciation here is perhaps not completely independent of a prior occasion (in an earlier session) when the hypnotist in talking with Jensen about his religion asked him if he went to "kirke".

H: Huh? Is there a church in Haverö? Huh? You know, you have been in Haverö. Is there a church there, where people go and pray to God? Huh? Come on, Jens, Jens, tell me. Is there a church? You know. What's the name of it? What's the name of the church? Don't you want to tell me? Huh? Who is your God?

Transcript	*Translation*	*Comments*
S: (emphatically) Hansen.		Here Jensen, spontaneously, declares that Hansen is his god, although elsewhere, even in this same session, he says Hansen is his chief or lord. In many instances the common people made little or no distinction between "god" and "lord"; hence Jensen is not inconsistent. Kings were often declared gods, whence the "divine right" asserted by some of them. Even in our own day, some rulers, e.g., in Japan, have been considered gods.
H: How do you pray to God? How do you pray to your God? Show me how. Did you ever hear of England? Did you ever hear of Norway? What do you know about Norway?		
S: Lite [t].	A little.	Jensen here adheres to the omission of final -t in "litet", when used adverbially in spoken Swedish. Today the short form occurs commonly in the written language also.
H: What?		
S: Lite [t]. (sighs)	A little.	One can hear a faint vowel sound in front of "lite", almost as if Jensen were influenced by English and half saying "a little". But there is no second "l" sound audible as in the English word.

H: What do you know about Norway? Tell me everything you have heard about Norway. Go ahead, tell me. I am your friend, I want to hear. What do you know about Norway? Huh? You know about Norway? Huh? You are a dumb man, Jensen. You don't know anything about Norway? Huh?

S: Norska.

Norwegian.

Jensen's reply to the bombardment of questions is the correct word for Norwegian (the language), as though he meant to say: "What I know about Norway is a little Norwegian". The interpreter had not used the word "norska" earlier in the session.

I: (repeating in the background) Norge? Norska?

Norway? Norwegian?

S: Norska.

Norwegian.

I: Ja, du förstår norska?

Yes, you understand Norwegian?

S: A lite [t].

A little.

The apparent addition of an English article here may be only a tired or hesitating sigh. See earlier comment on "lite".

I: A lite, ja.

A little, yes.

Here the Swedish interpreter includes the English article, perhaps in imitation of the vowel heard in front of Jensen's "lite" mentioned above.

Transcript	*Translation*	*Comments*
I: Förstår Ni norsk[a]? Förstår De Norsk?	Do you understand Norwegian? Do you understand Norwegian?	Here one of the interpreters begins to speak Norwegian to Jensen. In general he uses the more formal second person plural when speaking Norwegian to Jensen, but varies his usage sometimes.
S: Lite.	A little.	
I: Har De vart i Norge? Har De vart i Norge noen gang?	Have you been in Norway? Have you ever been in Norway?	
S: Mörby Hagar.	Mörby Meadows.	This association on the part of Jensen is unclear. Was "Mörby Meadows," in or near Norway? The interpreter does not hear Jensen's reply or does not understand its possible significance because he does not follow the lead offered.
I: Har De vart i Norge?	Have you been in Norway?	
S: Nej.	No.	
I: Kjenner De noen fra Norge? Tycker De noe av Norge? Kjenner De noen norrman? Deres mormor var fra Norge, har jeg blitt fortalt. Er det så? Mormor. Din mors mor fra Norge. Er det noen i Haverö som snakker norsk? Det er noen i Haverö som snakker norsk? Vem er det som snakker norsk?	Do you know someone from Norway? (Question not comprehensible.) Do you know any Norwegian person? Your grandmother was from Norway, I've been told. Is that so? Grandmother. Your mother's mother from Norway. Is there anyone in Haverö who speaks Norwegian? There is someone in Haverö who speaks Norwegian? Who is it that speaks Norwegian?	

S: [inaudible murmuring] ... norsk.

Norwegian.

I: (in background apparently repeating what S. has just said) Ja.
Snakk litt høyere.
Jeg har vært i Norge och jeg skulle gjerne treffe noen fra Norge i Haverö. Er det noen fra Norge i Haverö? Noen som snakker norsk? Er det noen norrman i Haverö? Kan De snakke lite høyere for meg?

Yes.
Speak a little louder.
I have been to Norway and I would be glad to meet someone from Norway in Haverö. Is there someone from Norway in Haverö? Someone who speaks Norwegian? Is there a Norwegian in Haverö? Can you speak a little louder for me?

The interpreter speaking Norwegian uses a few Swedish words, possibly to aid comprehension by Jensen, who seems to understand Swedish better than Norwegian.

V: (Voices in background) O.K. Yeah.

I: Når jeg tar deg på hodet, så ... kan De snakke høyere och da kan De forstå meg. Och da husker De om De er noen norrman eller om det er noen norske i Haverö. Snakker De noe norsk, lite norsk? Forstår de norska?

When I touch your head, then you can speak louder and you can understand me. And you remember then whether you are a Norwegian or whether there is a Norwegian in Haverö. Do you speak some Norwegian, a little Norwegian? Do you understand Norwegian?

The interpreter slips into the familiar "deg" instead of the more formal "Dem". At the end of the passage, "norska" is Swedish, not Norwegian, for "Norwegian language".

S: Lite.

A little.

Jensen responded better to Swedish than to Norwegian judging by this and a later occasion when another attempt was made to speak Norwegian with him. But his different responses might have been influenced by the different style and manner of the interpreter.

I: Lite. Hvor har De hørt norsk? Hvor har De hørt norsk, Jensen? I Haverö?

S: Oslomannen. Oslo[mannen].

I: Oslomannen? Oslomannen? Er det noen fra . . . ? Vem er Oslomannen? Var det det De sa? En norrman i Haverö, som snakker norsk?

H: When I touch your head you will talk. You will know what you want to say. Now you know what you want to say. Talk loud. Real loud. Go ahead. It's easy for you to talk. Go ahead. Talk loud. It's right there. It's on your tongue. Go ahead. All right, just relax. Now just relax, Jensen. You are having a good time. You are coming home from Haverö. You had a good time in Haverö, didn't you? Oh yea, you had a good time in the inn. Here is somebody on the road, you met him on the road. He is passing you. He is a nice man. He wants to ask you a couple of questions.

Translation

A little. Where have you heard Norwegian? Where have you heard Norwegian, Jensen? In Haverö?

The man from Oslo. The man from Oslo.

The man from Oslo? The man from Oslo? Is there someone from . . . ? Who is the man from Oslo? Was that what you said? A Norwegian in Haverö who speaks Norwegian?

Comments

The last part of Jensen's second "Oslomannen" is covered by the interpreter's next word. No one has suggested "Oslo" to Jensen.

I: [Inaudible words] Oslokarlen fra Kristiania. Du kjenner Oslomannen?

... The Oslo fellow from Christiania. Do you know the man from Oslo?

The interpreter probes for contact by using Christiania, the name imposed by the Danes on ancient Oslo in 1624 and retained until 1925 as the name of the city.

S: Oslomannen.

The man from Oslo.

I: Kan du forstå [kve] jeg säger?

Do you understand what I am saying?

Although the interpreter is heard as saying something like "kve" he may have tried to say "hva" in Norwegian (English: "what"). "Säger" is Swedish, not Norwegian.

S: Jag förstår Dem icke.

I don't understand you.

"Icke" is an older form of negation than "inte" in Swedish. "Ikke" is correct Norwegian.

I: (to the others present) Hon förstår dem icke.

She doesn't understand them.

The interpreter misunderstands "Dem" as Jensen shifts to Swedish and retains the Norwegian pronoun.

S: (very faintly) [Förstår dem icke.]

Don't understand them. (?)

I: Du förstår mig. Du förstår mig, Jens. Gör du inte? Du förstår mitt språk. Vi talar samma språk. Ja.

You understand me. You understand me, Jens. Don't you? You understand my language. We talk the same language. Yes.

An interpreter now continues the conversation in Swedish.

S: Ja, ja, då.

Yes, yes, surely.

I: Minns du när vi möttes i Haverö? Ja, vi gjorde. Var är Haverö? Är Haverö vid havet? Är det vatten vid Haverö?

Do you remember when we met in Haverö? Yes, we did so. Where is Haverö? Is Haverö on the sea? Is there water at Haverö?

S: Ja.

Yes.

Transcript	Translation	Comments
I: Och båtar?	And boats?	
S: Båtar . . fisk.	Boats . . . fish.	
I: Och husk?	And (?)	Jensen correctly pronounces "fisk" with a hard "k".
		The interpreter seems unsure of what Jensen said.
S: Fisk.	Fish.	
I: Fisk?	Fish?	
S: Fisk.	Fish.	
I: Mycket fisk?	A lot of fish?	
S: Fisk.	Fish.	
I: Vad heter fisken?	What is the name of the fish?	
S: Laxen, laxen.	The salmon, the salmon.	A good example of a new word introduced first by Jensen. An appropriate Swedish response to a Swedish question, although "lax" rather than the definite form would normally be expected.
I: (sotto voce) Good girl! Ah. Huh!		
I: Laxen?	The salmon?	
S: Laxen.	The salmon.	
I: Är det många stora båtar där? I Haverö? Varifrån kommer de?	Are there a lot of big boats there? In Haverö? Where do they come from?	

S: Hansen.

I: Från Hansen?

S: Ja.

I: Uppsala? Vet du var Uppsala är? Du vet inte vad det är. Haverö, det ligger vid havet? Och det kommer stora båtar dit? Tycker du om laxen?

S: Ja.

I: Du tycker om fisk?

S: Ja, fisk... Älvfisk[e].

I: Vad dricker du när du äter fisk? Säg mig, vad dricker du då?

S: Svisch.

Hansen.

From Hansen?

Yes.

Uppsala? Do you know where Uppsala is? You don't know what it is. Is Haverö on the sea? And large boats come there? Do you like the salmon?

Yes.

You enjoy fish?

Yes, fish... River fishing. (?)

What do you drink when you are eating fish? Tell me. What do you drink then?

(?)

Here Jensen spontaneously specifies what kind of fishing he prefers. The translation is perhaps doubtful since Jensen may have meant to say the kind of fish he liked—river or fresh water fish—not the kind of fishing.

Jensen pronounces the word fairly clearly, but if he is referring to a beverage, it has not been identified. According to R. Ejvegård "svisch" can be associated with a Slavic word for brandy. As I have listened to this word repeatedly, it seems to me that Jensen may be saying "fisk" indistinctly. This would then be another example of his tendency to perseveration.

Transcript	Translation	Comments
I: Säg det. Jag förstår dig inte.	Say that [again]. I don't understand you.	
S: Svisch.	(?)	
I: Vad dricker du?	What do you drink?	
S: Svisch. Svisch.	(?)	
I: Högre! (S. sighs) Du tycker om lax. Vad äter du mer än lax? Mer än laxen? Äter du andra mat? Äter du sill? Känner du till sill?	Louder . . . So you like salmon. What else do you eat besides salmon? In addition to the salmon? Do you eat other foods? Do you eat herring? Are you familiar with herring?	"Andra" should be "annan".
S: Makrill.	Mackerel.	An excellent example of an unexpected and appropriate response in Swedish to a question put in Swedish. The interpreter registers surprise in his repetition.
I: (with astonishment) Makrill? Vet du vad Danmark . . . Danmark är? Danmark? Har du hört om Danmark?	Mackerel? Do you know what Denmark . . . Denmark is? Denmark? Have you heard about Denmark?	Instead of following the lead of mackerel, the interpreter continues to search for geographical *points de repère*.
S: [Latvia.] Latvia. Latvia snackar. Latvia snackar.	Latvia. Latvia. Latvia is talking. Latvia is talking.	Jensen may have been reminded about Latvia by the talk of food or perhaps by a reference to Denmark. "Snackar" is rather colloquial for "talk" in Swedish of Stockholm. But elsewhere, especially in the country, "snackar" is the commonly used word for the English "talk" as the cognate "snakker" is in Norway.
I: Latvia?	Latvia?	

Since Jensen's home was apparently at "Mörby Meadows", the response of where Latvia is when Jensen is at Haverö seems quite appropriate.

S: Latvia.

I: Yes, where is she? Where is Latvia? Where is your wife?

S: Hansen.

I: In Hansen? Oh, she's at home in Hansen. And you're in Haverö alone.

S: Yes.

I: Oh! You leave your wife by herself?

S: Mörby Meadows.

I: I did not hear you. Repeat that.

S: Latvia talks. Talks.

I: What does Latvia do? Tell me! What does she speak? Norwegian?

S: Norwegian.

I: Latvia speaks Norwegian?

S: Yes, yes.

I: Does she? Does she speak Norwegian very well?

S: Very well.

S: Latvia.

I: Ja, var är hon? Var är Latvia? Var är din fru?

S: Hansen.

I: I Hansen? Oh, hon är hemma i Hansen. Och du är i Haverö ensam.

S: Ja.

I: O! Lämnar du din fru ensam?

S: Mörby Hagar.

I: Jag hörde dig inte. Säg det igen!

S: Latvia snackar. Snackar.

I: Vad gör Latvia? Säg det! Vad snackar hon? Norska?

S: Norska.

I: Latvia snackar norska?

S: Ja, ja.

I: Hon gör? Snackar hon norska bra?

S: Bra.

136   Xenoglossy

Transcript	Translation	Comments
I: Bra?	Very well?	
S: Bra. [Latvia.]	Very well. Latvia.	
I: När snackar Latvia norska? Snackar hon norska till dig? Det gör hon inte. Nej.	When does Latvia speak Norwegian? Does she speak Norwegian to you? She doesn't do that. No.	
Säg mig, när snackar Latvia norska? Vill du ha en annan drink?	Tell me. When does Latvia speak Norwegian? Would you like another drink?	
S: Nej.	No.	
I: En brännvin till?	Another brandy?	The interpreter slips into an ungrammatical phrase. He should have said: "Ett glas brännvin till?"
S: Nej. Nej.	No. No.	
I: Ingen mer?	No more?	
S: Nej.	No.	
I: Varför vill du inte det? Ta en till nu! Ja, ta en till! Den var inte så stark.	Why won't you have some? Take one more now? Yes. Take one more! It wasn't so very strong!	
S: Nej.	No.	
I: Nej, det var den inte. Så du vill ha en till nu? Ta den nu, Jens. Här har du en annan nu. Ta den! Jo, du måste ha en annan, en brännvinssup till.	No, it was not. So you want another one now? Take it now, Jens. Have another one here now. Take it! Yes, you must have another, one more dram of brandy.	
S: Nej, nej.	No, no.	

I: Är det nog för i dag? Var tror du du skall hitta din flicka?

Is that enough for today? Where do you think you will find your girl?

S: (sighs) [Jag är] så trött.

I am so tired.

I: Nej, du är inte trött. Du måste ha en flicka. Du måste ha en flicka i kväll. Säg mig, Jens, du är inte trött. Du är glad i kväll! Du är glad! Är det inte roligt här i Haverö?

No, you're not tired. You need to have a girl. You have to have a girl tonight. Tell me, Jens, you aren't tired. You are merry tonight. You are gay! Isn't it fun here in Haverö?

H: Now Jensen, listen to me very carefully. You feel very good. When I touch your eyes, you will be able to open them. And you are going to see things and you won't see anybody. But you will just hear a voice. You won't see anybody. You are Jensen. You won't see anybody. You will just hear a voice and that voice will talk to you. It is going to ask you what these things are. You are going to tell us because you know what these things are. You have seen these things before. And when I touch your eyes, you will be able to open your eyes and you will just see these things and you won't see anybody, but the things. Now watch that happen. Now you can open your eyes. You just see things. You can look at this. What do you see, Jensen? What is this?

The hypnotist here begins instructions preparing the subject to open her eyes and try to recognize various objects that will be shown to her. No list of the objects shown was made at the time, but I later learned of a number of them from persons present and others can be inferred from the remarks of the subject and the interviewers.

A watch was held up.

Transcript	Translation	Comments
S: Klocketif.	The clock (or watch). (?)	If "t" is meant to be the definite article, it is wrong and should be "n". Also the ending "if" is not understood.
H: What is it?		
S: Klocket.	The clock.	Jensen's article is again wrong. Correct Swedish would be "klockan".
I: Klocket?	The clock?	The interpreter repeats Jensen's word without correcting the article.
H: How does it work, Jensen? You can hold it, you can do anything you want with it. Have you ever seen that before?		
S: Ja. Ja.	Yes. Yes.	
H: Where? Where have you seen it? Have you ever seen one like it before? It is standing in the air, isn't it? All right, let's see you make it work. Go ahead, make it work. That's it. Now, what's it doing? Tell me, what's it doing? What's happening?		
I: Har du en sådan hemma, Jens? Har du den klockan hemma? Hur ofta vänder du den?	Do you have one like it at home, Jens? Do you have that clock at home? How often do you wind it?	The translation is correct for what was intended. The interpreter hit upon the wrong verb, using a cognate of "wind"

which actually means "turn". He should have said: "Hur ofta drar du upp den?" But Jensen seems to have understood his intent.

S: Dag.

S: Day.

I: En gång om dagen? Jag förstår det. Har du en sådan, Jens?

I: A day? Once a day. I understand that. Do you have one like it, Jens?

S: [Indistinct murmuring]

I: Du har en sådan i ditt hus? Hur gammal är den tror du? Hur gammal är den klockan? Hur många hade du? Hur många hade du hemma?

I: Do you have one like it at home? How old do you think this is? How old is this clock? How many did you have? How many did you have at home?

S: En lite. (sighs) ... [lite].

S: A little ... little.

Jensen's response is not intelligible unless he is trying to get across the idea that he does have a similar watch at home, but only a little one.

I: [Indistinct]

H: What's this, Jensen?

I: Vad heter det?

I: What is this called?

S: Flaxen. Flaxen.

S: The flax. The flax.

Here Jensen was shown a skein of dressed flax so his recognition was correct, but his word was not. Swedish for "flax" is "lin". Did the English word come into his mind somehow, to which (word) he then attached the suffixed definite article?

Transcript	Translation
I: Är det bra?	Is that good?
S: Bra.	Good.
I: Det är fint. Har du sådant hemma? Gör du dina kläder själv?	It is fine. Have you something like it at home? Do you make your clothes yourself?
H: Is it good flax, Jensen? What do you do with this flax, Jensen? What do you do with this flax, Jensen?	
I: Säg mig, vad gör du med den?	Tell me. What do you do with this?
S: (sighs) Klærne.	Clothes.
I: Du gör kläderna. Det förstär jag. Har du fina kläder?	You make clothes. I see. Do you have good clothes?

Comments

The value of Jensen's response is somewhat reduced by the interpreter's previous use of the word "kläder". I have given the Norwegian spelling, i.e., "klærne". Jensen's word sounds like "klærene" and is thus half-way between "klærne" (Norwegian) and "kläderna" (Swedish). The "d" in the Swedish word cannot be heard, but the vowels are clear and Swedish dialects often elide the "-de-" in "klä(de)rna", giving us Jensen's word in Swedish; however, his final vowel is "e", not "a". He is not imitating the interpreter's pronunciation of "kläder".

S: Ja.
Yes.

6 I: Många fina kläder? Titta här, Jens! Vad är detta här?
Many fine clothes? Take a look here, Jens! What is this here?

H: What is this, Jensen? Hold it. You know what it is. You have seen it. You have seen one like it. What is it, Jensen? What would you use it for if you had it?

A ship's model is shown.

S: Skuter. Skuter.
Ships. Ships.

A "skuta" is really a sloop, but to the landlubber it means almost any (old) sailing vessel. Jensen's plural is Norwegian, since correct Swedish would be "skutor". However, a slurred ending ("or" to "er") is often heard in Swedish. This is another instance of Jensen's producing a new (and rare) word, correctly pronounced with hard "k".

I: Jag förstår dig inte.
I don't understand you.

It is puzzling that the interpreter seems not to understand.

S: Skuter.
Ships.

I: Har du [glömt]?
Have you forgotten?

S: Skuter.
Ships.

I: Säg det högre!
Say it louder!

Transcript	Translation	Comments
S: (louder) Skuter, skuter.	Ships, ships.	Jensen speaks these words much louder showing his ability to understand the instruction to do so given in Swedish.
I: Gör du ost, Jensen? Vet du vad ost är? Från mjölken. Du gör aldrig ost?	Do you make cheese, Jensen? Do you know what cheese is? From [the] milk. You never make cheese?	
S: [Indistinct murmuring]		Jensen is shown a wooden cheese mold for shaping and draining cheese.
I: Kan du göra en sådan, Jensen?	Can you make something like this, Jensen?	
S: Ja.	Yes.	
I: Kan du det?	Can you really?	
S: Ja. Getter, getter. Skuter.	Yes. Goats, goats. Ships.	Note the appropriate association of goat to cheese. In Norway "gjetost" (goat's milk cheese) is very popular. Then Jensen reverts to saying "ships" again as if he is still thinking about them.
I: Vad är det för slags träd i det? Vad är det för trä? Är det bra trä i den?	What kind of a wood is in it? What kind of wood is it? Is there good wood in it?	Jensen is still shown the cheese mold.
S: (very faint) [Bra trä.]	Good wood.	
I: Tycker du det?	You think so, do you?	
S: [Indistinct muttering] [förstår inte.]	... don't understand.	
H: Jensen, what's this?		

	Swedish	English	Commentary
S:	Båt?	Boat?	As he does often, Jensen adds a vowel at the end. His word sounds close to "böte".
I:	Vad heter det? Ja, då har du sett den.	What is it called? Yes, you have seen it.	
S:	(faintly) Skuter. Skuter. Skuter.	Ships. Ships. Ships.	Here Jensen makes the "k" much softer and pronounces the word close to "skjuter" (shoot) which would, however, not make sense in the context.
I:	Har din hustru det? Har Latvia sådana? Hon har inte sådan? Har du får, Jensen? Har du några får, så du kan få ull?	Does your wife have this? Does Latvia have anything like these? She doesn't have that? Do you have sheep, Jensen? Do you have some sheep, so you can get wool?	Jensen is shown and handles a pair of wool carders.
S:	En djur, en djur.	An animal, an animal.	Jensen's article is wrong since "djur" is neuter. He may have said "En tjur" (English: "bull"), but this does not suit the context well.
I:	Jag förstår dig inte. Säg det högre! (S. sighs)	I don't understand you. Repeat that louder.	
S:	En djur. Pratar, pratar!	An animal. Talk, talk!	Here Jensen seems to complain of too much talk. Since the interpreters have not previously used the verb "prata" Jensen's introduction of it is quite remarkable.
I:	Vad pratar du?	What are you chattering about?	The interpreter has misunderstood Jensen's protest.
S:	Trött.	Tired.	Pronounced by Jensen as usual with an "e" at the end, like "trötte".

Transcript	Translation	Comments
I: Nej. Du är inte trött alls. O, nej.	No. You are not tired at all. Certainly not.	
H: Jensen, look at this. You like this. What is it?		Jensen is shown a saber here.
S: [I] krige[t].	In [the] war.	A good example of a correct association. Jensen omits the "-t" (definite article) which is quite common in Swedish dialects. The interpreter does the same as he repeats the word.
I: I krige[t], ja. Kommer du ihåg kriget? Var du i kriget, Jens?	In war. Yes. Do you remember the war? Were you in the war, Jens?	
S: [Krig . . .]	War.	Jensen's word is so faint as to be questionable.
H: All right, Jensen, you don't like it. No?		
S: Kriget.	The war.	
I: Du tycker inte om kriget. Känner du någon som var i kriget?	You don't like war. Do you know anyone who was in the war?	
S: Pers Petter.		Pers Petter is never identified, but seems to have been a friend of Jensen who was perhaps killed in a war.
I: Vem?	Who?	
S: Pers Petter.		
I: Vad hette han?	What was his name?	

S: Petter.		
I: Petter?		
S: (slowly and louder) Pers Petter, Pers Petter.		
V: (in background) Would she [Jensen] like to have it?		
I: Vill du ha det här svärdet?	Would you like to have this sword?	Meaning the saber.
S: (emphatically) Nej!	No!	
I: Du vill inte ha det?	You don't want to have it?	
S: (emphatically) Nej!	No!	
I: Vad vill du ha i stället?	What would you like instead?	
S: Pers Petter.		Another example of Jensen's perseveration.
I: Du vill ha ett ... sak? Ett spett?	Do you want a ... thing? A spit?	The interpreter seems to have lost the connection with the name "Pers Petter", and responds as if he heard "Per/spetter". The second part of this is the Swedish (plural) for "spits". Jensen keeps on repeating the name of "Pers Petter".
S: Pers Petter.		
I: Det är bättre. Jag förstår det, Jens. Det är bättre det. Vad hette ledaren i kriget?	That's better. I understand that, Jens. That's better. What was your leader in the war called?	The interpreter seems to have given up trying to understand Jensen's immediately previous references and now tries a question.

Transcript	Translation	Comments
S: Bättre, Pers Petter bättre.	Better. Pers Petter better.	Note the perseveration and even perhaps some echoing of the interpreter's words. Unfortunately throughout this section the rather faint words of Jensen are covered by the voice of the interpreter and it is difficult to make out the order in which they speak and what they say.
I: Ja, det är mycket bättre. Har du hört talas om en båge? Pilbåge? Skjuta pilar? Har du en bössa? Vet du vad en bössa är, Jens? Bössa? Du skjuter.	Yes, that's a lot better. Have you ever heard about a bow? Archery bow? Shoot arrows? Do you have a rifle? Do you know what a gun is, Jens? A rifle? You shoot.	
S: [Skjuter.]	Shoot.	
I: Hur slaktar du? Hur slaktar du Din ko?	How do you slaughter? How do you slaughter your cow?	Another dead end is reached here.
S: [Min ko.] Med stenar ... stenar.	My cow. With stones, stones.	
I: Tala högre, Jens!	Speak up, Jens!	
S: Med stenar.	With stones.	
I: Med stenar?	With stones?	
S: Ja. En ... skjuter.	Yes. One ... shoots.	Jensen reverts to the topic of shooting.
I: Så du vet vad en pilbåge är i alla fall. Du vet vad ... Titta här, Jens!	In any case, you know what an archery bow is. You know what ... Look here, Jens!	Jensen is now shown a toy archery bow.
S: [För] gammal.	Too old.	

	English	Notes
I: Du har sett den. Du har sett den. (S. laughs) Vad?	You have seen it. You have seen it. You have seen it. What?	Jensen laughs derisively at the small bow.
S: Gammal, gammal, gammal.	Old, old, old.	
I: Ja, har du skjutit den? Ta den och skjut nu! Visa mig hur du använder den! Visa mig nu! Ta den nu! Du ser den. Ta den nu!	Yes, have you shot one? Take it and shoot now! Show me how you use it! Show me now! Take it now. You see it. Take it now.	
S: Nej, nej.	No, no.	
I: Ja, visa mig hur du skjuter, Jens! Visa mig! Du kan det. Vad skjuter du på? Vad skjuter du på? (S. laughs) Är den bra? Den är dålig.	Yes, show me how you shoot, Jens. Show me. You can do it. What are you aiming at? What are you aiming at? Is that good? It's no good.	Jensen discards the toy bow with contempt as being quite beneath his dignity.
S: Ja.	Yes.	
I: Ja, Så den är ingenting att ha. Nej, den var dålig, var den inte? (S. laughs) Har du haft en sådan? Har du haft en sådan någon gång?	Yes. So it is nothing. No, it was bad, wasn't it? Have you had something like it? Have you ever had something similar?	Jensen continues throughout this section to chuckle, evidently amused at the toy bow.
S: (laughs) Gammal. Gammal. (laughs)	Old. Old.	In the end Jensen sights with the bow and shows familiarity with its use.
I: Huh?		
S: Nej.	No.	
I: Du har inte det.	You have not had that.	The interpreter evidently means that Jensen has never had a bow like the toy one shown him.

Transcript	Translation	Comments
S: Nej.	No.	
I: Du tycker inte om det.	You don't care for it.	
S: [Jag] brukar sperte.	I use [a] spear.	Not being sure of the word "sperte" I have spelled it as Jensen pronounced it— "sperte". From the context Jensen is trying to say he used a spear rather than a bow and arrow in hunting. Correct Swedish for "spear" is "spjut" and Norwegian is "spire" or "spyd". "Brukar" (English: "use") is a new and correct word from Jensen.
I: Du brukar sperte. Du brukar sperte.	You use [a] spear. You use [a] spear.	
S: Sperte. Sperte.	Spear. Spear.	
I: Ja, det är mycket bättre. Ja.	Yes, that's much better. Yes.	
V: (*sotto voce* in background) Has she ever seen one [like it]?		
I: Ja. Har du sett någon [som har] haft en sådan? Har du sett någon? Har [du] någon båge? Ja, känner du någon?	Yes. Have you ever seen anyone who has had something like it? Have you seen one? Have you any bow? Yes, do you know any such person?	Here, as occasionally elsewhere, I have filled out the heard interpreter's words to make grammatically correct and full sentences. By "any such person", the interpreter means someone familiar with bows and arrows.
S: Latvia en Lester. [Inaudible word] Lester, Latvia. Lester.		Latvia is known to be Jensen's wife from previous sessions. Lester is unidentified. The "en" heard between "Latvia" and

I: Latvia, och vem mer?

S: Latvia.

I: Vad?

S: Min fru.

I: Din fru? Har hon en båge?

S: Lester.

I: Och Lester? De har båge.
Men du brukar sperte? Ja.

S: Ja. Jag brukar sperte, sperte, sperte.

I: Har du varit i krig?

S: Nej.

I: Vad dödar du? Vad kan du döda med spjut?

S: En djur.

I: Latvia, and who else?

S: Latvia.

I: What?

S: My wife.

I: Your wife? Has she a bow?

S: Lester.

I: And Lester? They have [a] bow.
But you use [a] spear? Yes.

S: Yes. I use [a] spear, spear, spear.

I: Have you been in [a] war?

S: No.

I: What do you kill? What can you kill with a spear?

S: An animal.

"Lester" is not understood. It may be a variant of English "and". The Swedish equivalent would be a short "o".

A good example of a correct response.

Here occurs one of a number of instances when the interpreter adopts Jensen pronunciation, in this case of "sperte", evidently to improve communication with him.

More perseveration by Jensen.

As often, Jensen's "nej" is drawn out into "neej".

If the translation is correct, Jensen's article is wrong. Correct Swedish would be "ett djur". Jensen may have been saying the Norwegian "dyr" (English: "animal"; also "deer"). But his article would still be wrong.

Transcript	Translation	Comments
I: Djur? Ett djur?	Animal? An animal?	
S: Djur.	Animal.	
I: Vilka djur har du här?	Which animals have you here?	
S: (faintly) Djur.	Animal.	Note Jensen's tendency to keep on repeating a word.
I: Vilka djur tycker du om?	Which animals do you like?	
S: Björnjakter.	Bear hunts.	This response impresses me as being an appropriate association on the part of Jensen, but not a fully correct conversational answer to the question.
I: Björnjakter? O!	Bear hunts? Oh.	The interpreter is quite startled by Jensen's saying "björnjakter".
S: Ja.	Yes.	
I: O, har du dödat många björnar, Jens? Har du dödat någon björn?	Oh, have you killed many bears, Jens? Have you killed any bear?	
S: [Ja, björnjakter.]	Yes, bear hunts.	
I: Björnjakter? Dödade du någon björn då? Med spjerte?	Bear hunts? Did you kill any bear then? With [a] spear?	The interpreter again bends towards Jensen's pronunciation in saying "spjerte".
S: [Indistinct murmuring] [Skjuter. Skjuter. Skjuter.]	Shoot. Shoot. Shoot.	

I: Vad? Tala högre, Jens! Jag hör dig inte. Säg mig nu! Ja, säg det, Jens! Tala om björnjakten!	What? Speak up, Jens! I can't hear you. Now tell me. Yes, say it, Jens! Tell us about the bear hunting!	
S: [Indistinct murmuring]		Jensen's repeated complaints of being tired are ignored or rejected throughout, with rare exceptions.
I: Säg det igen!	Repeat that, Jens!	
S: (sighs deeply) [Jag är] så trött.	I'm so tired.	
I: Nej. Du är inte trött, Jens. Du kan inte vara trött, nu inte.	No. You're not tired, Jens. You can't be tired, not now.	
S: [Ja.]	Yes.	Unfortunately, we do not know what Jensen is being shown here.
I: Nej då! Titta här, Jens! Här har du något. Har du sett den förr?	Absolutely not! Look here, Jens. Here is something. Have you seen this before?	
H: Know what this is, Jens?		
S: Ja, ja. En skuta jeder skaka . . . jeder skaka.	Yes, yes. (Untranslatable)	Jensen seems to speak loudly enough, but the words pronounced do not make an intelligible sentence. "Jeder" is German (English: "every") but Jensen's pronunciation has a slight "g" sound in it suggestive of Norwegian "jeger", and Swedish "jägare" (English: "hunter").
I: Vad heter den? Vad kallar du den?	What is its name? What do you call it?	

Transcript	Translation	Comments
S: Bord.	Table.	As he often does, Jensen ends the word with a vowel making "borde". Jensen is the first person to use this word.
I: En bord?	A table?	The article here is incorrect. The correct phrase is "ett bord".
S: Stol . . Ja.	Chair . . Yes.	Jensen adds a vowel at the end, pronouncing "stole". In session six, an interpreter had used the word "stol" so, although Jensen uses it first in this session, he had heard it in the earlier session.
I: Den är fin, är den inte?	It's fine, isn't it?	
S: Ja, den är bra.	Yes, it's good.	
I: Du skulle vilja ha en sådan. Den är bra. Den är bra.	You would like to have one like it. It is fine. It is fine.	
S: [Bra. Bra.]	Fine. Fine.	
I: Vad gör du med den? Säg. Vad gör du med den?	What do you do with it? Say. What do you do with it?	
S: Stuga.	Cottage.	"Stuga" may also mean a "cabin" or even "hut".
I: En stuga?	A cottage?	

Swedish	English	Commentary
S: En bord.	A table.	Jensen puts a vowel at the end of the word, pronouncing "borde". Jensen's article is wrong. "Ett bord" would be correct.
I: Bord. Har du en sådan hemma, Jens?	Table. Have you one like it at home, Jens?	Jensen is shown another object as the interpreter fails to pursue Jensen's rather startling introduction of "en bord" (with wrong article). Unfortunately, we do not know, and the discussion that follows does not tell us, what it is. The interpreter's consistent use of "den" shows that it cannot be the table, which as a neuter object calls for "det".
S: Ja.	Yes.	
I: Du har det?	You have?	
S: Ja, ja.	Yes, yes.	
I: Vill du ha den?	Would you like it?	
S: O, ja!	Oh, yes!	
I: Du vill ha den. Den är fin, ja.	You want it. It's a good one, isn't it?	
S: Bra!	Excellent!	
I: Ja, den är bra. Vad skall du göra? Det kostar pengar, Jens. Hur mycket? Vad kan jag få för den? Säg mig, Jens, vad kan jag få för den?	Yes, it is very good. What will you do? It costs money, Jens. How much? What can I get for it? Tell me, Jens, what can I get for it?	
S: Min fru.	My wife.	
I: Din fru? (laughter in background) Vill du ge bort din fru? Tycker du inte om din fru? Tycker du inte om Latvia?	Your wife? Are you willing to give your wife away? Don't you like your wife? Don't you like Latvia?	

Transcrip	Translation	Comments
S: Nah. Latvia [är] bra.	No. Latvia is good.	Jensen's negation is off his usual "Nej" or "Nej" and between "Nah" and "Näh", also perfectly good dialectal negatives.
I: Är hon bra? Så, vad skulle du göra med den om du hade den hemma? Vad skulle du göra då?	She is good, is she? So, what would you do with this if you had it at home? What would you do then?	In this section Jensen is apparently being shown various kitchen and other household objects.
S: En plass.	A seat.	
I: En?	A?	The context is uncertain here, but since the speakers refer to a table before and after this sequence it is reasonable to conjecture that Jensen is saying the Norwegian word for "a seat". Cognate Swedish is "en plats". English "chair" is "stol" in both languages and Jensen's usage suggests a reference to a bench to sit on when at a table.
S: En plass.	A seat.	
I: En plass? Och vad skulle du göra mer?	A seat? And what would you do besides?	
S: Ja, me[d] bordet.	Yes, with the table.	Jensen has now put in the correct suffixed definite article "-et", without any previous correction by the interpreter.
I: Ja, med bordet. (S. sighs deeply.) Du tycker inte om din fru.	Yes, with the table. You don't care for your wife.	

The hypnotist rather abruptly changes the topic and shows Jensen a steelyard of the type used in Sweden. These consisted of a long bar (graduated) having a rather heavy weight at one end and a hook at the other. A handle had an attachment to the bar so that it could be slid along the bar until the weight at one end and whatever was attached to the hook at the other end, e.g., a fish or piece of meat, were in balance when the operator held the handle.

H: Jens, look at this. Have you ever seen one of these before? Hold it, hold it. Look at it, look at it close. What is it used for? What's this hook up here?

You know what this is, don't you, Jens?

I: Du vet vad det är, Jens, vet du inte?

You know what this is, don't you, Jens?

S: Nej.

No.

Jensen is still being shown the old-fashioned steelyard.

H: What does this say, Jens? Read the numbers.

S: [Indistinct murmuring]

I: Du förstår inte.

You don't understand.

S: [Indistinct murmuring] . . . förstår.

. . . understand.

I: Förstår du det? Förstår du numren?

Do you understand that? Do you understand the numbers?

S: Nej.

No.

I: Nej. Du förstår inte det. När du väger något, vet du vad det är? Vad tror du den skall vara till?

No. You don't understand that. When you weigh something, do you know what that is? What do you think this is used for?

Transcript	Translation	Comments
S: Tung.	Heavy.	A good example of an appropriate association, although not answering the question directly. Jensen simply comments on the heaviness of the steelyard which has a fixed weight at one end.
I: Väger du någon gång saker? Om du väger....	Do you sometimes weigh things? If you weigh....	
S: Tung.	Heavy.	
I: Ja, du vet hur man gör när man väger. Vet du? Du sätter en fisk här? Sätter du laxen här?	Yes, you know what one does when he weighs. Do you know? Do you put a fish here? Do you put the salmon here?	
S: Ja, ett djur.	Yes, an animal.	
I: Ett djur? Du sätter ett djur där och hur gör du?	An animal? You put an animal there and then what do you do?	
S: (faintly) [Fjær.] Fjær.	Spring. Spring.	Jensen's pronunciation omitted the "d" of Swedish "fjäder" and sounded like Norwegian "fjær". "Fjær" here may refer to a type of spring scale used for weighing articles, especially fish. But Jensen was not being shown such a spring scale. Is this another response by association?
I: Vad?	What?	
S: Fjær.	Spring.	

I: Fjær. Vad kallas den? Vad kallas det? Vad heter det? Säg mig, vad tror du det är? Vet inte?

   Spring? What is it called? What's its name? Tell me, what do you think it is? Don't you know?

S: Nej.

   No.

I: Jag vet inte heller! Jag vet inte heller, Jens. Här har vi någonting.

   I don't know either! I don't know either, Jens. Here's something, now.

H: What is this, Jensen? Did you ever see one of these before? What do you use it for?

I: Har du sett den, Jens? Vad är det?

   Have you ever seen that, Jens? What is it?

S: [Indistinct murmuring]

I: Säg mig!

   Tell me!

S: (slowly and with effort) Fyr. En brand.

   Fire. A torch.

Jensen pronounces "brante" with a "t" sound and a vowel at the end. His pronunciation is here closer to the Swedish word "brand" than to the Norwegian cognate "brann". He provides the correct article for "en brand". "Fyr" is a prefix for "fire".

"Fyrsticka" may be a burning splinter for lighting a fire or a tobacco pipe. "Brand" (as in English) is an old, now rare word for "fackla" (English: "torch"). (Cf. English "firebrand".) "Fyrsticka" was also a word for "match" when matches first appeared and is still heard in dialects or humorously.

Transcript	Translation	Comments
I: Jag hör dig inte. Säg det högre! Vad är det? Säg mig nu! Vad är det? Är det järn?	I can't hear you. Repeat that louder! What is this? Tell me now! What is it? Is it iron?	N. Sahlin did not remember what Jensen was being shown at this point. I conjecture from the context that it may have been a hammer or a mallet.
S: Nej, järn. Är trä.	No. Iron. It is wood.	
I: Är det trä?	Is it wood?	
S: Nej, inte trä.	No, not wood.	
I: Nej, det är inte trä. Vad är det då? Är det kol?	No, it's not wood. So what is it then? Is it coal?	
S: Nej, inge[t] kol. Inge[t] kol.	No, no coal. No coal.	The final "t" of Jensen's "inget" is not heard, but neither is that of the repetition by the interpreter.
I: Inge[t] kol?	No coal?	
S: . . . [förstår.] . . .	. . . understand. . .	
I: Vad är det för metall? Vad är det här? Har du sett det förut?	What kind of metal is it? What is this here? Have you ever seen it before?	
S: Stenet.	The stone.	Correct Swedish would be "stenen", not "stenet". R. Ejvegård heard the word as "stener", a south Swedish and Danish form of the plural "stenar".
I: Sten?	Stone?	

S: Nej.

I: Nej, det är inte sten heller. Och inte trä?

No, it's not stone either. And not wood?

S: Inte trä.

Not wood.

I: Och inte kol?

And not coal?

S: Nej, nej.

No, no.

I: Vad är det då?

So what is it then?

S: [Inaudible murmuring]

I: Du vet inte. Du har aldrig sett det förut.

You don't know. You have never seen it before.

S: Nej.

No.

I: Nej. Har du hört järn? Har du järn?

No. Have you heard of iron? Do you have iron?

Jens, är det här järn?

Jens, is this iron?

Är det järn? Känn på det! Är det järn?

Is this iron? Feel it. Is it iron?

The second interpreter takes over for a time here.

S: Skjuter.

Shoot(?)

If this faintly spoken word is correctly identified, its meaning is not understood.

I: Vet du vad man gör här? Vad användes det för? Har du stöpt ljus? Förstår du ljus?

Do you know what one does here? What is this used for? Have you molded candles? Do you understand what candles are?

Jensen is shown a metal candle mold.

S: Jag förstår inte.

I don't understand.

Transcript	*Translation*	*Comments*
I: Du förstår det inte.	You don't understand it.	
S: Förstår inte. (sighs deeply)	[I] don't understand.	
I: Vad har du i huset för att få ljus?	What do you have at home to get light?	
S: En brand.	A torch.	Again pronounced like "brantè".
I: Vad har du?	What do you have?	
S: En brand.	A torch.	
I: En brand? Ja, det har du. En stor brand?	A fire? Yes, you have that. A big fire?	Here, as occasionally elsewhere, the interpreter imitates Jensen's pronunciation and says "brande". Because "brand" also means "fire" in Swedish, the interpreter has not clearly understood Jensen to be referring to a torch; hence he asks his question about a big fire. In the next exchange Jensen tries to get the interpreter back to the idea of torches and himself introduces the word "sticker" for the first time.
S: (softly) Brand. Ja.	Torch. Yes.	
I: Är det allt ljus du har?	Is that all the light you have?	
S: Är sticker.	[There] are sticks.	Jensen's word sounds intermediate between "sticka" (singular) and "sticker". The correct plural would be "stickor", although one can often hear "sticker" in colloquial spoken Swedish. Evidently, he means to

Swedish	English	Commentary
V: (in background) [Sticker.]	Sticks.	indicate here pieces of wood lit to make torches. The interpreter thinks so too, since he talks about sticks put on walls as torches would have been.
I: Sticker? Du har sticker på väggarna?	Sticks? Do you have sticks on the walls?	The interpreter also pronounces the word "sticker" instead of the formally correct plural "stickor", but such a pronunciation could be commonly heard in spoken Swedish.
S: Ja, [och] brand [och vante].	Yes, and fire .. and mitten. (?)	It is difficult to hear the second of Jensen's nouns in this response. He may have been saying "vante" (English: "mitten") but this makes less sense than supposing that he was simply repeating "brante".
I: Och vante?	And mitten?	
S: Ja. En skute.	Yes. A ship.	
I: Säg det igen!	Repeat that!	
S: [En] skute.	A ship.	
I: Skroe?	(?)	Word not identified.
S: Skute.	Ship.	
I: Är det varmt i skute?	Is it warm in the ship?	The interpreter uses Jensen's word. Correct Swedish would be "i skutan".

Transcript	Translation	Comments
S: Brand.	Fire.	
I: Säg det högre igen!	Say that louder again!	
S: Brand.	Fire.	
I: Brand?	Fire?	
S: Ja.	Yes.	
I: Hur många rum har du i ditt hus? Hur många rum har du i huset?	How many rooms do you have in your house? How many rooms do you have in the house?	Here the interpreter shifts subjects because the previous exchange, after the talk about torches, was obviously leading nowhere.
S: Inte, inte.	Not, not.	
I: En?	One?	
S: Inte.	Not.	
I: Är det stort?	Is it large?	
S: Nej.	No.	
I: Du har ett litet hus?	You have a small house?	
S: Nej, lite[t] hus.	No, small house.	The "t" at the end of Jensen's "litet" is not heard.
I: Litet hus?	Small house?	
S: Litet hus.	Small house.	
I: Vem bor i huset? Mer än du?	Who lives in the house? Besides you?	

S: Latvia.

Latvia.

This response shows the subject's understanding of Swedish. Latvia has not been mentioned for some time.

I: Latvia, din fru, ja?

Latvia, your wife, yes?

S: Ja.

Yes.

I: Har du några barn?

Do you have any children?

S: Nej, barn, barn.

No, children, children.

I: Inga barn? Vem bor i huset mer? Någon annan? Har du några grannar? Nej . . . . Har du några folk i närheten?

No children? Who else lives in [your] house? Someone else? Do you have any neighbors? No . . . . Have you any people nearby?

S: En skute.

A ship.

I: Vem bor intill?

Who lives nearby?

S: [Indistinct murmuring]

I: Nu skall du få se på något annat, Jens. Du skall känna dig mycket bättre när du får se det.

Now you are going to see something else, Jens. You're going to feel much better when you see this.

S: Ja.

Yes.

I: Ja, du skall få se en riktigt fin sak nu. Ja. Titta här! Titta! Se på den, Jens! Vad är det? Har du sett en sådan förr?

Yes, you're going to see something really fine now. Yes. Look here. Look! Look at that, Jens! What is that? Have you ever seen anything like it before?

Jensen is here shown an old birchbark horn, such as used by herdgirls tending cattle in the summer on the slopes of hills and mountains.

S: Nej.

No.

Transcript	Translation	Comments
I: Det har du inte. Du har aldrig sett en sådan. Har du satt den till din mun och blåst? En lur? Vet du hur man gör när man blåser? Man blåser i den. Ja, man blåser i den. Så gör man. Ja. (S. chuckles) Varför gör man det tror du? Gör det igen! Gör det igen, Jens! (S. tries to blow.) Ja, du förstår. Ja, gör det nu igen! Låt mig höra!	No, you haven't. You have never seen anything like it. Have you put it to your mouth (lips) and blown it? A horn? Do you know what to do when you blow it? One blows in it. Yes, one blows in it. One does it thus. Yes, why does one do that, do you think? Do it again! Do it again, Jens. Yes, you understand. Yes, do it again now. Let me hear!	The interpreter blows the horn himself.
H: Jens, what is this?		
I: Titta här, Jens! Vad är det?	Look here, Jens. What is this?	
V: (in background) Sharp. Sharp. Very sharp.		
H: Very sharp. Jens, very sharp. What is it? You ever seen and used that before? It has a very sharp point. Very sharp. Don't touch it. What do you use it for?		Jensen is here shown the saber again. The interpreter wants to learn whether Jensen still knows the word for "war" and has the same reaction as before.
I: Vad är det, Jens?	What is it, Jens?	
S: I krige[t].	In the war.	The "t" at the end of Jensen's "kriget" is not heard, but neither is that in the interpreter's repetition.
I: Krige[t], ja. Det har de i kriget. Du tycker inte om kriget, Jens . . . . Nej. Säg mig! Krigar ni mot ryssarna?	The war. Yes. This is used in war. You don't like war, Jens . . . No. Tell me. Do you wage war against the Russians?	The "ni" is plural and means "you and your people".

S: Nej.

No.

I: Vem krigar ni emot?

Against whom do you fight?

S: Galter ryska. Galter ryska.

Boars Russian. Boars Russian. (?)

Spoken faintly, but distinctly. Jensen's meaning is unclear unless he means to insult Russians by equating them with boars.

H: Have you ever seen one of these, Jensen?

Jensen is shown a wooden bucket with one stave extended into a side handle.

S: Ja, ja.

Yes, yes.

H: What is this, Jensen?

S: [Indistinct word] Mjölk... inte.

Milk... not.

Jensen's word has a vowel at the end, and he pronounces "Mjölke". Jensen's reference to milk is quite appropriate since pails of this type were sometimes used as milking pails, especially when a cow was drying up. But his "inte" remains puzzling unless he somehow did not approve of this use of the pail.

H: What is it? Do you have one of these at home?

S: Ja.

Yes.

I: Du har en sådan?

You have something like it, have you?

Transcript	Translation	Comments
H: Do you like it? Do you want to keep it?		
I: Vill du ha den, Jens?	Would you like to have it, Jens?	
H: Would you like to give it to Latvia? Would she like it?		
S: Ja, ja, ja.	Yes, yes, yes.	
H: What would Latvia do with it? What would Latvia use it for?		
S: For vannet.	For the water.	Here Jensen's phrase seems Norwegian since he says "For vannet" instead of the correct Swedish "för vatnet". However, in southern Sweden (Skåne) one also hears "vannet" (from the Danish influence) so Jensen's word is acceptable Swedish.
I: For vannet? Ja. Har du gott vatten? Har du gott vann?	For the water? Yes. Do you have good water? Do you have good water?	
S: Ja.	Yes.	
I: Var har du det?	Where do you have it?	
S: I fjalle[t].	On the mountain.	Presumably Jensen refers to a mountain spring. The expected final "t" is not heard. See text (p. 41) for comment by N. Jacobson on use of "fjäll".
I: Var har du ditt vatten?	Where do you have your water?	The interpreter repeats the question without apparently having understood Jensen's answer.

	Swedish	English	Commentary
S:	En backe.	A slope.	Jensen pronounces this word with an "r" sound as "barke".
I:	Var?	Where?	
S:	En backe.	A slope.	
I:	Säg mig!	Tell me!	
S:	En dal, en dal.	A valley, a valley.	Jensen pronounces this word with a vowel at the end, saying "dale". In this section we have a remarkable display of associated words—"fjäll", "backe", and "dal", all appropriate to the theme of spring water in hilly country. The words are in no way suggested by the interpreter and show as much as any sequence that Jensen, although he never achieves fluency, has a more than superficial knowledge of Swedish.
I:	I dalen?	In the valley?	
S:	I fjälle[t], fjälle[t].	On the mountain, the mountain.	
I:	I fjället? Bor du på fjället?	On the mountain? Do you live on the mountain?	
S:	I fjället.	On the mountain.	The repetition of "fjället" here gives another example of Jensen's tendency to perseveration.
I:	Har du mycket vatten där? Är vatnet långt från ditt hus, Jens?	Do you have a lot of water there? Is the water a long way from your house, Jens?	

Transcript	*Translation*	*Comments*
S: Mörby Hagar. [Hagar.]	Mörby Meadows. Meadows.	Instead of answering the question Jensen gives an association, the name of the hamlet where he lived.
I: Säg mig! Jag hör dig inte, Jens. Var har du vatnet? Är det långt från ditt hus?	Tell me. I can't hear you, Jens. Where do you have the water? Is it a long way from your house?	
S: Nej.	No.	
I: Förstår du det? Förstår du det? Vad är det?	Do you understand that? Do you understand that? What is this?	
S: (S. sighs deeply.) [Jag är så trött.]	I am so tired.	Although Jensen has often said he was tired he adds a very idiomatic "så" for emphasis.
V: [Indistinct in background]		
I: Hur gammal tror du den är?	How old do you believe this is?	
S: O, gammalt.	O, old.	It is interesting that Jensen does not repeat the interpreter's word, but offers the neuter form with suffixed "–t".
I: Är det gammalt?	Is it old?	
S: Ja.	Yes.	
I: Tror du den är gammal den?	You think it is old?	
S: Ja.	Yes.	
I: Kan du göra en sådan, Jens?	Can you make one like it, Jens?	
S: (faintly) Nej.	No.	

I: Varför inte? Säg mig! Varför kan du inte göra den?	Why not? Tell me. Why cannot you make it?	
S: Nej. [Det är icke] möjligt. Möjligt. Möjligt.	No. It isn't possible. Possible. Possible.	E. Hellström considered this phrase one of the ones best pronounced by Jensen. Unfortunately, I cannot clearly hear the portion in brackets on the copy of the recording I have.
I: Möjligt?	Possible?	
S: Möjligt.	Possible.	
I: Hur skulle du göra då?	How would you do it then?	
S: [Det är så] tung, tung.	It is so heavy, heavy.	Jensen pronounces the word closer to "tyng", and his sentence is ungrammatical, for he could have said correctly either "Det är så tungt", or "Den är så tung".
I: Tung?	Heavy?	
S: Tung.	Heavy.	
I: Hur skulle du göra?	How would you work it?	From the context and later remark of the interpreter it seems that here Jensen is being shown an iron nail.
S: En skate ... skjuta.	(?) ... shoot.	The translation and meaning are quite uncertain. Jensen pronounces "skate". He could be saying Swedish "skata" (English: "magpie").
I: Tala högre! Har du gjort en tunna någon gång? Har du gjort en bagge?	Speak up! Have you ever made a barrel? Have you made a tub?	"Bagge" (English: "tub") is a somewhat archaic word.

Transcript	Translation	Comments
S: Ja.	Yes.	
I: Det har du gjort.	You have done that.	
S: Ja, ja.	Yes, yes.	
I: En sådan? Har du gjort en sådan?	One like this? Have you made something like this?	
S: Ja, det har jag.	Yes, I have.	
I: Det har du. Har du sådant också?	You have that. Do you also have something like this?	
S: Ja.	Yes.	
I: Har du järn här?	Do you have iron here?	
S: Nej.	No.	
I: Nej, det har du inte.	No, you don't have that.	
S: Nej, nej.	No, no.	
I: Nej, det har du aldrig sett förr.	No, you have never seen that before.	
S: Nej . . . då . . . . for laxen [Indistinct murmuring] Laxen. . . . [Laxen.]	No . . . (?) for the salmon. The salmon.	The meaning is not clear. The iron nail may have reminded Jensen of a fish hook. Jensen here pronounces Norwegian "for" rather than Swedish "för".
I: Det är en fin sak, är det inte? Ja du, det sitter fast. Vad heter det? Vad kallar du den? En spik? (S. is uttering low	That's a fine thing, isn't it? Yes, it catches tight. What's it called? What's its name? A nail?	Jensen does not give the object a name.

(indistinct sounds here, suggestive of wonder or amazement at what Jensen is being shown.)

H: Did you ever see iron before? Did you ever see this?

I: Du har sett den förr?

Have you seen that before?

S: Nej.

No.

I: Det har du inte. Du har inte sett järn förut.

You have not. You have not seen iron before.

H: In Haverö? Don't you see this?

Here Jensen is apparently being shown an iron or pewter cup or mug.

S: (rather loudly) Sterte!

(?)

Here I have spelled Jensen's word close to the pronunciation, although it is not clearly identified. R. Ejvegård pointed out that a Swedish dialect word "stert" refers to a big party that goes on all night. This fits the context here. Brandy is the main drink consumed at such parties. If this is correct then Jensen's "sterte" could be regarded as short for "stertet" (the definite form) or a distinctive pronunciation of "stert" (the indefinite form).

I: Stark?

Strong?

The interpreter thinks Jensen may be trying to say Swedish "stark" (English: "strong"). Jensen's word is closer to the Norwegian cognate "sterk", but the second "t" sound is clearly heard as well as the final vowel.

Transcript	Translation	Comment
S: (fainter) Sterte.	(?)	
I: Har du brännvinet i den? Ja, det har du.	Do you have brandy in it? Yes, you do.	
S: Ja.	Yes.	
I: Vill du ha litet av det? Vill du dricka litet ur den? Ja, ta dig en klunk du, Jens! Ta dig en klunk ur den!	Would you like to have a little from it? Would you like to drink a little out of it? Come on, have a swig, Jens, Take a swig from it!	
S: Ja.	Yes.	
I: Ja, Ja, Jens. (S. laughs) Den var tung, Jens. Vi lurade dig. (S. laughs)	Yes. Yes, Jens. That was heavy, Jens. We deceived you.	Evidently Jensen was surprised that the mug was so heavy.
H: But Jensen, if you never saw this ... did you ever see this? This is hard, too.		
S: Sten ... sten.	Stone ... stone.	
I: Sten?	Stone?	
S: Sten.	Stone.	
H: Did you ever see this, Jensen?		
S: Sten.	Stone.	Here occurs another example of Jensen's tendency to perseveration, repeating a word more or less automatically as if he cannot get it off his mind.
I: Sten?	Stone?	
S: Sten ... sten.	Stone ... stone.	
H: Is this strong, Jensen? Try to bend it. Did you ever see one of these before?		
S: Ja, ja. [Är stark.]	Yes, yes. [It] is strong.	

H: Did you ever see soldiers before?		
S: Nej, nej.	No, no.	
I: I kriget? Har de inte sådana i kriget?	In wartime? Don't they have such in wartime?	
S: Kriget.	War.	Here Jensen is perhaps repeating what the interpreter has just said.
I: Ja, de har sådana i kriget.	Yes, they have these in war.	
S: En gud i kriget... en gud.	A god in war... a god.	
I: Gud? Har du hört några stora krig? Mig... Tala om för mig! Vad heter de? Vad heter kriget? Säg mig!	God? Have you heard of some big wars? Me... Tell me about it! What are they called? What is the war called? Tell me!	
S: Min mor.	My mother.	Jensen puts a vowel on the end of the word giving "mora", which as it happens is a frequent dialect form.
I: Min mor? Jag förstår dig inte! Vad heter kriget?	My mother? I don't understand you. What is the war called?	The interpreter is puzzled by Jensen's sudden mention of his mother when they have been talking about war.
S: Min mor tarai.	My mother... (?)	We have not identified or made sense of what Jensen says here about his mother.
I: Säg det igen!	Repeat that!	
S: Min mor tarai tu.	My mother... (?)	
I: Mördar man? Säg! Vad heter kriget?	Does one murder? Tell me. What is the war called?	The interpreter evidently thinks Jensen is talking about murder in relation to war.
S: Min mor.	My mother.	

Transcript	Translation	Comments
I: Din mor?	Your mother?	
S: Ja.	Yes.	
I: Din mor? Var hon i kriget?	Your mother? Was she in the war?	
S: [Min mor] . . . . [Jag vet inte.]	My mother . . . . I do not know.	
I: Vem var ledaren i kriget?	Who was the leader in the war?	
S: Räde[r].	Afraid. (?)	This translation is quite conjectural. Jensen says something like "räder", but his second "r" is not well heard. He may be trying to say "[Jag är] rädder" (English: "I am afraid"). "Rädder" is a dialect form of standard Swedish "rädd" (English: "afraid"). Another, more far-fetched conjecture is "röd" (English: "red") as the name of his leader, or nickname as in "Erik den Röde" (Eric the Red).
I: Vad hette han?	What was he called?	
S: Räde[r].	Afraid. (?)	
I: Vad hette han? Räder?	What was he called? Räder?	The interpreter thinks Jensen is trying to give the name of his leader which perhaps he is.
S: Räder. Räder juske.	Afraid. Afraid. (?)	Jensen's word "juske" is not identified. "juske" may be a mispronunciation of "ryska". In the sixth session Jensen said repeatedly "rädd ryska", indicating a fear

I: Räder juske? Var han ... var han en kung?

Afraid. (?) Was he ... was he a king?

of Russians, and he may be trying to say this phrase here also.

S: Kung.

King.

I: Kungen?

The king?

S: Ja, en kung. Förste man Hansen.

Yes, a king, Chief Hansen.

A good example of Jensen's associative responses. The phrase, literally "first man", is spoken very distinctly.

I: Förste man Hansen?

Chief Hansen?

S: Ja.

Yes.

I: Vet du några andra namn?

Do you know some other names?

S: Mörby Hagar.

Mörby Meadows.

Here Jensen, apparently by association, says again the name of his small village.

I: Vem?
(The tape recording is briefly interrupted here.)

Who?

Apparently the interview went on without the participants realizing for some time that the tape had run out. It must have been during this period that several objects and pictures recognized by Jensen (according to N. Sahlin) which are not mentioned in the recorded part of the interview were shown to Jensen. These objects included an hour-glass which he called correctly "timglas" and a stick used for measuring the amount of grain or seed in a barrel and which he correctly identified.

Transcript

H: O.K. I want to give you a glass of water.
You are going to feel better.

S: [Jag är trött.]

H: You are going to feel better.
Here is the glass of water. Here you are.
Here is some water. (S. sighs) Drink it
down. You will feel better. Ah. You feel
better. Ah. Now you are going to talk.
Now you feel very good, Jensen. (S.
sighs) Now you feel very good.

I: Känns det inte bättre nu igen Jens? Ja,
det känns mycket bättre.

V: [Indistinct in background]

I: Ja. Var han träl?

S: [Träl.]

I: I kriget?

S: I kriget.

Translation

I am tired.

Don't you feel better now, Jens? Yes, you
feel much better.

Yes. Was he a serf?

Serf.

In the war?

In the war.

Comments

Because of the interruption in the tape
recording, we do not know the context for
the next question and response. Evidently
the interpreter is trying to ask Jensen for
more specific information about someone
referred to during the interruption of the
recording.

H: Now Jensen, you can open your eyes and tell me what you see here. What is this? Did you ever see one of these before?		Here Jensen is shown a model of a naval sailing ship with guns.
S: Skuta.	Ship.	Jensen pronounces the word as "skute" giving a Norwegian ending.
I: Skuta?	Ship?	The interpreter imitates Jensen's pronunciation and also says "skute" here.
V: (*sotto voce*) Good girl!		
S: [En skuta.]	A ship.	Jensen's second and third repetitions of "skuta" are partially covered by the interpreter's voice.
I: Har du sett en skuta?	Have you seen a ship?	
S: En skuta.	A ship.	
I: Var såg du den?	Where did you see it?	
S: [Indistinct murmuring]		
I: I Haverö?	In Haverö?	
S: Ja då.	Yes, certainly.	
I: Har de skuta i Haverö?	Have they [a] ship at Haverö?	The interpreter should perhaps have given the plural "skutor" here, but evidently repeats Jensen's singular "skuta" to aid communication with him.
S: Skuta.	Ship.	Jensen again pronounces the word "skute" on the Norwegian side.

Transcript	Translation	Comments
I: De har inte så stora där?	But they don't have such big ones there, do they?	
S: Stora där. Lite[n skuta].	Big there. Little ship.	
I: En liten skuta i Haverö.	A small ship at Haverö.	
H: What are these things sticking out of them, out here, on a big one? You know, you have seen it. What do you call these things that stick out? What do they do, what are they?		The hypnotist is pointing to the cannon protruding from the ship.
S: Skjuta.	Shoot.	Another appropriate response in Swedish to a question posed in English, although in this instance Jensen had a visual stimulus also.
I: Skjuta? Skjuter de här?	Shoot? Do these shoot?	
S: Ja, ja.	Yes, yes.	
H: What do they shoot? Were you ever on one of these?		
S: Nej.	No.	
H: Were you ever on any boat?		
I: Vet du vad det är? Vad är det?	Do you know what this is? What is this?	
S: I krige[t].	In war.	A correct association. It is not clear, however, whether Jensen's references to war indicate a particular war or wars in general.
I: I kriget? Har de sådana i kriget?	In war? Have they things like this in war?	

H: What do you call this, Jens?

I: Vad är det?

    What is this?

H: How does this go?

Jensen's recognition of a naval ship with cannon fired through ports helps to fix the date of his life as probably not earlier than 1500. Although guns were used on ships before then they were not mounted on lower decks and fired through ports until the sixteenth century.

S: Vindar.

    Winds.

Apparently someone is pointing to the ship's sails.

I: Vindar, ja.

    Winds, yes.

S: Ja.

    Yes.

Jensen pronounces the "d" like a "t" saying "vintar".

I: Vad är det, Jens? Ankaret.

    What is that, Jens? The anchor.

S: Morsom.

    Interesting.

I: Morsom?

    Interesting?

Here Jensen again comes out with the Norwegian word "morsom". Although it mostly means "funny", "amusing", "divert-ing", or "enjoyable", it can also mean just "interesting" or "curious" and one of these last two is almost certainly the correct translation, since Jensen would not find the anchor "funny" in the sense of laughable.

Transcript	Translation	Comments
V: (*sotto voce* in background) Hmhm. Norwegian.		
I: Är den morsom?	Is it interesting?	
S: (chuckles) Bra.	Good.	
H: What's this Jens?		
V: (*sotto voce* in background) Where did she learn to talk?		
I: Var lärde du dig att tala?	Where did you learn to speak?	
S: Min broder . . . min mor.	My brother . . . my mother.	An appropriate response by Jensen, but as often, he does not answer the question fully, seeming to give a minimal response only. Jensen pronounces "d" as "t" again, saying "bruter".
I: Din mor? Bra?	Your mother? Good?	
S: Min mor . . . min broder.	My mother . . . my brother.	
I: De lärde dig att tala?	So they taught you to speak?	
S: Ja, minsann!	Yes, really!	The interpreter is charmed by Jensen's spontaneous use of the interjection "minsann".
I: Du talar bra, Jens!	You speak well, Jens!	
S: [Indistinct murmuring]		

V: Ask her if she would like to go to Norway on it?

I: Vill du ta en tur på den skutan? / Would you like to take a trip on the ship?

S: Nej. / No.

I: Vill du inte? / You don't want to?

S: (emphatically) Nej! / No!

I: Varför inte? Tycker du inte om sjön? / Why not? Don't you like the sea?

S: Nej. / No.

I: Varför tycker du inte om vatten? / Why don't you like water?

S: Nej. Kriget [om] vatten. / No. The war (?) water.

I: Kriget på vatten? / War on water?

S: Ja. / Yes.

I: Tycker du inte om vatten? / You don't like water?

S: Ja. / Yes.

I: Fiskar du inte? / Don't you fish?

S: Lite. / A little.

Jensen's "om" sounds a little close to English "on", but this makes no sense. Moreover, Jensen has spoken no English since the beginning of the interview. It seems more likely that his phrase "om vatten" is an echoing of the phrase spoken just before by the interpreter.

Transcript	Translation	Comments
I: Lite? Vad fångar du för fisk? Vad heter fisken?	A little? What sort of fish do you catch? What is the name of the fish?	
S: Kriget, kriget. (sighs) Trött.	The war, the war. Tired.	Note the perseveration of "kriget" here. Jensen still has war on his mind despite the interpreter's effort to get him to talk about fishing. Perhaps the topic of war which he finds distasteful makes him feel more tired.
I: Nej, du är inte trött, Jens. Nej du, säg inte mig att du är trött. Nej, inte alls. Vi skall inte tänka på kriget nu.	No, you're not tired, Jens. Come on now, don't tell me you're tired. Not one bit. We won't think about the war now.	
I: (in background) Kan du sjunga nu? Kan du sjunga nu?	Can you sing now? Can you sing now?	
I: Har du sett? Titta, Jens! Vad är det?	Have you seen? Look, Jens! What is this?	Here Jensen is apparently being shown some leafy vegetable.
S: En blad.	A leaf.	Jensen, as often, pronounces the "d" like a "t" and says "blate". His article is wrong. Correct Swedish is "ett blad".
I: Blad?	Leaf?	
S: [En blad.]	A leaf.	
I: Kan du äta den?	Can you eat it?	
S: En mat, en mat.	A food, a food.	Again Jensen adds a vowel at the end, saying "mate". Jensen's use of "mat" here

makes an appropriate response, but the phrase "en mat" without other qualifying words is rarely found in modern Swedish.

Here Jensen's pronunciation of the first vowel gives "blömster". The interpreter in repeating the word corrects the vowel pronunciation, but Jensen continues with his sound. Jensen's article here is incorrect since "blomster" is neuter.

I: Vad? — What?

S: Mat. — Food.

H: What is it, Jensen? Did you ever see this in Haverö?

S: [Nej.] [Indistinct words] — No.

H: No? What do you do with it? Do you eat it?

S: En blomster. — A flower.

I: Blomster? — Flower?

S: Blomster. — Flower.

I: Vi kan inte äta det, Jens. (S. sighs deeply.) Du skall få se på något annat här. — We can't eat that, Jens. You are going to see something else here.

H: Jensen, did you ever see this?

I: Har Du sett den, Jens? Har Du sett den någon gång? — Have you seen that, Jens? Have you ever seen that?

Transcript	Translation	Comments
H: You never saw that?		
I: Jens, nu skall du få se på något!	Jens, now you are going to see something!	
H: Jensen, look at this.	Jensen, look at this.	
I: Var är det? Vad är det, Jens?	What is this? What is this, Jens?	
S: [Äta] potäter.	Eat potatoes.	Correct Swedish for "potato" is "potatis", but "potäter" is an acceptable plural (of "potat"), especially in dialects. Jensen's verb sounds like "äte" and is closer to Norwegian "ete" than Swedish "äta". The translation of the passages in which potatoes are mentioned is difficult, first because we do not know if Jensen was shown one potato or several and secondly because "potatis" is a collective noun in Swedish.
I: Vad är det?	What is it?	
I: Äta potäter.	Eat potatoes.	
S: Har du sådana hemma?	Do you have something similar at home?	
S: Ja, ja, Hansen . . . hemma.	Yes, yes, Hansen . . . at home.	"Hansen" is a correct association to "home" since it is both the name of Jensen's lord or chief and of the area where they lived.
I: Har du det? Har du sådana? Har du många?	You have them? You have the same? Do you have a lot?	

S: I Amerika. — In America. — Jensen's "Amerika" is not clear. As will be seen later there is a possibility that Jensen is trying to say "i marken" (English: "in the ground").

I: I Amerika? — In America?

S: Amerika. — America.

I: Säg det en gång till! Vad är det? — Say that once more. What is it?

S: En skörd, [en] skörd. — A crop, a crop. — Jensen adds a vowel at the end, saying "skörde". The response is quite appropriate in talking about potatoes.

I: Tala högre! — Speak up!

S: Skörd. — Crop.

V: [Indistinct in background]

I: Jens, jeg snakker norsk men men De forstår lite norsk. Gjør De inte det, Jens, forstår lite norska? — Jens, I speak Norwegian, but you understand Norwegian a little. You do, don't you, Jens, understand a little Norwegian? — The interpreter who speaks Norwegian comes in again. He again uses some Swedish words in speaking Norwegian.

S: Lite. — Little.

I: Har De sett noget som det? Hva er det? Hva er det? Hva er det? Hva er det? Hva er det? Hva er det? — Have you seen something like that? What is it? What is it? What is it? What is it? What is it? What is it?

S: En mat, en mat. — A food, a food. — The use of the article with "mat" is inappropriate in Swedish, although not in the corresponding English.

I: Mat? Det är mat, men hva er det? — Food? It is [a] food, but what is it?

Transcript	Translation	Comments
S: Ja.	Yes.	
I: Ja. Men vad heter det? Men hva kaller De det i Haverö? Hva kalles det?	Yes. But what do you call it? But what is the name of this in Haverö? What is it called?	
V: [Indistinct in background]		
I: Har du sådana hemma?	Do you have something similar at home?	An interpreter now begins to speak Swedish again.
S: Ja.	Yes.	
I: Har du sådana hemma, Jens?	Have you something similar at home, Jens?	
S: Ja.	Yes.	
I: Har du mycket?	Do you have a lot?	
S: Mycket, ja. Är skörd. Är skörd.	Much, yes. Is [a] crop. Is [a] crop.	As often, Jensen adds a vowel sound at the end of "skörd" saying "skörde", but his "k" is appropriately soft, giving approximately the English "sh" sound for Swedish "sk".
I: Var får du dem ifrån?	Where do you get them from?	
S: [Amerika. Amerika.]	America. America.	
V: (*sotto voce*) [Marken.]	The ground.	Just what Jensen says is not clear. The interpreter here evidently thinks he is talking about America again, but the other interpreter in a minute suggests Jensen is saying he gets this food from the ground.

I: Amerika?

S: Nej.

America?

No.

Here Jensen seems clearly to deny that he was talking about America which denial makes it more likely that the sound heard as "Amerika", even by the interpreter, was "från marken".

I: Vad säger du?

V: Från marken.

I: Från marken?

What are you saying?

From the ground.

From the ground?

Jensen never does say clearly "Från marken", but his denial earlier that he was talking about America in this connection supports this translation. Indeed some doubt remains about whether even earlier he mentioned "Amerika" although most auditors of the tape believe he did. Since potatoes come "from the ground" either response could have been appropriate in the context if Jensen and the interviewers are still talking about potatoes.

S: En skörd.

A crop.

Jensen pronounces "skörd" with a soft "k" but with a vowel at the end, saying "skörde". The response seems appropriate in view of the foregoing remarks.

I: Skörd?

S: En skörd.

Crop?

A crop.

Transcript	Translation	Comments
H: Did you ever see this before, Jensen? Did you ever see that? What is that?		Here the hypnotist shows something else to Jensen, evidently an apple.
S: Äpple.	Apple.	Jensen pronounces "apple" with a suggestion of an "f" sound so that his word approaches the German "Apfel". He does not pronounce the word close to the Norwegian "eple". Nor is his pronunciation close to Swedish "äpple" in which the first vowel approximates a short "e" and the last vowel is sounded.
I: What?		
S: Äpple.	Apple.	
I: Äpple.	Apple.	
H: Do you raise them on your farm?		
S: Ja, ja.	Yes, yes.	
H: How many do you raise?		
S: På trär.	On trees.	An example of Jensen's ability to answer appropriately in Swedish questions that have been asked in English. His answer, however, is a more appropriate response to the second last question than to the last one. "Trär" is dialect Swedish. Jensen has no "d" sound in his word as would occur in the correct Swedish "träd". He may be saying the Norwegian cognate "trær".

H: Talk louder, Jensen, I can't hear you.		
S: På trär, trär.	On trees, trees.	
I: Yes, på trär.	On trees.	
S: På trär.	On trees.	
I: (interpreting for H.) On the tree.		
H: I see. How many trees do you have on your farm that have apples? Talk louder.		
S: Många, många.	Many, many.	Another correct response in Swedish to a question posed in English.
H: Huh?		
S: Många, många.	Many, many.	Jensen gives this word the sound of German "manche". His pronunciation is also close to Norwegian "mange". Since the interpreter has already spoken Swedish "många", we have here one clear example of Jensen *not* simply copying the interpreter's pronunciation. Jensen's repetition of "många, många" provides another good example of his tendency to perseveration.
V: He must have lots of trees. Många, många. (I. repeats and comments to H. *sotto voce*.)		
S: Många, många.	Many, many.	
V: [Indistinct in background]		
S: Många, många.	Many, many.	

Transcript	Translation	Comments
H: Did you ever see this, Jensen? No? Did you ever see this, Jensen? Never saw that in your life?		
S: Apfel. Apfel.	Apple. Apple.	Jensen here seems again to give the word a German sound by including the "f" sound. Here we have transcribed it as he seemed to pronounce it.
H: Did you ever see this?		
S: Apfel.	Apple.	
I: Apfel.	Apple.	The interpreter here imitates Jensen's pronunciation, including the German "f" sound in "Apfel".
H: Now the apples that you grow on your farm, are they this color? What color is this?		It is not clear what Jensen is being shown here.
S: Gult.	Yellow.	Again Jensen shows he can give a Swedish answer to a question spoken in English. Jensen's pronunciation is close to "gult". But the final "t" is the correct Swedish ending, assuming he is referring to the color of "ett äpple".
I: (repeating) Gult?	Yellow?	
H: And what color is this?		
S: Grön.	Green.	

I: Grön?

H: And what color is this? This little one?

I: Säg, vad är den färgen?

S: [Orange.]

I: Säg den igen!

S: Orange.

Green?

Say, what is that color?

Orange.

Repeat that!

Orange.

The interpreter is not sure he has heard correctly and indeed Jensen never does pronounce this word as clearly as one wishes. It is certain, however, that he pronounces it generally in the Swedish manner with accent on the second syllable. But he adds a vowel sound at the end giving something like "oran'che". Pronunciation of the Swedish word "orange" may be approximated by "or anj'". Jensen's pronunciation is far off the English cognate with accent on the first syllable. It is perhaps closer to the German cognate than to either the English or Swedish word.

I: Orange? Vad är det för färg? Vad heter den?

S: [Orange, orange.]

H: What's this, Jensen?

I: Är den gul, Jens? Är den gul?

S: Nej.

Orange? What kind of a color is that? What is it called?

Orange, orange.

Is it yellow, Jens? Is it yellow?

No.

Transcript	Translation	Comments
I: Nej. Vad är den?	No. What is it?	
S: Orange, orange.	Orange, orange.	
H: What's this, Jensen? What color is it? Would you like to eat it? Huh?		
S: Mat.	Food.	Jensen again pronounces "mate".
H: Taste it. Taste it. Go ahead. Taste it. See if you like it. Go ahead. Taste it. Taste it. Go ahead.		
S: [Mat.] Mat.	Food. Food.	
I: Har Du sådant? Bite it.	Do you have something similar?	
H: Bite it. Go ahead.		
I: Bit i den! (Sounds of biting something like an apple.) Så där ja!	Bite it. There you are!	
H: Do you like it? What does it taste like?		
S: En fru[k]t.	A fruit.	The "k" sound is barely audible and Jensen adds a vowel at the end making "frukte".
H: What does it taste like?		
S: En fru[k]t.	A fruit.	
I: En frukt, en frukt.	A fruit, a fruit.	
H: Is it a fruit? Never saw it before in your life? Do you like it? (Sounds of S. chewing. Sounds suggest an apple being		

chewed.) You like it, huh? Would you like to raise it on your farm? How would you plant it if you want to raise it on your farm? What would you do? If you wanted to raise that on your farm, how would you plant it? You are a good farmer, Huh?

S: En planta. Plant[a].

Jensen's pronunciation of this word is on the Norwegian side, close to "plante".

H: What?

S: En skörd?

I: En skörd?

"Skörd" may also be translated as "harvest".

V: [*Sotto voce* background comment about "harvest".]

H: Tell me, what do you harvest on your farm? What's the thing you grow the most of?

S: Batty seed.

Here Jensen refers to the unidentified plant from which he derived a seed made into cakes and an apparently intoxicating drink. It is provisionally identified as "poppy seed", but pronounced by Jensen closer to "batty seed". (See discussion in text.) Jensen's pronunciation of "seed" is English. The Swedish cognate is "säd".

Transcript	Translation	Comments
V: (chuckles in background)		N. Sahlin recalled (but was not positive) that the hypnotist here showed Jensen a banana. His remarks then about "opening it up" are facetious and teasing.
H: Did you ever see this? Ah, this you know. What's this? Did you ever see this before in your life? Open it up. How do you open it up? Open it up. Open it up. Go ahead, you are a strong man. Go ahead, you are a strong man. Open it up! What's the matter? Oh. Now, what... what what is that, Jensen? Hmhm? What is it? What do you think it is? Do you think it is a fruit or a vegetable? Huh?		
I: Eat it. Ät det!	Eat it.	
H: Eat it.		
I: Ät det! Det är gott.	Eat it. It's good.	
S: [Det är] mat.	It is a food.	What one hears here is close to "De e mate". Except for the final "e" in "mate" it is good spoken Swedish.
I: Det är gott. Det är mat.	It's good. It is a food.	
H: Do you like it? Jensen, you are a strong man. Squeeze my hand. Squeeze it real hard. Go ahead. Squeeze it. Go ahead. Let's see if you are strong. You are a strong man. All right. O.K. All right, Jensen.		

I: Håll min hand också. — Hold my hand also.

H: Oh, you are a strong man, Jensen. O.K. Let go, let go. All right, not too hard, all right. O.K. All right. You are a strong man.

I: Du är stark, Jensen! — You're strong, Jensen!

H: Yes, sir, you are the strongest man in Hansen. Yeah. Do you like to fight, Jensen?

S: (emphatically) Nej! — No!

H: Why? If somebody came up to you and started to fight, what would you do? What would you do?

S: Borta. — Away.

H: What?

I: Bort. (interpreting to H.) She would go away. — Away.

V: [Indistinct in background]

Note the continuing ability of Jensen to answer English questions with correct Swedish responses. Jensen's pronunciation is again on the Norwegian side and close to "borte".

Transcript	Translation	Comments
H: Did you ever fight in your life? Think, and you will know if you ever had a fight. Now when I snap my finger, you will remember a fight. Ah! Now you remember a fight. Tell me about it. Who were you fighting? Did you ever fight anybody in your life?		
S: Nej.	No.	
H: Nej? Everybody like you? When you ever go into Haverö, do you ever get in a fight? No? Are you a big man or a lit. . . Ha? What?	No?	
S: Sku[lle] . . . bort.	Should . . . [run (?)] . . away.	Jensen's pronunciation is "borte".
H: What?		
I: (repeating) Bort. (interpreting for H.) Away.	Away.	
H: Tell me, are you a big man or a little man, Jensen? Look at yourself. Are you a big man or a little man? Huh?		
S: Lite[n].	Little.	The "n" at the end of Jensen's "liten" is not heard.
I: Mhm.		
H: What color is [sic] your eyes?		

S: Stora.

Big.

One hears here "störe" and the "t" sound does not give a word making sense unless possibly Jensen is trying to say "största" (Swedish: "biggest") but in that case the "s" sound is missing.

I: Ja, stora.

Yes, big.

The interpreter imitates Jensen's pronunciation and says "störta".

H: What color is your eyes? What do they tell you is the color of your eyes? Hmhm? What color is your hair?

S: [Inaudible]

In this inaudible passage Jensen has evidently communicated that he is bald, perhaps by gestures.

V: (laughter in background) Fall [en!]

H: Do you have no hair? Huh? Do you have any hair left?

S: Skägge[t].

The beard.

It is well to recall in reading this section that the subject is an attractive housewife! "Skägge" is spoken first by Jensen, spontaneously and with properly pronounced soft "sk".

V: Beard.

H: You like the beard, huh?

I: Är skägget rött, Jens? Är skägget rött och styvt?

Is your beard red, Jens? Is your beard red and stiff?

V: [Indistinct in background] (faintly) Did he have a beard that he can remember?

Transcript	*Translation*	*Comments*
H: Now, Jens, how do you cut that beard? Did somebody cut it for you when you went to Haverö? Or your mother or your brother cut it, or Latvia cuts it? What does she use when she cuts it? Huh? She has a knife? How does she cut it? Tell me how.		
S: Klippen . . . sten . . . klipp[er].	Clips (?) . . . stone . . . she clips.	Exact translation is difficult here because of the fragmentary utterances of Jensen. He seems to be trying hard to find the correct Swedish verb for a proper response. He gets the stem of "klippa" (English: "to cut"), and adds an "-en" ending that may derive from some German–Yiddish the subject knows. He then seems to arrive, more or less, at the right form, i.e., "klipper" (English: "she clips"). The middle word "sten" cannot be fitted into the present context.
H: What?		
S: Klipper.	[She] clips.	
H: How? What does she use? What does she use?		
I: Skär de skägget eller klipper de skägget?	Do they cut the beard off or just clip it?	
S: [Klipper.]	[They] clip [it].	

I: Ja, det var det jag sade.　Yes, that was what I said.

H: Now, Jensen look at this.

I: You are a good boy, Jensen. You are a good boy, Jens.

H: When you look at this, you are going to feel good. What is this? You eat that! What is it? It's hard. It's old.

I: Vad kallar du det?　What do you call this?

S: [Ett] bröd.　A bread.　Jensen's correct article "ett" is not well heard. As so often, Jensen pronounces a vowel at the end of "bröd", saying rather "bröde".

I: Ja.　Yes.

H: What kind of bread is it?

I: (*sotto voce*) She answered a good question.

S: Bröd.　Bread.　Here on a second saying of the word, Jensen says "bröd" without an extraneous terminal vowel sound, and the interpreter did not give him a lead.

H: What kind? What do you call it?

S: Löske.　(?)　Word not identified.

I: Är det rågbröd, Jens? Är det råg?　Is it rye bread, Jens? Is it rye?　Was Jensen trying to say something about how the bread was baked?

Transcript	Translation	Comments
S: En löske.	(?)	Word not identified.
I: Är det råg eller vete?	Is it rye or wheat?	
S: En löss.	(?)	
I: Är det rågbröd eller vetebröd? Mhm?	Is it rye bread or wheat bread?	
H: Jensen, what is this?		
S: Faretje.	(?)	Word not identified.
I: [Kornet?]	The grain?	
H: Did you ever see that before in your life?		
S: Nej.	No.	
H: Never saw that before?		
S: Nej.	No.	
H: Taste it. Tell me what it tastes like. Taste it. Did you ever see that before in your life? What does it taste like? Did you ever raise that on your farm?		
S: Nej.	No.	
H: Does that look like poppy seed?		
S: Nej.	No.	
H: Now, what's this? Did you ever see that before in your life?		

Here the interviewers are actually showing Jensen some poppy seed to see if he would recognize it and identify it perhaps as the "batty seed" to which he referred.

Jensen's pronunciation here is close to "fra" and quite far off the interpreter's "frö". And his word has an extraneous "shj" sound occurring just before one hears "frö". Of importance, however, is Jensen's use of the word "frö" instead of the cognate "säd". (See comment by N. Sahlin in text, p. 37.)

Here one can hear Jensen say "frö" without the "shj" sound noted above.

I do not understand this remark in the background, unless it refers to an expectation on the part of the interviewers that Jensen would recognize a seed presented to him as his "batty seed" or "poppy seed".

I: Tell us what it is. What do you call that? What do you call that? Hm?

S: Ja. Frö.   Yes. Seed.

I: Hm?
S: Frö.   Seed.
I: Ja. Uhm. Hm.   Yes.
S: Frö.   Seed.

I: What is it?

I: Frö. Det är ett frö, inte sant? Men vad kallas fröet? Du vet inte.   Seed. That is a seed, isn't it? But what kind of seed? You don't know.

H: Tell me, did they put this in bread?

V: (in background) We were way off on that [poppy seed].

Transcript	*Translation*	*Comments*
H: Did you ever see this?		
S: Nej. [Hansen.]	No. Hansen.	
H: Taste it, taste it. Go ahead. Bite it. You like to taste everything. Taste it. See if you like it. Go ahead.		
I: Är det ett äpple, hm? Är det ett äpple?	Is it an apple? Is it an apple?	
S: Nej.	No.	
I: Nej.	No.	
H: Did you ever see this? What do you use this for? You never saw this in your life?		
S: [Skeden.]	The spoon.	Jensen's "k" is incorrectly hard, and the final "n" is not heard, but Jensen says the word spontaneously. It has no cognate in English or German.
I: Vad heter den? Vad gör du med den?	What is this called? What do you do with it?	
S: [Skede . . . skede.]	Spoon . . . spoon.	In these very faint words, Jensen's "k" seems to be soft.
I: Vad är namnet? Vad kallas det? Är det en sked?	What is its name? What do you call it? Is it a spoon?	
S: (Sounds of Jensen straining as if trying the hardness of something.)		

I: Är den tung?	Is it heavy?	
H: Tell me, did you ever see this? How do you cut your food when you are going to eat? When you catch a deer?		
S: Stenen... stenen... stenen.	The stone... the stone... the stone.	Jensen's reference to a stone here is not understood. Is he just possibly referring to a stone implement of some kind?
H: You cut it with stone?		
S: Stenen.	The stone.	
H: You know what this is? What do you use this for?		
I: Go ahead, break it. It's only ten cent store stuff.		The interpreter apparently addresses this remark to the hypnotist or someone else present as they are preparing objects to show Jensen.
H: What's this? Did you ever see anything like this? In Haverö? No? (*sotto voce*) How do we get the time in this?		
I: Det är en sked. Ser du inte det, Jens? En sked. Du har träsked, har du inte? (*sotto voce*) You didn't bring a wooden spoon, did you?	That's a spoon. Don't you see it, Jens? A spoon. You have [a] wooden spoon, haven't you?	The last question is addressed to the other interpreter.
H: Yes, what's this, Jens?		

Transcript	Translation	Comments
S: En sked.	A spoon.	Jensen adds a vowel at the end, saying "skede". But his pronunciation of "k" is soft giving a correct Swedish sound close to English "shed". The interpreter, however, had just pronounced the word.
H: Huh?		
S: En sked.	A spoon.	
H: A what?		
S: En sked.	A spoon.	
I: Vad kallar du den? Ett ägg?	What do you call that? An egg?	The interpreter inadvertently gives the word away, but Jensen does not repeat it. Instead he gives another example of a correct associative response.
S: En höna.	A hen.	Jensen's pronunciation is close to the Norwegian "høne".
I: Höna? Vad kommer det ifrån?	Hen? What does it come from?	
S: En höna.	A hen.	Again Jensen says "høne".
I: Hm hm. Har du många hönor, Jens?	Do you have many hens, Jens?	
S: Ja.	Yes.	
I: Hur många?	How many?	
S: Sex.	Six.	Jensen pronounces this word very clearly.

8	I: Sex. Har du bara sex hönor? Hur många ägg får du?	Six. You have only six hens? How many eggs do you get?	The next question is put before Jensen answers this one.
	H: What's this? What is it?		
	S: En sked.	A spoon.	Here Jensen again adds a vowel at the end of the noun, saying "skede", but his "k" is appropriately soft.
	I: En sked.	A spoon.	
	V: (in background) That is Swedish for [a piece of] "cutlery".		
	H: (to the interpreters) It's not Norwegian?		
	V: No.		
	H: What do you use this for?		
	S: Spisa.	Eat.	Jensen's pronunciation of the word is close to Norwegian "spise". Another example of an appropriate response in Swedish to a question asked in English.
	I: Spisa. Uh huh. (interpreting) To eat.	Eat.	
	H: Does Latvia have it?		
	S: Ja.	Yes.	
	H: How many of these do you have at home? Huh?		

Transcript	Translation	Comments
S: (indistinctly) Mång[a].	Many.	Here Jensen's pronunciation of "många" is much improved and this may be an example of his learning from the interpreter.
H: How many? Do you only have one?		
S: Nej.	No.	
H: How many? Huh?		
I: Kan du göra den själv? Kan du göra en sådan själv, Jens? Gör du den själv? Vad har du då? Hur gör du?	Can you make it yourself? Can you make one like it yourself, Jens? Do you make it yourself? What do you have then? How do you make it?	
H: Go ahead.		
I: Kan du använda den? Bruka den?	Can you use it? Use it?	The interpreter offers Jensen two synonyms for English "use".
V: (in the background) That is not one of ours, is it? I'll give it to you. (laughter)		
I: Ja, den är bra.	Yes, that one is good.	
S: Bra.	Good.	
I: Ja.	Yes.	
H: You like it, eh? Do you want to keep it? Don't you have anything on your farm like this? To cut with?		

I: En sten? — A stone?

S: Ja. — Yes.

V: [Background voices heard discussing potatoes and the date "1720" is mentioned.] — Potatoes were introduced first into Sweden in the 1720s. (See text.)

H: Tell me, now when you have a spear, what is the spear made out of?

S: Skogen . . . sten. — The woods . . . stone.

The puzzling introduction of "stone" here, a word on which Jensen insists, seems to become clearer as discussion continues, although some doubt remains. In Jensen's "skogen," one hears an extraneous "t" sound as if he says "skogten". The use of "skogen" ("the wood" or "the forest") here seems less appropriate than "trä", which refers to wood used in making objects, e.g., houses, furniture, weapons.

H: What is a spear made out of?

S: Skogen . . . sten. — The woods . . . stone.

In his second pronunciation of "skogen" Jensen does not include the "t" sound mentioned above.

I: Sten? — Stone?

S: Sten. — Stone.

I: Och vad har du mera? — And what else besides?

Transcript	Translation	Comments
S: Skog.	Woods.	As usual Jensen adds a vowel at the end. He also includes an extraneous "r" sound, saying "skorge".
I: Skorte?	(?)	The interpreter does not follow what Jensen is saying.
S: Skog.	Woods.	
I: Skolde? Är det trä?	(?) Is that wood?	The interpreter is confused because Jensen seems to use the word "skog" in the sense of wood for use in furniture, tools, weapons, etc. For these purposes "trä" is the correct Swedish and "skog" refers to standing wood in trees, i.e., "woods".
S: Ja.	Yes.	
I: Är det trä, och så sätter du en sten på den?	Is it wood and you put a stone on it?	
S: [Ja.] . . . [stort.]	Yes. . . . Big.	Jensen adds a vowel at the end of the word and says "storte". But "stort" is correct if he is talking about a spear ("ett spjut") with a wooden shaft onto which a stone blade or point was fitted.
H: In Haverö, did you see this . . . this thing?		
S: Nej.	No.	

H: You know what this is, don't you?

S: Nej.

      No.

H: Oh, sure you do, you know what this is.

S: Nej.

      No.

S: What do you do with this?

S: Nej. En mat.

      No. A food.

      Jensen again adds an "e" sound at the end and pronounces "mate". As mentioned in an earlier note, "en mat", is inappropriate usage.

I: Nej.

      No.

S: En mat.

      A food.

I: Nej. Nej. Nej, Jens, titta på mig! Öppna ögonen! Öppna ögonen! Titta på mig!

      No. No. No. No, Jens, look at me! Look at me! Open your eyes! Open your eyes! Look at me!

H: Do you see him, Jens? Do you see any-body?

S: Nej.

      No.

V: She doesn't see him. [Other remarks not understandable.]

H: Jens, now look! Is this going in my mouth?

      H. has lit a cigarette.

Transcript	Translation	Comments
S: Ja, en brand.	Yes, a fire.	Again Jensen pronounces the word like "brante". Compare the discussion on "torch", pp. 157—162.
I: En brand. En brand.	A fire. A fire.	
S: [Han] röker. Han röker.	He is smoking. He is smoking.	Another example of a correct spontaneous response.
H: Do you like smoke, Jens?		
I: Röker?	Smokes?	
S: [Röker.]	Smokes.	
H: Smoke it, you will see how you feel. Go ahead. (sotto voce) She is a chain-smoker.		
S: Röker.	Smokes.	Here occurs another example of Jensen's perseveration—repeating a word or phrase rather automatically.
H: Didn't you ever see anybody have smoke in the mouth? Didn't you ever see anybody have smoke in their mouth?		
I: Jens, vet du vad det är?	Jens, do you know what that is?	
S: (exclamations of astonishment) O! O!	Oh! Oh!	
I: That is pretty darn interesting, isn't it?		

Swedish	English	Commentary
S: O! O!	Oh! Oh!	
I: Vad kallar du det? Vad heter det? Vad kallas det? Kan du blåsa ut det? (Sound of someone blowing out smoke.) Så där ja!	What do you call this? What is its name? What's it called? Can you blow it out? So there you are.	
S: O! (Exclamation still suggests astonishment and fear.)	Oh!	
I: Jens, vad är det?	Jens, what is this?	
S: Potäter.	Potatoes.	As mentioned earlier, "potäter" instead of "potatis" is essentially a dialect form.
I: Äter du den?	Do you eat it?	
H: (*sotto voce*) How many years has she been raising potatoes?		
I: Kan du äta den? Vad är det? Kan du äta den? Säg mig, vad är det?	Can you eat it? What is it? Can you eat it? Tell me, what is it?	
S: [Amerika.] .... Potäter.	America .... Potatoes.	Jensen's pronunciation of "Amerika" is indistinct and doubt remains about whether he may have said "från marken" (English: "from the ground") instead. But in either case he shows a spontaneous association to the idea of potatoes.
I: Potäter? Äter du den?	Potato? Do you eat it?	The interpreter here imitates Jensen's pronunciation of "potäter".
S: [Nej.]	No.	

Transcript	*Translation*	*Comments*
I: Är det mat?	Is it [a] food?	
S: Ja, ja. Ett spilske.	Yes, yes. (?)	"Ett spilske" has not been identified. No Swedish word resembles it, even remotely.
I: Vad gör du?	What do you do [to eat this food?]	
S: Ett spilske?	(?)	
I: Spilske?	(?)	
S: Ett spilske.	(?)	
I: Vad är det? Jag förstår dig inte, Jens.	What is this? I don't understand you, Jens.	
S: Ett spilske.	(?)	
I: Hur gör du när du äter den? Har du sett den förut, Jens?	How do you do when you eat it? Have you seen this before, Jens?	
I: Vad kallas det? Vad är det?	What's this called? What is it?	Something else is evidently shown here.
S: En skinn.	A skin.	Jensen pronounces the word "skinne". His article is wrong since the word is neuter. He also incorrectly pronounces the "k" hard, as if pronouncing the English cognate "skin".
I: Skinn?	Skin?	The interpreter imitates Jensen's hard "k" and gives the word an English pronunciation.

H: (in background) Ask her how she used to peel the potatoes if she did not have a knife.

I: Jens, do you peel the potatoes?

S: No.

I: You eat it. How do you eat it? Show me how you eat it. Can you eat it now?

S: Yes. Eat now.

I: Can you eat it now?

S: Eat.

I: Don't you cook them first?

S: ...understand...understand.

Because he has said the phrase before, we can surmise that Jensen is probably trying here to say "Jag förstår dig inte" (Swedish) or the Norwegian "Jeg förstår Dem ikke", but only one word of the entire phrase is clearly heard and it faintly.

I: Show me!

S: ...understand....

I: Speak up, Jens! Do you eat them every day? Speak up, Jens!

S: Food...food...food...potatoes.

Jensen can be heard muttering indistinctly throughout this section.

H: (in background) Ask her how she used to peel the potatoes if she did not have a knife.

I: Jens, skalar du potatisen?

S: Nej.

I: Du äter den. Hur äter du den? Visa mig hur du äter den! Kan du äta den nu?

S: Ja. Äta nu.

I: Kan du äta den nu?

S: Äta.

I: Kokar du den inte först?

S: [Indistinct muttering] [förstår] ... [förstår].

I: Visa mig!

S: [Indistinct muttering] ... förstår....

I: Tala högre, Jens! Äter du den varje dag? [Background voices] Tala högre, Jens!

S: Mat ... mat ... mat ... potäter.

Transcript	*Translation*	*Comments*
I: Är det en potater?	Is this a potato?	It is difficult throughout this section to decide if one potato or several are being referred to.
		The interpreter should have said "en potatis" or "en potat" but the forms of this word—singular or plural, standard or dialect—are confusing even to the native speaker.
S: Ja, ja, potater . . . [ja potater . . . potater].	Yes, yes, potatoes . . . yes, potatoes . . . . . . potatoes.	Here Jensen modifies his vowel sound, evidently imitating the interpreter, and says "potater" instead of "potäter" as he pronounced the word earlier.
I: Vad har man den till? Kan du äta den? Nej. Du vet inte.	What does one do with it? Can you eat it? No. You don't know.	
S: (sighs deeply) [Jag är] trött.	I am tired.	
H: What's this, Jensen? What's this? Did you ever see that?		Jensen has been saying this repeatedly, but his protests are usually ignored or refuted by the interpreters.
S: [Indistinct muttering]		
H: What? Talk louder! I don't hear you. What?		
S: En bröd.	A bread.	Jensen's article for "ett bröd" is wrong. He also adds a vowel at the end and pro-nounces "bröde".

I: Vad är det? Säg mig, vad heter den? What is it? Tell me, what is it called?

S: En skuta. A ship.

I: Skuta? Ship?

H: Did you ever see this, Jensen?

S: Morsom, morsom. Curious, curious.

> When Jensen used the Norwegian word "morsom" earlier I translated it first (p. 121) with the word "funny". When it occurred again (p. 127), I translated it by "interesting". English has no exact equivalent but the German word "komisch" has a very similar meaning. Here I have adopted the translation of "curious" as best reflecting Jensen's apparent attitude of puzzled interest concerning the object he is being shown.

I: Morsom. Curious.

S: Morsom, morsom, morsom. Curious, curious, curious.

H: Look, what's this?

S: Är kornet. [It] is the grain.

> This phrase is ungrammatical. There is no need for the suffixed definite article. "Det är korn" would be correct for "It is grain".

I: Kornet? Har du sett det kornet? Vad heter det? The grain? Have you seen this grain? What's it called?

H: Did you ever see this before?

S: Ja, i huset. Yes, at home.

Transcript	*Translation*	*Comments*
I: Vad heter ditt korn? Råg?	What is your grain called? Rye?	
H: Did you ever see this. Hold it. Hold it. What do you use it for? What's this, what do you call this material? This . . . uh. . . . ? What's it made of?		
S: Skata.	(Not translatable.)	The word "skata" means "magpie" in Swedish. This does not fit the context here in any way. Nor does the closely similar word "skada" (English: "damage").
V: [In background, indistinct]		
H: What's this? What do you call this? You are a strong man. Try to break it. (S. makes sounds as if straining.)		
S: Stort.	Big.	Jensen pronounces the word "störte".
H: Would you like to keep it? Could you use it on a farm? What's this? What do you use that for?		Jensen is here being shown a pair of steel pliers. He apparently applies them too strongly to someone's finger, probably the interpreter's.
S: [Indistinct muttering]		
V: Aj! Aj!	Ouch! Ouch!	Someone is being hurt by something here (probably the pliers) and exclaims with pain, in Swedish.
S: O! . . . O! . . . storte . . . O!	Oh! . . . Oh! . . . big . . . Oh!	There is doubt about who says this indistinct word here. It is much drawn out so that it sounds like "stoo . . . orte".

H: Put your own finger in here, you will see how strong it is. And now, don't hurt yourself.

S: O! Vad är d[et]?

    Oh! What is it?

I: Vad är det?

    What is it?

S: Vad är det? [Vad är det?]

    What is it? What is it?

I: Du vet inte det, Jens. Du vet inte vad den är gjord av heller.

    You don't know what it is, Jens. You don't know what it is made of either.

S: Ja.

    Yes.

H: You broke it, Jens.

S: Ja.

    Yes.

H: Try to break it, Jens, try to squeeze it.

I: Oh. You are strong. That's the boy.

H: See, you can't take it out.

        Jensen does not know how to use pliers and evidently gets his finger caught in them.

S: Ah.

H: See. (exclaiming) Hold it, hold it, hold it, hold it, hold it! Would you like to keep these, Jensen? Did you ever see one of these before, Jensen? What do you call this? See, you can see my fingers in there.

Transcript	Translation	Comments
V: [In the background, indistinct]		I do not know what Jensen is shown here and translation of the following passage is thereby made difficult. N. Sahlin thought he remembered (but not with certainty) that Jensen was being shown a mirror. If so, Jensen's next response makes perfect sense.
H: Now Jensen, tell me. What is this thing made of? What is this?		
S: [Plattan.] Plattan. Plattan.	The plate. The plate. The plate.	
H: Huh?		
S: Plattan.	The plate.	Here Jensen pronounces the word as "plåten". His definite article is correct, but unneccesary. Since the hypnotist asked "What is this thing made of?" Jensen's responses may be an effort on his part to indicate that the object shown (mirror?) is made of metal, for Swedish "platta" does mean a plate of metal, and has nothing to do with English "plate", as a piece of table-ware. Jensen may also know and try to fit in the adjective "platt" (English: "flat").
H: Now, you saw this before. Didn't you ever see one of these before?		
S: Ja, ja.	Yes, yes.	
H: Now what is this made out of? What do they call the stuff?		

S: Plattan.

I: Plattan?

S: Plattan.

H: If you drop this, will it break?

S: Nej, nej, nej.

H: No? How do they make it? From what do they make this? You are a smart man. Do you have one at home?

S: Ja.

H: Huh? Do you have two of them or one of them?

I: Ja [Indistinct murmuring] . . . inte.

H: What's inside of it?

S: En sand.

I: Sand?

The plate.

The plate?

The plate.

No, no, no.

Yes.

Yes . . . not.

A sand.

Sand?

Jensen pronounces the word with a "t" sound and vowel at the end as "sante". The usage "en sand" seems perhaps incorrect here. However, Jensen could be trying to indicate that the object contains one kind of sand. An abrupt change of topic seems to have occurred at the place where he mentions "sand". It is possible that the interviewers showed Jensen the hourglass again and asked him to name the sand in it.

Transcript	*Translation*	*Comments*
I: Har du sett den förut? Drycker?	Have you seen that before? Drinks?	Here they seem to have shown him a drinking vessel of some kind. The translation is difficult in this section because of doubts about what the interviewers were showing Jensen. It is not easy to decide whether the speakers are using the verb "dricka", (English: "to drink") or the noun "dryck" (English: "drink"), plural "drycker".
S: Drycker?	Drinks?	
I: Drycker från den.	Drinks from it?	
S: [Ja? Drycker?]	Yes? Drinks?	
I: Ja, du dricker brännvin från den.	Yes. You drink brandy from it.	
S: Drycker.	Drinks.	
I: Ja.	Yes.	
S: Ja. Drycker.	Yes. Drinks.	
I: Ja, vad heter den? Har du inte sett den?	Yes, what is it called? Have you not seen that?	
S: O!...O!...	Oh!...Oh!...	Jensen seems to be making exclamations of wonderment here.
H: What do you call this? Did Latvia ever have one of these? How does Latvia make your meals? Your...your food? How does Latvia cook? What did she use to cook?		

S: En sten.	A stone.	Jensen's response may refer to a hearthstone on which cooking might have been done.
I: På sten?	On stone?	
V: [Partially audible voices discuss the response.]		
H: Do you know what this is? Here you are. Hold it. You know what that is.		
S: [Indistinct murmuring]		
I: Vad heter det, Jens? Vad är det, Jens?	What do you call this, Jens? What is it, Jens?	
S: Mat.	Food.	Jensen adds a vowel at the end, saying "mate".
I: Vad heter det?	What is it called?	
S: Mat.	Food.	
I: Tomater?	Tomatoes?	Jensen's end vowel makes the interpreter misunderstand what he said.
S: (groans) Nej.	No.	Jensen corrects him firmly.
I: Vad sade du?	What did you say?	
H: What's this?		Before Jensen can answer this last question the hypnotist offers him something else to look at.

Transcript	Translation	Comments
S: En fisk.	A fish.	Jensen pronounces "fiske". He applies the correct indefinite article.
H: What kind of "fisk"?		
S: Älvfisk.	River fish.	An excellent example of a correct and completely spontaneous response. Jensen has previously used the word "älvfisk", but he was the first to do so at any time.
H: What kind?		
S: Älvfisk.	River fish.	
I: Älv. Från älven?	River? From the river?	
S: Mat. Mat.	Food. Food.	Jensen again adds a vowel at the end, pronouncing "mate".
H: What do you call this?		
S: Et tøi.	A cloth.	A Norwegian word. Jensen's article is correct.
I: En øye?	An eye?	If the interpreter is trying to repeat what Jensen said, his "t", in "tøi" is not heard.
H: And this?		
S: En nåt.	A seam.	Jensen pronounces the word with a vowel at the end, saying "nåta". The indefinite article is correct.

Speaker	Original	Translation	Commentary
I:	Nåt?	Seam?	The interpreter is nonplussed by Jensen's use of the rare word "nåt", which means "seam in a sail".
H:	And this in here?		
S:	Jag känner [det] inte. Jag känner [det] inte.	I don't know [it]. I don't know [it].	
H:	And this, what do you call this?		
S:	En sked . . . sked.	A spoon . . . spoon.	Jensen pronounces the word "sked" with a soft "k", but with a vowel at the end and a partial "t" sound instead of "d". He thus says something like "shaiteh" in English pronunciation.
H:	What?		
S:	En sked.	A spoon.	
H:	What happened to this fish, what did they do to it?		
S:	Dräpa.	Kill.	Another example of a correct and spontaneous response by Jensen. "Dräpa" is correct, but not so common in modern Swedish as "döda" when meaning "to kill".
I:	Dräper den?	Kill it?	
H:	How does Latvia make the fish? What does she do?		

Transcript	Translation	Comments
S: Jag torrer.	I dry [it].	The phrase is not well heard, but Jensen makes sense, if the translation is correct. To dry fish, especially sun-dry, is an age-old way to preserve fish. Even today, dried cod is a Norwegian export to foreign countries, including the United States. "Tørre" is Norwegian for "dry". The cognate Swedish is "torkar" but no "k" sound is heard in Jensen's word.
H: Huh?		
S: Jag torrer.	I dry [it].	
H: What?		
S: [Jag] torrer.	[I] dry [it].	
H: I want to show you something. You are going to be very happy. You like it. You like it very much. Watch. Now you are happy. What is this?		
S: En fisk.	A fish.	Here Jensen has no vowel at the end of the word.
H: What kind of "fisk" is this?		
S: En fisk.	A fish.	
H: Where do they get this "fiske"?		Here the hypnotist imitates Jensen's previous pronunciation of "fisk".

I: Du vet vad den heter? Vad heter fisken? Vad kallas fisken?

You know what it is called. What is the name of the fish? What is the fish called?

S: [Indistinct word] Mak....

Here Jensen seems struggling to say the word "makrill".

I: Du vet det ... Ma...? Vad heter den? Det vet du, Jens. Du vet namnet på fisken.

You know it. Mak....? What is it called? You know it, Jens. You know the name of the fish.

H: What's this on my finger?

S: (very faintly) Fisk.

Fish.

Another example of Jensen's perseveration because the hypnotist is now showing him something else.

H: Huh? ... What, what do you call this?

S: En vete.

A wheat. (?)

The translation is uncertain. The word "vete" does not take the indefinite article "en", and, in any case, the usage "ett vete" is just as inappropriate in Swedish as would be the corresponding phrase in English, "a wheat".

H: What—this here?

S: En vete.

A wheat.

V: [Indistinct in background]

H: (to someone else present) What do you want to do? All right. (to Jensen) Now look, what do you wear for clothes?

Transcript	Translation	Comments
S: Klærne.	Clothes.	Jensen again uses the Norwegian word for clothes. Since the interpreter has in the meantime spoken the Swedish cognate with a "d" sound, this is another example of Jensen *not* modifying his usage to imitate the interpreter.
I: Kläderna? Clothes. Kläderna? Vad har du för kläder? Har du ylle? Ull?	Clothes? Clothes? What kind of clothes do you have? Do you have wool? Wool?	Swedish has two words for "wool". "Ull" refers to the wool or fleece on a sheep and "ylle" to woolen yarn, cloth, or clothes.
S: Ull, ull, ull.	Wool, wool, wool.	
I: Får du fram ...? Har du ...?	Do you get ...? Do you have ...?	
S: Skön, skö.... En stante.	Beautiful, beautiful. (?)	
I: Säg det igen!	Say that again.	
S: En stante.	(?)	The word is not recognized.
I: Jag förstår dig inte, Jens. Tala högre!	I don't understand you, Jens. Speak louder!	
S: [Indistinct muttering] Skö[n].	Beautiful.	
I: Sko?	Shoe?	Here the interpreter suggests that Jensen is trying to say the Swedish word for "shoe".
S: [Indistinct]		
H: Look Jens, I want to show you this. Tell me what it is. What is it? Feel it.		

S: En sköld.

A shield. (?)

Doubtful translation. Jensen may still be saying "skön" in his somewhat automatic way.

H: What is it? What is that, Jens?

S: En skö[l].

(?)

H: Would you like it? What do you call this, Jensen? Do you see these pictures?

Illustrations in a book are now shown to Jensen.

S: (Seems to grunt in puzzlement.) [Skön.]

Beautiful.

The "n" at the end of "skön" is not heard.

I: Vad är det, Jens? Ja, vad är det?

What is that, Jens? Yes, what is it?

H: Did you ever see that before, Jens? Huh?

S: (Laughs softly suggesting surprise.)

V: (*sotto voce*) She has never seen a picture before.

The "she" referred to here is Jensen, not the subject in her ordinary state.

I: Vad är det? Det är djur?

What is that? They are animals?

S: (Soft ejaculations suggesting wonderment.)

I: Säg mig, vad är det?

Tell me, what is it?

S: (Continuing ejaculations suggesting surprise or curiosity.)

H: Did you ever see that before?

S: (Ejaculations as before.)

Transcript	Translation	Comments
I: Vad är det? Vad är det? Vad är det? Vad är det? Säg mig, Jens, vad är det?	What is that? What is that? What is that? Tell me, Jens, what is that?	
V: [Background voices indistinct]		
S: [Skra.]	(?)	
I: Vad? Vad heter det?	What? What is it called?	
S: [indistinct words] Bra.	Fine.	
H: Jens, do you like this? What is this?		
S: Skinn. Skinn.	Fur. Fur.	As often, Jensen adds a vowel at the end, saying "skinne". But his "k" is correctly soft for Swedish in contrast to hard the "k" pronounced in the English cognate. Jensen's pronunciation has also improved on his own earlier sounding of this word with a hard "k".
I: What? Säg det igen!	What? Say that again.	
S: Skinn.	Fur.	
I: Uhm. Hm. Skinn. Uhm. Hm. Skin.	Fur.	The interpreter repeats Jensen's pronunciation with the soft "k" sound and final (superfluous) vowel and then he gives the English cognate for the benefit of the hypnotist.
H: Do you wear that on your clothes? Do you put this on your body?		

I: Har du sådana kläder?	Do you have clothes like that?	
S: Ja.	Yes.	
I: Kläderna?	The clothes?	
S: Ja, ja.	Yes, yes.	
H: How do you make it? How do you make it. Tell me how you make it. What?		
S: Jag tørrer dem.	I dry them.	"Tørrer" is correct Norwegian for "dry". One does not hear any "k" sound such as occurs in the cognate Swedish "torkar". Jensen used this word earlier in saying he dried fish. His pronunciation is similar on both occasions.
H: Huh?		
S: Tørrer [i] sol.... Tørrer....	Dry [them in the] sun.... Dry....	Jensen here introduces the word "sol" (English: "sun") for the first time in this session. He had used this word before in session six. On that occasion he spoke the word before interpreters did so.
I: (faintly in background) That's right.		
H: What do you do when you take the skin off of the animal? What do you do with it?		
S: Tørrer. Ja[g] tørr[er].... Ja[g] tørrer....	Dry. I dry.... I dry....	Jensen's responses in this group show again his ability to reply in Swedish to questions put in English.

Transcript	Translation	Comments
I: (in the background) She dries it.		The interpreter's "she" refers to the subject, T.E., a woman, not to the male Jensen personality.
H: How do you dry it? Tell me how you dry it.		
S: I solen.	In the sun.	Jensen has the correct definite article suffixed here.
I: I solen.	In the sun.	
H: And then what do you do to it?		
S: Klippe[r].	Clip.	R. Ejvegård suggested that Jensen may here refer to "klippor" (English: "cliffs"), often pronounced "klipper". The reference would then be to drying the pelt, after removal from the animal, on cliffs. Fish are also sometimes dried on cliffs which has led to the word "klippfisk" (English: "klipfish"). But Jensen may equally have meant to say "[Jag] klipper" (English: "[I] clip [it]") referring to trimming from the pelt excess hair, etc.
H: Do you do all that yourself?		
S: [Nej. . . .] Ja.	No. . . . Yes.	

H: You don't know how to do it, Jensen. | | The hypnotist here feigns incredulity over Jensen's claims of being able to make his clothes from pelts.

S: Ja, ja. | Yes, yes.

H: You don't know how to do it.

S: Ja, ja. | Yes, yes.

H: You don't know how to do it.

S: Ja. | Yes.

H: You go into Haverö and buy it. That's what you have been doing. Where do you get the animals? Where do you get the animals? What's the name of this animal? From what animal does this come? Huh?

S: En häre. | A hare. | Jensen pronounces this word close to "häre", that is, closer to the pronunciation of the English cognate than the Swedish. He uses the correct indefinite article in saying "en häre".

I: Vad? | What?

S: En häre. | A hare.

I: Häre? Häre. Är det häre? Vet du [om] räven, Jens? | [A] hare? [A] hare. Is it [a] hare? Do you know the fox, Jens? | The interpreter first repeats Jensen's pronunciation, then suddenly realizes what Jensen means and gives the word a correct Swedish pronunciation.

Transcript

S: (sighs deeply)

H: Jens, what is this animal? Do you like
that? Did you ever see this, Jensen?
Huh? What kind of fur is this, Jensen?
Did you ever see this? From what kind
of animal? What kind of animal is this?
Huh? What's this? What's this? What
do you think it is? You know. When
I snap my finger (snap) you know
what it is. What is it? Huh? What is it?
What could it be? You know! Did you
ever see it before? What do you think
it is?

V: [Background talking in English]

H: Now, if you have a little piece of fur and
you want to make a big piece of fur . . .
you have a lot of little pieces, what do
you do with it? We have a lot of
little pieces of fur and you want to
make a big piece? Huh?

S: [Indistinct word]

H: What?

S: [Indistinct word] förstår [inte].

V: [Indistinct background voices]

Translation

. . . do not understand.

Comments

I do not know what Jensen is being shown
here.

H: Now tell me, Jensen, I am going to show you something you are going to like. You are going to feel good. Tell me, Jensen, did you ever see anything like this?

S: [Indistinct murmuring]

Jensen is here being shown pictures in a book.

I: (*sotto voce*) She is fascinated by the books.

H: Did you ever see anything like this, a house that looks like this? Did you?

I: (speaking English to Jensen) What is that, Jens, what is that? Hhm? What is that?

S: [Indistinct phrase] [Morsom.]

Curious.

Jensen's first mention of "morsom" in this passage is not clear, but the interpreter evidently recognizes the word and in an aside to the hypnotist he gives it the translation of "peculiar". In his next responses Jensen speaks the word much more distinctly. As on the last two occasions when Jensen used the word (see p. 179 and p. 215) he expresses with it his sense of puzzled interest in what he is being shown. For the translation here "curious" seems appropriate as also the interpreter's "peculiar".

Transcript	*Translation*	*Comments*
I: (*sotto voce*) Mhm. Hm. Peculiar. Very nice.		
S: [Morsom. Morsom.]	Curious. Curious.	
H: What is this man doing, Jensen?		
S: Morsom. Morsom.	Curious. Curious.	
H: Oh, what's this, Jensen? What are they doing?		
S: [Indistinct murmuring] En gutt.... En gu[tt]....	A boy.... A boy.	Jensen uses the Norwegian word "gutt" (English: "boy") instead of Swedish "pojke" and pronounces it with a vowel at the end as "gutte".
H: What's that?		
I: Gutt. [... back in Norway.] Boy.	Boy.	In this section, as sometimes elsewhere, the interpreter's remarks are often intended to translate Jensen's responses for the hypnotist.
H: Is this a boy, too?		
S: Nej, pike.	No, girl.	Jensen does not pronounce the Norwegian word for "girl" very distinctly and it sounds somewhat like "piet". But the interpreters obviously recognize the word. The Swedish cognate "piga" means "maid-servant" (on a farm) but is now in disuse

I: Piga. Hhmm.

H: What's that?

I: [Piga.] A girl. Girl in Norway.

S: En sko.

I: Sko? Har du sådana skor, Jens? Har du sådana skor, Jens? Säg mig, har du trä [skor]?

S: [Indistinct murmuring]

H: What's this, Jensen? Do you like her? Is she nice?

S: Ja.

I: Would you like to sleep with her?

S: (with enthusiasm) O, ja!

V: (laughter in background)

Girl.

Girl.

A shoe.

Shoe? Do you have similar shoes, Jens? Do you have similar shoes, Jens? Tell me, do you have wooden [shoes]?

Yes.

Oh, yes!

---

as derogatory. Jensen comes close to Danish "pige" with its almost unspoken "g" in his pronunciation.

The sudden transition from girl to shoe here is presumably explained by Jensen's being shown a series of pictures or having his attention drawn to items in a composite picture. He correctly pronounces the "k" in "sko" hard, in contrast to the English cognate "shoe". His article is also correct.

Transcript	Translation	Comments
H: Would you like to lay with her?		
S: Ja.	Yes.	
H: What's her name? Do you know her? Look at her. You know her. Look at her. Have you ever seen anybody with hair like this? Is this what the girls in Haverö look like?		
S: Nej.	No.	
H: What do the girls in Haverö look like? Huh?		
S: [Indistinct murmuring]		
I: What is this? Vad är det för någonting?	What sort of thing is that?	
S: En häst.	A horse.	Jensen ends the word with a vowel, pronouncing "häste". His indefinite article is correct.
I: Vad?	What?	
S: En häst.	A horse.	
I: Right. Häste[n]?	The horse?	The interpreter's word is not clearly heard. He may be just repeating Jensen's "häste" with a final vowel sound.
H: What is this?		
I: Vad är det?	What is that?	

9

S: (Laughs and seems to exclaim with wonderment and pleasure.)

H: What's that?

S: Häst. — Horse.

V: (Voices in background mention "picture of a horse", but their words are otherwise mostly indistinguishable.)

> The transcript cannot convey adequately the strong emotional response Jensen showed to the picture and thought of a horse.

H: And what is this? Have you ever seen one of these?

S: (laughs) [Lycklig.] — Happy.

H: Tell me.....

S: Morsom. — Curious.

H: What do you call this? What is the "häste" pulling? What is he pulling? What is he pulling, what's this? What's that? Did you ever see one of these?

S: Häst. — Horse.

> Another example of Jensen's perseveration occurs here.

H: Huh?

S: Häst. — Horse.

H: What's this? You know.

I: Djur? Är det djur?

I: (*sotto voce*) No. She does not know.

V: [Indistinct in background]

S: Häst. [Häst.] Häst. Häst.

H: All right. All right. Oh, you know what this is, don't you? What does this look like? Have you ever been to a place that looked like this?

I: Vad är det?

S: En . . . skuta.

I: Det är skuta?

S: Ja, brygga.

Translation

Animal(s)? Are these animals?

Horse. Horse. Horse. Horse.

What is that?

A . . . ship

That is [a] ship?

Yes, bridge.

Comments

The interpreter's "djur?" seems to ask a question as if repeating what Jensen had said but nothing definite can be heard on the recording from Jensen just before the interpreter's words.

While the others present carry on a conversation, Jensen can be heard softly perseverating with his "häste".

Jensen correctly pronounces the "k" in "skuta" hard and his indefinite article is correct.

Since we do not know what object Jensen is being shown (in a picture in a book) the translation is uncertain. The Swedish "brygga" means variously "bridge", "dock", or "pier".

I: Brygga? Bridged.

Here the interpreter concludes that Jensen meant "bridge".

S: [Mast.]

Mast.

The word "mast" is correct Swedish as well as English.

V: [Indistinct in background] Boat.

H: Tell me, does Haverö look like this? (S. sighs deeply.) Did you ever see pictures like this? Huh?

S: [Indistinct murmuring]

I: Vad är det? Vad är det?

What is that? What is that?

S: En hand . . . en hand.

A hand . . . a hand.

Jensen's first pronunciation of this word adds a vowel at the end and gives a "t" sound to the final consonant so that he says something like "hante". His second pronunciation is better. His indefinite article is correct.

I: Ja, en hand. Hmhm. Och vad är det?

Yes, a hand. And what is that?

Although I do not know what the interviewers are showing Jensen here, the interpreter is evidently satisfied as indicated by his murmuring "Hmhm" with Jensen's responses.

S: En sko.

A shoe.

I: En sko, hm, hm.

A shoe.

Jensen correctly pronounces the "k" hard (in contrast to the English cognate) and his indefinite article is correct.

Transcript	*Translation*	*Comments*
H: Tell me		
I: Vad är det? Vad kallar du det? Titta här uppe, Jens!	What is that? What do you call that? Look up here, Jens.	
S: [Hjässan.]	The top of the head.	If this very faintly heard word has been correctly identified it is remarkable that Jensen knows it, for it is quite rare.
I: Vad har de på huvudet?	What do they have on their heads?	
S: [Gult.]	Yellow (?)	Jensen is probably trying for "gul" meaning "yellow", in the neuter form "gult". The difference between "-d" and "-t" is often difficult to distinguish. In this case one hears "guld" (English: "gold") rather than the "t" sound of "gult", but the latter word makes more sense in the context. It is evidently what the interpreter expected to hear judging by his "Hmhm" and his clear pronunciation of "gult". (See next responses and further comment below.)
I: Vad kallas det?	What do you call that?	
S: [Indistinct word] . . . Gult . . . . Gult	. . . Yellow . . . . Yellow	Jensen's word has a vowel at the end and a "t" sound in the final consonant so that it sounds close to "gulter". The interpreter then thinks he is saying "gult här", and perhaps he is.

I: Hmhm. Gult hår.
S: Gult hår.

Yellow hair.
Yellow hair.

Now Jensen pronounces the phrase more distinctly, but by this time he may be repeating what the interpreter has said.

I: (*sotto voce*) Yellow. Yellow.
S: Gult . . . .

Yellow . . . .

A possible repetition of "hår" is covered by the hypnotist's next phrase.

H: Jens, tell me, what color are these people? Did you ever see people this color?

Here the interviewers are evidently showing Jensen pictures of Negroes.

S: [Indistinct murmuring]

H: Huh?

S: (very indistinctly) [Svart.]

Black.

The word is pronounced so indistinctly that it must be considered doubtful.

H: Did you ever see people with dark skin, black skin? Are there any people with black skin, Jensen? Huh?

S: Är trött. (sighs deeply) [Jag är] trött.

[I] am tired. I am tired.

H: Look Jensen, all right, now you are feeling good.

S: (Seems to groan with fatigue.)

H: All right. All right. Do you want to go to sleep? Do you want to take a nap?

Transcript	Translation	Comments
S: [Så . . . .]	(?)	Possibly Jensen is trying here to say "sova" (English: "sleep"), but only the first syllable is heard and that indistinctly.
H: All right, take a nap. All right, take a nap. All right, take a nap. And when I come back, you will wake up. You will feel very good. You will feel good. And you are going to take a nap. For how many hours? For how long do you want to take a nap?		
I: Hur många timmar? Hur länge vill du sova?	How many hours? How long do you want to sleep?	
S: En dag.	A day.	A good example of an appropriate response in Swedish to a question posed in Swedish. The question was, however, also posed in English just before by the hypnotist.
I: En dag. A day.	A day.	
H: All right, you take a sleep for a day and when I come back you [will] feel good and rested. Like you slept for a day. All right, just sleep and you feel good. (A short pause.) Now I am back. The day is over. You feel refreshed.		Jensen repeatedly complains of being tired and sleepy, but the interviewers for the most part ignore or contradict his remarks on this theme. Here he is given suggestions of sleeping and feeling refreshed when he awakens.
V: [Indistinct in background]		

H: Now when you wake up, you are going to feel so good that you are going to want to sing.

S: Nej.   No.

V: (laughter)

H: Yea, yea.

S: Jensen . . . sjung.   Jensen . . . sing.

H: (coaxingly) All right, now, Latvia is going to sing a song. . . .

S: Latvia?

H: Yea, and Latvia is going to ask you to sing and you are going to sing with Latvia.

S: Nej, nej.   No, no.

H: Yea, you are going to sing with Latvia. All right you . . . you are going to sing a song that your mama sang to you. Do you remember any song that your mama sang to you? Do you? All right, now, just think. When I snap my fingers, you will remember a song your mama sang. Think. Here we go. (snap) Now you remember a song your mama sang, and you want to sing it. Go. You want to sing it to Latvia. Go ahead.

Transcript	*Translation*	*Comments*
S: (laughs gently) Nej.	No.	
H: Go ahead.		
S: (emphatically) Nej!	No!	
H: Go ahead.		
S: Nej, nej.	No, no.	
H: All right, Latvia is going to sing. And after Latvia you are going to sing. Right? Listen to Latvia. (H. sings) Now it is your turn. Go ahead.		
S: Latvia?		Jensen's "Latvia?" expresses incredulity that the hypnotist should expect him to confuse the crude singing he has just heard with the voice of his wife.
H: Yea, that's how Latvia sings.		
S: Nej.	No.	
H: No? All right. Now you want to sing a song. Go ahead.		
S: Nej.	No.	
H: All right.		The hypnotist gives up the attempt to persuade Jensen to sing again.
V: [Indistinct in background]		

H: Now look, I am going to show you these pictures and you are going to tell me what they are. You can open your eyes. Look at this. What do you see? What do you see up here? What do you see? What do you call them?

S: [Indistinct]

I: [Hönor?]

Hens?

H: What are these men doing? What are they doing to her? Huh? What are they doing? Look. . . . Look at the men down here. Look at them. Here, here at the bottom. Look at them. Look at them. What are they doing? What are they doing? What are they doing? What are they doing? Huh? What are these men doing?

V: [Indistinct in background]

H: Oh, Jensen!

I: Jensen, Jensen, Jensen.

H: Jensen, what do you see? Huh? What do you see, Jensen?

I: What is this, Jens?

H: What do you call that? What do you call that?

Again we do not know what the inter-viewers are showing Jensen.

Transcript	Translation	Comments
I: Är det en fisk? Ser du det?	Is that a fish? Do you see it?	
S: [En fisk.]	A fish.	
I: Ja. Vad är det här? Vad är det? Hmhm? Vill du sova hos henne? Vill du sova hos henne? Är det en fru? Är det en piga? Är det en piga? Heh?	Yes. What is this here? What is that? Hmhm? Would you like to sleep with her? Would you like to sleep with her? Is that a woman? Is that a girl? Is that a girl? Heh?	
S: (very faintly) [En piga.]	A girl.	"Piga" usually denotes in Swedish a maid-servant. "Flicka" is the more usual expression for "girl". But, since Jensen seemed previously to have used the word "piga" himself, the interpreter has picked it up and uses it here. This is one of numerous examples where the interpreter has skillfully accommodated to Jensen's usages.
V: [Indistinct in background]		
H: What is this man doing?		
I: Hm, det här är en piga. Är det Latvia?	Hm, this is a girl. Is it Latvia?	
S: Nej!	No!	Jensen's "Nej" is drawn out to give emphasis to his denial. His word sounds close to "Neeej".
I: Är det inte Latvia?	Is it not Latvia?	
S: (laughs) Nej.	No.	
H: This is Latvia over here. This is Latvia.		
S: Nej. (laughing)	No.	

H: Did Latvia look like her? Huh? Did Latvia look like her?		
I: Är Latvia gammal?	Is Latvia old?	
S: Ja, gammal.	Yes, old.	
I: Gammal.	Old.	
H: How old is Latvia?		
I: Hur gammal är Latvia?	How old is Latvia?	
H: How old are you? If you are forty years old, how old is Latvia? How old were you when you got married?		
S: [Sjutton. Sjutton.]	Seventeen. Seventeen.	Jensen includes a distinct "f" sound in this word so that he seems to pronounce "sjyfte". He repeats it several times and eventually the interpreter thinks he is saying "sjutton" (English: "seventeen").
H: How old were you when you got married? You will know when I snap my fingers. (snap) You will know. How old were you?		
S: Sjutton. Sjutton.	Seventeen. Seventeen.	
I: (*sotto voce*) Fifteen.		Here the interpreter must have thought Jensen had said "femton" (English: "fifteen").
V: (in background) Seventeen. Sjutton.	Seventeen.	

Transcript	Translation	Comments
I: Sjutton.	Seventeen.	
H: When I snap my fingers, you are right there. You are getting married. You are marrying Latvia. You feel very good. Now listen. I am going to snap my fingers. You are marrying Latvia. (snap) You are marrying Latvia. How old are you? You feel good. You are happy. You love Latvia. You love Latvia.		
S: [Älska.]	Love.	Jensen here gives the Swedish word for "love" after hearing the English word for it.
H: Does Latvia love you?		
S: Älska, älska.	Love, love.	
I: (sotto voce) Älska. Love.	Love.	
S: Älska.	Love.	
H: How old is Latvia?		
S: Älska.	Love.	Jensen continues to perseverate with the word "älska" almost as if to himself and ignoring the hypnotist's questions.
H: Huh? You know how old.		
S: [Älska.]	Love.	
H: How old is Latvia?		

S: Äls[ka]. — Love.

H: Huh?

V: [Indistinct in background]

S: Latvia.

H: Is Latvia an old girl when you marry her or a young girl? Is Latvia a young girl?

S: Ja. — Yes.

H: How young? Is she five years old?

S: (emphatically) Nej. — No.

H: Is she ten years old? How old? Is she thirteen years old? Is she fourteen years old? Is she fifteen?

S: Förstår dem icke. — [I] do not understand them.

Jensen uses the negative "icke" instead of "inte". "Icke" is less common than "inte" in Swedish, but "ikke" is common usage in Norwegian and Jensen's tendency to prefer it to "inte" suggests the Norwegian influence in his language. This phrase was earlier translated as "I do not understand you" on the assumption Jensen was using "Dem" (Norwegian: "you").

I: Jag förstår inte. She doesn't understand. Vet du.... Vet du hur många är sedan du föddes? Hur många är sedan? — I don't understand. Do you know.... Do you know how many years it is since you were born? How many years since then?

Transcript	*Translation*	*Comments*
S: [Indistinct]		
I: Vet du det?	Do you know that?	
S: [Indistinct]		
I: Vet du vad ett år är? Hur långt är ett år?	Do you know what a year is? How long is a year?	
S: [Indistinct]		
I: Vet du en sommar? Du vet vad sommar är då solen skiner. Det är varmt.	Do you know summer? You know what summer is when the sun shines. It is warm.	
S: Vinter . . . är kallt.	Winter . . . is cold.	
I: Är det kallt? O! Det är kallt. Är det snö? Snö också?	It is cold, is it? O! It is cold. Is there snow? Snow also?	
S: Snö.	Snow.	Jensen's pronunciation of "snö" is unlike the English cognate, but here he could have imitated the interpreter's previous pronunciation.
I: Mycket snö?	Much snow?	
S: Mycket s[nö].	Much snow.	
I: Hur mycket? Hur mycket snö?	How much? How much snow?	
S: [Hög snö.]	High snow.	
I: Hög snö? Åker du skidor? Skidar du? Har du skidor? Skidor?	High snow? Do you go skiing? Do you ski? Do you have skiis? Skiis?	

S: S . . .

V: (faint in background) Ski.

I: Ski.

   Ski . . . på snö? Har du snö? — Ski . . . on snow? Do you have snow?

   Here the interpreter hardens his "k" and pronounces the word as in English.
   Here the interpreter again uses the soft "k" sound.

S: [Indistinct murmuring]

I: Hur många månader, hur många mån . . . månader är Latviä? — How many months, how many . . . months [old] is Latvia?

   Jensen was found previously to reckon time in months, so the interpreter phrases his question accordingly.

S: Stor. — Big.

I: Vet du det? — Do you know that?

S: Stor. — Big.

   Jensen's word sounds like "störte". On other occasions also Jensen has pronounced "störte" when from the context it can be supposed that he meant "stor".

I: Säg det högre! — Say it louder!

H: All right, just relax and take another little nap and when I do this you will feel very good. Just relax and go to sleep again, Jensen. Just relax and go to sleep. (A short pause.)
All right now, when you wake up now and open your eyes, you are going to see something, Jensen. What is this? You can open your eyes. What do you see, Jensen? Take a look at it. Hold it. Hold it. What is that? Did you ever see that before? Huh?

   I do not know what Jensen is being shown here.

Transcript	Translation	Comments
S: Pengar.	Money.	
I: Vad är det?	What is it?	
S: Pengar.	Money.	
I: Pengar?	Money?	
S: (faintly) [Pengar.]	Money.	
H: What is this? Don't you like "pengar"?		
S: Krig tar pengar. Krig tar . . .	War takes money. War takes	
I: Krig tar pengar.	War takes money.	The interpreter, as often, repeats Jensen's phrase, but Jensen clearly says the phrase first.
S: (sighs deeply)		
V: (faint in background) (sotto voce) War takes the money.		The voice resembles that of H. It seems that one of the interpreters has translated for him (out of range of the microphone) and he repeats the translation.
I: Har du . . . ?	Have you . . . ?	
H: Look at this. Oh, you like this. You can get a lot of wine. You can go into town. Go ahead, keep it and go into town.		Apparently the hypnotist here shows and gives some coins to Jensen.
S: [Indistinct murmur] Mhm . . . pengar.	Mhm . . . money.	
I: No pengar.	No money.	
S: [Indistinct murmur] Mhm . . . pengar.	Mhm . . . money.	

H: Why don't you want it? You can go into Haverö and have a good time. You can get a lot of women with "pengar". Huh? Do you need "pengar" to get women in Haverö?

S: Nej... pengar.

No... money.

H: What do you need?

S: Nej. Pengar.

No. Money.

H: What do you need?

I: Om du vill ha en flicka i Haverö behöver du inte pengar då? Hon vill ha pengar, Jens.

If you want to have a girl in Haverö, don't you need money then? She wants money, Jens.

S: (sighs deeply) Pengar.

Money.

I: Vill inte hon? Flickan? Hon vill ha pengar. Jens, vad ger du flickan? Vad ger du flickan?

Doesn't she? The girl? She wants money. Jens, what do you give the girl? What do you give the girl?

V: (in background) Ask him what king....

I: Vad heter... vet du vad kungen heter? Kungen?

What do you call ... Do you know what the king's name is? The king?

S: Kungen?

The king?

Here Jensen is apparently not responding to the questions. He is partly trying to express a negative thought and partly perseverating with the word "pengar".

Transcript	Translation	Comments
I: Ja, vad heter kungen? I Hansen? Vad heter kungen där?	Yes, what is the king called? In Hansen? What is the king called there?	
S: Hansen [är] förste man.	Hansen is [the] chief.	Another example of an appropriate associative response.
I: Hansen är förste mannen? Heter han Hansen? Tycker du om honom?	Hansen is the chief? Is he called Hansen? Do you like him?	
S: Hansen . . . min kung.	Hansen [is] my king.	Jensen's verb cannot be heard. Although Jensen here says Hansen is his king, the interpreter may have suggested the answer by his earlier question about the king.
I: Hans?	Hans?	
S: Stor.	Great.	
I: Heter han Johannes? Heter han Johannes?	Is he called Johannes? Is he called Johannes?	The second interpreter now brings up a new topic trying to clarify whether Jensen's chief was called Hansen or Johannes.
S: Stor.	Great.	Again Jensen pronounces "störte".
I: Är han stor?	Is he great?	In repeating, the interpreter accommodatingly imitates Jensen's pronunciation.
S: Ja.	Yes.	
I: Var bor han?	Where does he live?	

S: I fjälle[t].	On the mountain.	Another good example of an appropriate response in Swedish to a question asked in Swedish.
I: I fjället?	On the mountain?	
S: Ja.	Yes.	
I: Är det långt från här?	Is it far from here?	
S: Ja.	Yes.	
I: Hur kan jag gå och möta honom?	How can I go and meet him?	
S: Ja.	Yes.	
I: Kan jag gå till honom?	Can I go to him?	
S: Ja.	Yes.	
I: Till förste mannen? Hur många dagar vill det ta?	To the chief? How many days will it take?	
S: [Hansen.]	Hansen.	Instead of answering the questions Jensen continues to mutter "Hansen".
I: Jensen, Jens, har du hört om Oden? Vem är Oden? Oden och Tor?	Jensen, Jens, have you heard of Odin? Who is Odin? Odin and Thor?	
S: [Hansen.]	Hansen.	
I: Förstår du det?	Do you understand that?	
S: Nej ... förstår	No ... understand	

Transcript	Translation	Comments
I: Vad heter din gud? Vad heter din gud, Jens?	What is your god called? What is your god called, Jens?	
S: Hansen.	Hansen.	
I: Har du en gud? Är förste mannen din gud? Den förste mannen?	Do you have a god? Is your chief your god? The chief?	
S: Stora . . . stora Hansen.	Great . . . great Hansen.	Jensen again pronounces "störte", although the second "t" sound is inappropriate.
I: Vad heter han?	What is he called?	
S: (faintly) Johansen.	Johansen.	
I: Johansen?	Johansen?	
H: What does "Ho" mean . . . in my language?	What does "Ho" mean? What does "Ho" mean? What do you mean by "Ho"?	
I: Vad betyder "Ho"? Vad betyder "Ho"? Vad menar du med "Ho"? Helig?	What does "Ho" mean? What does "Ho" mean? What do you mean by "Ho"? Holy?	The interviewers are here trying to learn whether "Jo" or "Ho" is part of the chief's name or perhaps an honorific. R. Ejvegård has suggested that perhaps Jensen is saying "Jo, Hansen" which could mean "Well, Hansen", or "Oh, yes. Hansen".
S: (emphatically) Ja, helig.	Yes, holy.	Jensen's answer was suggested by the interpreter's word spoken first.
I: Helig? Hhmhm.	Holy?	
S: (sighs deeply) Ja, Hansen.	Yes, Hansen.	

I: Säg det igen! — Repeat that.

S: Johansen. — Johansen.

I: En gång till! Högre! — Once more! Louder!

S: (louder) Johansen. — Johansen.

I: Vem är det? Säg mig, Jens, vem är Johansen? — Who is that? Tell me, Jens, who is Johansen?

S: Min förste man. — My chief.

I: Min förste man. Är det din förste man? — My chief. Is he your chief?

S: Ja. — Yes.

I: Och du tycker om honom? Är han bra? Har han en fru? Har han en fru? — And you like him? Is he a fine person? Has he a wife? Has he a wife?

V: [Indistinct in background]

I: Är han gift? Svara mig nu, Jens! Är han gift? Har han en fru? Tala högt nu! Ja. — Is he married? Answer me now, Jens. Is he married? Does he have a wife? Speak up now! Yes.

S: [Ja.] En fru. — Yes. A wife.

I: Har han det? Vet du det? — Has he one? Do you know?

S: [Indistinct murmuring]

I: Har han söner? — Has he [any] sons?

S: [Söner.] — Sons.

Transcript	Translation	Comments
I: Har han söner? Har han guter?	Has he sons? Has he boys?	
S: Snäll.	Good.	Jensen has previously (in session six) applied the word "snäll" to Latvia. It indicates a character: good, kind, dear.
I: Snäll? Snäll. Tycker du om honom?	Good? Good. Do you like him?	
S: En barn.	A child.	Jensen adds a vowel at the end, pronouncing "barne". His indefinite article is wrong, since correct Swedish would be "ett barn". But the noun itself is an appropriate response in Swedish to the question posed earlier about whether the chief had any sons.
I: Säg högre! Jag hör dig inte.	Speak louder! I can't hear you.	
S: En barn . . . [den] bäste Johansen.	A child . . . [the] best Johansen.	
I: Är han den bäste? Var bor Johansen?	Is he the best person? Where does Johansen live?	
S: I fjälle[t].	On the mountain.	
I: I fjället.	On the mountain.	
V: (*sotto voce*) In the mountains. He lives in the mountains.		
H: How do you go to him? Do you ever see him?		
S: Nej.	No.	

H: Then how do you know that he is in the mountains?

S: [Indistinct murmuring]

H: How do you know it?

S: (softly) Johansen.

Johansen seems pronounced as one word. On other occasions it has seemed to listeners that Jensen said "Ho Hansen".

H: Tell me were you scared of the dark when you walk in the dark? At night when you have to go out in the field, are you scared? What are you scared of? Do you get scared when you go out in the dark? Huh? Or does Hansen protect you? Does Hansen save you? When you say "Hansen" you feel good, don't you?

Here the hypnotist probes to learn whether Hansen is conceived by Jensen to have god-like powers that provide supernatural protection to his followers.

S: Ja.

Yes.

H: Does Hansen have any children?

S: Ett barn.

A child.

As often, one hears a vowel at the end of the word so that Jensen seems to be saying "barna" or even "barnare". Jensen here gives the correct neuter indefinite article, correcting his earlier error in saying "en barn".

I: Barnet?

The child?

S: Ja.

Yes.

Transcript	Translation	Comments
H: How many children?		
S: [Tu.]	Two.	The word is pronounced partly as if Norwegian. The Swedish cognate is "två". No "v" sound occurs in Jensen's word. However, Jensen's pronunciation is closer to American "two" than to the Norwegian cognate which can be better represented by English "toe".
I: Hur många?	How many?	
S: Tu.	Two.	
I: Säg det igen!	Say that again!	
S: Tu.	Two.	
I: Hur många barn har han?	How many children does he have?	
S: Tu.	Two.	
H: What are their names? What are the children's names? Are they good children?		
S: Ja.	Yes.	
H: Does Hansen have a house?		
S: Slotte[t].	The castle.	Jensen's final "t" for the neuter definite article is not heard. Another example of a correct Swedish response to a question posed in English.

I: Slottet.　　The castle.

V: (in the background) Good girl!

I: Bor han på slottet? ... och ... slottet?　　He lives in the castle? ... and ... the castle?

S: (sighs deeply) Ja ... [i] fjälle[t].　　Yes ... on the mountain.

I: Känner du någon som har varit på slottet? Känner du någon som har varit på slottet?　　Do you know anyone who has been to the castle? Do you know anyone who has been to the castle?

S: [Slottet.]　　The castle.

I: Vet du det? Vet du någon?　　Do you know that? Do you know anyone?

S: [Indistinct murmuring]

I: Högre! Säg det högre!　　Louder. Say it louder.

S: [Mörby] Hagar.　　Mörby Meadows.　　An interesting association of Jensen. One gains the impression that "Mörby Meadows" was in a valley dominated by the mountain on which Hansen's castle was located.

I: Jag hör dig inte, Jens!　　I can't hear you, Jens!

S: [Indistinct murmuring] ... [Hante.]　　(?)　　Word not identified.

I: Johansen.

S: [Indistinct murmuring] [Hante.]

I: Johansen bor på slottet?　　Johansen lives in the castle?

Transcript	Translation	Comments
S: [Min] hord. Min hord.	My clan. My clan.	Jensen again places a vowel sound at the end of the word, saying "horde". The word "hord" is cognate with English "horde" and best translated as "tribe" or "clan". Jensen's pronunciation, however, is off from correct modern Swedish.
I: Du hörde?	You heard?	The interpreter, apparently misled by Jensen's accent, thinks he is saying something about being heard. Actually if Jensen said "min hord", as seems most likely, he provided one more example of an appropriate response at least by association since presumably Hansen, as the local ruler living in a castle, would be leader of the surrounding clan.
H: All right, now just relax and go to sleep again and you'll feel better, Jens.		
S: (sighs, murmurs) O . . . [ante].		
I: All right, just go to sleep.		
V: [In background]		
H: Just go to sleep. You'll feel better when I come back to you. When I come back here again you will feel wonderful. Just go to sleep.		

V: [Indistinct in background] (A short pause.)

H: All right. Now I am back and you feel good, Jensen. You can open your eyes. Tell me. What do you see here? What do you see? What do you see? You can open your eyes. Do you see anything here? Huh? What do you see here? Tell me. What's he doing? (Sounds of pages of book being turned.) Do you have one of these?

Evidently a picture of some spear-like weapon or part of a spear is being shown to Jensen in a book.

I: Tala! Tala högre, Jens! Hmhm?

S: För ett spjut.

Jensen again puts a vowel at the end of the word and pronounces something like "spjute".

I: (approvingly) Hmhm.

Although we do not know exactly what Jensen was shown, the interpreter's murmur indicates his approval of Jensen's response as being correct.

S: För ett spjut. För ett spjut.

H: (*sotto voce*) She's familiar with spears.

S: För ett spjut.

Transcript

I: (*sotto voce*) She got the right word, too, there.

S: För ett s . . . (sighs deeply). Ah . . . [är] trött.

H: All right.

I: Nej. Du är inte trött alls.

H: All right. Now just relax and you are going to sleep.

S: [Indistinct murmuring and sounds like groaning]

H: All right. Just go to sleep and relax. (H. now gives suggestions to S. to resume her normal personality and then to go to sleep.)

Translation

For a . . . . [I] am tired.

No. You're not tired at all.

Comments

Following these suggestions and the "recall" of the subject's normal personality, the recording includes short statements by Dr. Nils Sahlin and Mr. Lennart Ekman in which they testify to the subject's ability to speak Swedish with some elements of Norwegian in her language.

Index